Bomber Aircrew
in
World War II

Libraries and Information

- 4 OCT 2019

- 4 OCT 2019

- 3 MAY 2020 24

183977 Designed and Produced by Wakefield Council. Communications 11/17 ♻recycle

This book should be returned by the last date stamped above.
You may renew the loan personally, by post or telephone for a
further period if the book is not required by another reader.

www.wakefield.gc

D1354054

0000000170420 4

- 4 JAN 2013

Bomber Aircrew
in
World War II

Bruce Barrymore Halpenny

Pen & Sword
AVIATION

This edition first published in
Great Britain in 2004
By Pen & Sword Aviation
An imprint of Pen and Sword Books Ltd
47 Church Street,
Barnsley
South Yorkshire
S70 2AS
England

Copyright © Bruce Barrymore Halpenny, 2004

ISBN 1 84415 066 6

The right of Bruce Barrymore Halpenny to be identified as the Author of
this Work has been asserted by him in accordance with the Copyright,
Designs and Patents Act 1988

A CIP record for this book is available from the British Library

First published as *To Shatter the Sky* by Patrick Stevens, Cambridge, in
1984.

All rights reserved. No part of this book may be reproduced or
transmitted in any form or by any means, electronic or mechanical
including photocopying, recording or by any information storage and
retrieval system, without permission from the Publisher in writing.

Typeset in the UK by Mac Style Ltd, Scarborough, N. Yorkshire
Printed and bound in the UK by CPI UK

Pen & Sword Books Ltd incorporates the imprints of Pen & Sword
Aviation, Pen & Sword Maritime, Pen & Sword Military, Wharncliffe
Local History, Pen & Sword Select, Pen & Sword Military Classics and
Leo Cooper.

For a complete list of Pen & Sword titles please contact
Pen & Sword Books Limited
47 Church Street, Barnsley, South Yorkshire, S70 2AS, England
E-mail: enquiries@pen-and-sword.co.uk
Website: www.pen-and-sword.co.uk

CONTENTS

Foreword

Much has been written about the role of Bomber Command in World War II. Many writers were not born until after the war. They have written with the benefit of hindsight, not realising the mood of the time, and the effect of the offensive on British morale, and the outcome of the war.

Only those who were involved will understand the atmosphere that prevailed on a bomber station. Whether aircrew or ground staff, most had experienced the Blitz, seen the thousands sleeping in Underground stations, and, in some way, been affected by it. The Baedeker Raids on our cultural centres continued, and the enemy presence in our skies could be heard almost nightly. The threat of invasion was real and, for many months, the invasion barge concentrations were a vital Bomber Command target. On my own station, just south of the Humber, we sometimes watched a raid on Hull, while waiting to take off. As the bomb flashes lit the night sky we had few doubts about the rectitude of our role.

This book recounts a collection of experiences of bomber aircrew. Theirs was a cold, tiring and perilous task, undertaken at hours at which the human spirit is at its lowest ebb. It did not then seem prudent to think further ahead than the target for tonight, and hope to return. Not many, I suspect, would have chosen to be in bombers, but I think most of us are proud to have flown in Bomber Command. During critical years of the war in Europe, only the bomber stations could carry the war back to our powerful enemy. What would have happened to British morale had German cities not been seen to be receiving the terrible retribution eventually exacted by Bomber Command? The price was high, but it had to be paid.

This book gives the reader who did not know those days some idea of the experiences and feelings of bomber crews. Those experiences and feelings were well understood by those who remained behind, on the bomber station. They saw the laden aircraft heave themselves into the night, and their imagination filled the silent hours. They counted the returning aircraft, and saw the ravages of the German defences, and the hazards of weather. For those of us who were there, this book will rekindle the memories that will always be with us.

Wing Commander K.H. Wallis
CEng, FRAeS, FRSA, RAF, Ret'd.

Acknowledgements

I t is not possible to mention by name all the many people who
have helped me with the loan of letters, flying log-books, diaries,
photographs and other material for my many books. This book
came about with the overflow of material and from the response of
my other books. I decided that the best of the stories should be
published as a sincere tribute to the men who served on the wartime
bomber stations. My grateful thanks to all those who have helped
me. My special thanks to Philip Moyes of MacDonald & Janes for
the extract of the Airmen of RAF Bomber Squadrons who were
awarded the Victoria Cross in the book *Bomber Squadrons of the RAF
and their aircraft*.

The author would also like to thank the Controller of HM
Stationery Office for granting permission to reproduce in full from
issues of The London Gazette, the Victoria Cross citations which
appear in Part Three.

For the factual accounts and many of the photographs I wish to
thank 'Andy' Andrew, Doug Bancroft, Ron Buck, Alan Cuthbertson,
A.F. Dales, Ralph Dargue, Henry Drozdz, Jack Dunn, Les Fuller,
Henry Van Geffen, Jack Halstead, Gilbert Haworth, R.G. Hutton,
Jack Lazenby, Mrs Levy, the sister of Sergeant Henry Conrad for the
last letter, Arthur Palmer, Reg Payne, Bill Perry, Gordon Ritchie, Reg
Stidolph, Ken Wallis, Tom Wardle, Richard Whiting.

I also wish to thank Ken Border for his valued help with research
and material for the chapter on the Development of the Bomber
Airfield; my long-time friend Ted Evans for his valued support – a
very loyal friend who was there when I needed him during my
recent illness; Dr Paris, Sliema, Malta, for his medical care and
friendship, making it possible for me to write this book; Charles E
Whitmore, Hantsport, Nova Scotia, Canada; Brian Forway who
accompanied me to London and helped with the research at MOD
(AHB); my good friend Neville Franklin for some of the bomb
photographs; E. Hine from the Department of Photographs,
Imperial War Museum; George Hubbert who gave me crash

information relating to the Ken Wallis story; Berny Kennedy for the poem *Bomber Command War Theme*; Honourable J. Gilles Lamontagne (Ex 425 Squadron RCAF) Minister of National Defence, Ottawa, Canada for his help with photographs; Air Commodore H.A. Probert MBE, MA, RAF (Rt'd), Head of Air Historical Branch (RAF) and the staff at AHB; Nick Roberts for drawing the map; my good friend Margaret Morris for typing sections of the book; and a mention also for my son Baron whose smile and enthusiasm gave me the idea for this book. I'm sorry I could not use the pictures that he did for the book. Again my very special thanks for all who loaned me material and donated photographs, with apologies to any that I might have forgotten.

The author would be interested to receive any photographs or other material for incorporation in any future publications.

Introduction

Bomber Aircrew in World War II, is not the story of one specific airfield but a composite picture from many airfields of Bomber Command. Told in three parts, the first part sets the scene with the development of the bomber airfield. The cold wind whistled through the crevices of the well dispersed Nissen huts. Clothing and beds were perpetually damp. This was a wartime bomber airfield and thousands of men and women laboured under these conditions with skill and devotion to maintain the ever increasing demands as the pace of war increased.

The second part is the bulk of the text and is a unique collection of first-hand stories of those who served on the bomber airfields. The bomber stations were our front line and the bomber crews were a special breed of men which is evidenced by the deeds and experiences related in this book. Many stories are still untold and many will never be told. There are many mysteries which will never be solved. One mystery that remains unsolved for ex-Sergeant Charles Whitmore who flew with 429 Squadron RCAF is: who was Sergeant 'Must We', WAAF, of the Royal Air Force?

Charles Whitmore did a tour of 37 bomber operations on No. 429 (Bison) Squadron from Leeming aerodrome in Yorkshire in 1943–44. The aerodrome control tower RT (Radio Telephone) code name was 'Must We' so their WAAF Sergeant operator was always called

Was this 'Sergeant Must We'?

'Sergeant Must We'. On returning to Leeming it was always reassuring when they reached RT range of the control tower to hear the cool, calm, clear cultured English voice of 'Sergeant Must We' cutting through the static of the airwaves into their earphones with their landing instructions. Even in times of poor visibility and most difficult landing conditions with many under and over 'shoot' passes at the runway, each using an extra minute or more of their very limited reserve fuel supplies, and also in times of disaster, 'Sergeant Must We' continued with her duty getting them all landed as safely as possible with never a falter or hesitation in her finely modulated English voice.

Bomber Command was made up of ordinary men from all walks of life who became in a short time proficient pilots, navigators, air gunners, etc, to fly the ever increasing number of bombers while others became fitters, riggers, etc, to keep the aircraft in the air. For the bomber crews it was a strange way of life. The contrast between the very civilised behaviour and relative remoteness from the war in the mess, and being over 'Happy Valley', the Ruhr, an hour or two later, took a bit of getting used to. The bomber airfield was built to house the ever increasing number of bombers which were needed to sow devastation across the Nazi homeland. It is strange that Bomber Command did not know of the *Schräge Musik* method used by the German night fighters and just proves how bad their intelligence was. *Schräge Musik* was first used in force on the Nuremberg Raid on 30/31 March 1944 and 'A' Able in the story 'Failed to Return' was shot down by this method. *Schräge Musik* did not use tracer since the idea was not to reveal the location of fire, ie, its source.

One or two Canadian COs, one being Wing Commander Pattison of 429 'Bison' Squadron, knew there was something but it was all presumption, not fact. They took out the mid-upper turret and the displaced mid-upper gunner lay on a mattress on the floor and looked through a perspex blister for night fighters coming up from below. Wartime photographs are relatively sparse. However, I have been able to find enough to give a picture of the crews and their mounts.

The third part of the book lists all the airmen of RAF Bomber Squadrons who were awarded the Victoria Cross during World War II. The Victoria Cross is the highest possible decoration available for award to citizens of Britain and the Commonwealth and since its institution on 29 January 1856 it has been granted to just 51 airmen. Lieutenant W.B. Rhodes Moorhouse was the first air VC. These then are the individual tales of those who served on a bomber airfield at war.

Bruce Barrymore Halpenny, Malta 1982

Glossary

AASF	Advanced Air Striking Force	IFF	Identification Friend or Foe
A/c	Aircraft	ITW	Initial Training Wing
ACRC	Aircrew Receiving Centre	LAC	Leading Aircraftman (RAF)
AC1	Aircraftman 1st Class (RAF)	LMF	Lack of Moral Fibre
		MC	Military Cross
AC2	Aircraftman 2nd Class (RAF)	Me	Messerschmitt AG
		MM	Military Medal
9 AFU (P)	No 9 Advanced Flying Unit (Pilot)	MoD	Ministry of Defence
		MTB	Motor Torpedo Boat.
AMPG	Air Miles Per Gallon	MUG	Mid-upper gunner
22 APC	No 22 Armament Practice Camp	N	North
		NAAFI	Navy, Army and Air Force Institutes
AVM	Air Vice-Marshal		
CGM	Conspicuous Gallantry Medal	NCO	Non-Commissioned Officer
CO	Commanding Officer	Op(s)	Operation(s)
'Cookie'	4,000 lb high-capacity bomb	OTU	Operational Training Unit
Cpl	Corporal	PFF	Pathfinder Force
DAHE	Delayed Action High Explosive	P/O	Pilot Officer
		RAAF	Royal Australian Air Force
DFC	Distinguished Flying Cross	RAF	Royal Air Force
DFM	Distinguished Flying Medal	RCAF	Royal Canadian Air Force
DSC	Distinguished Service Cross	RNZAF	Royal New Zealand Air Force
E	East	R/T	Radio Telephone
EFTS	Elementary Flying Training School	SEAAF	South East Asia Air Forces
EVT	Educational & Vocational Training Instructor	Sgt	Sergeant
		S/Ldr	Squadron Leader
		Sortie	Operational flight by a single aircraft
F/Lt	Flight-Lieutenant		
F/O	Flying Officer	Sqdn	Squadron
F/Sgt	Flight Sergeant	Stn	Station
FTR	Failed to Return	UK	United Kingdom
GEE	Medium-range radio aid to navigation and target identification with ground transmitters and airborne receiver	U/S	Unserviceable
		USAAF	United States Army Air Force
		VC	Victoria Cross
		WAAF	Women's Auxiliary Air Force
Gp/Cpt	Group Captain	W/Cdr	Wing Commander
HCU	Heavy Conversion Unit	WO	Warrant Officer
H_2S	Airborne radar aid to navigation and target identification	WOP	Wireless Operator (RAF)
		W/T	Wireless Telegraphy

Part One

CHAPTER ONE

Development of the Bomber Airfield

The earliest military aerodromes in the United Kingdom were little more than areas of rough grassland, mainly in the vicinity of the Army garrisons at Aldershot and on Salisbury Plain. Tents provided accommodation for the men and wood-framed canvas shelters were erected although they appear to have been almost as flimsy as the aeroplanes that they were intended to protect. By the time World War I started in 1914 several aerodromes had received aeroplane sheds of wooden construction, rather like oversized garden sheds, plus some hutted accommodation.

The war caused an enormous expansion in the aviation services and many new aerodromes had to be opened to train pilots and

Hampden bombers at Waddington in 1939 just before the outbreak of World War II.

Wartime triangular pattern of a bomber airfield with three intersecting runways. The main one was usually 2,000 yds in length with the two subsidiaries being 1,400 yds each.

observers for the new squadrons. Initially these were little different in layout from the pre-war aerodromes but soon a fairly standardised training aerodrome evolved. A completely new type of hangar was designed, the Aeroplane Shed RFC 1915 pattern, made mainly of wood with a curved roof and six large sliding doors at each end and a couple of years later this was superseded by an improved design, the Aeroplane Shed, General Service, 1917 RFC pattern. Similar in outline, this had brick walls with external buttresses and curved roof supported by elaborate wooden Belfast trusses which provided the GS Shed with its popular name – the Belfast Hangar.

Most of the training aerodromes had seven hangars of either the 1915 or 1917 pattern, six in three pairs as the squadron hangars and the seventh as the aeroplane repair shed for all units. At the edge of the aerodrome, which was often undulating to assist with drainage, were these hangars, rows of huts used as workshops, barracks, etc. They were usually adjacent to a road

Concrete pill-boxes, housing machine-guns and crews, were erected at RAF bomber stations as part of the airfield defences.

and were sometimes provided with a siding from a convenient railway line.

Soon after the end of the war the armed forces began to contract to their peacetime establishment and most of the aerodromes were abandoned. A few were retained and these were the bomber airfields of the 1920s with a very gradual programme of building replacement starting towards the end of the decade.

In 1924 a new type of hangar was designed for the Royal Air Force and eventually over 30 were built on airfields in various parts of England. This was the type 'A' hangar and was steel framed with brick walls, the vertical girders being outside the walls, and the multi-gabled roof was covered with toughened asbestos sheets. Other aerodrome buildings were designed around this time, particularly barrack blocks and messes, grim looking red brick buildings but nevertheless providing far better facilities than the worn out old temporary huts that they replaced. Early in the 1930s a modest expansion programme was approved for the Royal Air

On the left, the familiar water tower that dominates this group of buildings. The round-roofed Nissen huts are living huts, the other huts are the ablutions. These are at Skipton-on-Swale and photographed August 1945, and were the general layout for living quarters.

The well planned-roads and pathways characterise the permanent station. The permanent two-storey buildings were used for billets and administration. Photograph taken at RCAF Station Leeming in August 1945.

Force and one or two new bomber aerodromes were constructed. One of these was Mildenhall and here the first buildings to be completed were in accordance with these drawings dating back to the previous decade, including a pair of 'A' hangars.

However, about this time a completely new range of buildings was being designed for the airfields being planned under the later expansion schemes. These buildings were very well designed and proportioned, the theme of the barracks, messes, etc, being Georgian with facings carefully selected to match in with the locality, and they were erected on virtually all the airfields constructed for Bomber Command between 1935 and 1939. The new general purpose hangar specified for these expansion-period bomber bases was the 'C' type, an attractive looking steel-framed structure with brick walls and tiled roof, 150 ft wide and 300 ft long, each end covered by six sliding doors. The earliest version had a plain gable roof and looked rather

Barrack block at Topcliffe.

'C1' Type hangar at Topcliffe.

like an overgrown 'A' type; it was called the 'C' type, gabled, and few were built (these included three at Mildenhall) before the plans were refined. The definitive pattern was the 'C' type hipped, the gable ends being cut back or hipped, and there were many detail improvements in design. These hangars were built in large numbers, over 100 on bomber bases alone, to standard plans with very few variations other than in the number and position of the offices and stores attached to the side walls.

Not only were the buildings on the bomber stations constructed in the mid-30s standardised but so was their layout to a great extent. It centred on a well drained grass field large enough to contain a 'bombing circle' of 1,100 yards' diameter and on the edge was an arc of four 'C' type hipped hangars, often with a fifth of the same type behind the arc. Between, and slightly forward of, the middle hangars was a watch office, a brick building of the 'Fort' pattern which was the forerunner of the control tower, and grouped neatly behind the hangars were all the other buildings essential for a bomber airfield. There were barrack blocks, messes, armouries, tyre bays, sick quarters, guard rooms, etc, all substantial brick buildings, dominated by the station headquarters and, of

Fort-type control tower at Catterick.

Control tower at Podington, February 1945. Note the array of radio and navigational aids and the meteorological box. Podington was originally built as an RAF bomber station then used by the American Eighth Air Force.

course, the parade ground. Even married quarters, graded according to the rank of the occupants, were included in the complex, the whole forming a small town complete with water tanks, sewage works, roads, lighting and other services – and providing a compact target for enemy bombers.

By about 1937 shortages of money and some traditional building materials caused the simplification in the plans of some of the buildings, for example flat concrete roofs were introduced instead of the elaborate pitched types.

Thus Bomber Command entered World War II in 1939 with practically all its front line squadrons based on airfields which had been purpose-built to a standard layout during the preceding five or six years. Many were on the sites of earlier aerodromes and a few, eg, Waddington, retained some of the original hangars in addition to the new ones. Perhaps the greatest deficiency of these bomber airfields was an almost complete lack of paved runways, a fault that had to be remedied with the arrival of the heavy bombers.

World War II saw the development of the Royal Air Force airfield from the construction of a grass landing ground to a complex engineering task. By 1942 the average cost of one heavy bomber airfield exclusive of any buildings or services was over £500,000. During the years 1939–45 some 444 Royal Air Force airfields were

'Ops' block at Driffield.

constructed in this country with paved runways, perimeter tracks and hard-standings at a cost of over £200,000,000 excluding any building construction. The 444 airfields were constructed as follows: 203 with concrete paving; 122 with concrete paving with parts macadam or tarmacadam; 14 with stone pitching with asphalt; 23 with stone pitching with asphalt, bituminous or tarmac; 74 with stone pitching with asphalt or tarmac surfacing and 8 with sand mix. In 1942 a peak labour force of 60,000 men was employed in the UK exclusively on the civil engineering task of airfield and runway construction for the Royal Air Force.

During the six years of war some 175,000,000 square yards of concrete, tarmacadam, or other hard surfacing were laid in paved runways and connecting tracks. In 1939 only nine airfields had runways and these were of maximum dimensions 1,000 yds by 50 yds designed to take the load of the heaviest machine in service – the Wellington bomber with an all-up weight of 32,000 lb and tyre pressures of 45 lb/sq in. In 1945 runways at selected bomber airfields were constructed with main runway dimensions of 3,000 yards by 100 yards of high grade concrete 12 in thick and designed to take machines of a total load of 140,000 lb with tyre pressures of 85 lb/sq in.

With the outbreak of war the airfield construction programme continued at full speed although there was a greater emphasis on

'B1' Hangar at Dalton.

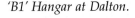

'T2' Hangar at Middleton St George.

design simplification. Even the 'C' type hangar was a victim and on those bomber stations completed in 1939–40 it was built in an austerity version with much of the walls clad in asbestos sheeting; this variant was the 'C1' and was very distinctive with the asbestos roof falling away steeply from the summit of the final gable to doortop level. For a while there was little change in the standard layout of these early wartime airfields and they could only be distinguished by the increasing theme of austerity apparent in their buildings and by the lack of landscaping and other non essential features.

It soon became obvious that even the 'C1' hangars could not be built in sufficient numbers under wartime conditions for the expansion scheme bomber stations still to be completed, so a completely different type of permanent hangar was adopted. This had been designed in 1939 by Sir William Arrol & Co Ltd and was the 'J' type. Similar in size to the 'C' it was steel framed, clad with steel sheeting and had a curved roof which made it look vaguely like the old GS sheds of 1917. Initially groups of 'J' hangars were erected, eg, three at Swinderby but this dwindled to two, eg, Syerston, and finally one, eg, Elsham Wolds. It was very unusual for permanent hangars of different types to be built on an airfield but there was an exception at Middleton St George where a 'C1' and a 'J' were built on the

Wartime menu – Christmas Day 1940. Note the buildings and Hampden bombers.

Hampden bomber at Waddington at the start of the war.

technical site, now part of Teesside Airport and still in good condition over 40 years later. Many of these airfields had some permanent accommodation but the temporary huts were appearing in ever increasing numbers, soon to take over completely in the next generation of bomber field.

In the years immediately before World War II several designs of temporary, or transportable hangar had been put into production and had been erected on a number of airfields, mainly training bases. The most numerous was the 'Bellman' type, steel framed with corrugated iron cladding but this type of hangar was little used on bomber bases. In 1940 the Teesside Bridge & Engineering Works Ltd designed a series of transportable sheds, appropriately called the 'T' series, one of which went into mass production. This was the 'T2' of which several hundred were produced for the airfields of Bomber Command and later the USAAF bomber forces and it was quite similar in appearance to the 'Bellman'. It, too, was steel framed and covered with corrugated iron sheets but it can be distinguished from the 'Bellman' by having a more steeply sloped roof and by having a strip of end wall visible either side of the closed doors; the clear height and width over the doors were 25 ft and 113 ft respectively but the length was governed by the requirement of the individual airfield being a multiple of the bay length of 10 ft 5 ins.

First year of the war – Hampden and Wellington bombers at Swinderby.

How to swamp a Hampden bomber. Note the familiar water tower on the right.

Some of the earliest 'T2's were erected on the last of the airfields to have been provided with permanent hangars of the 'J' type, and these airfields conformed largely to pre-war thinking as far as layout was concerned with hutted accommodation replacing the brick built accommodation. Several airfields were then constructed where all the buildings were temporary but were still grouped together in accordance with pre-war thinking, for example Bovingdon which was constructed during 1941–42 by John Laing & Son Ltd with a row of 'T2's on the eastern edge of the airfield and most of the other buildings clustered nearby.

The beginning of the war introduced very early a demand for large numbers of new airfields. The increasing weight of aircraft and the necessity for all-weather operations without any possibility of airfield unserviceability, together with the impossibility of preparing and seeding grassed surfaces in time, soon turned the airfield problem primarily into the task of constructing hard and adequate all-weather runways. Speed of construction was a paramount consideration. A material had to be utilised which could be supplied by the biggest range of contractors and with plant universally available. Obviously, only concrete could meet the wholesale demand. It was a known and predictable material and could be specified and supervised with precision. Concrete was the usual and almost standard construction for airfield runways in the UK. Other types of surfacing were tarmacadam and asphalt. The ultimate development in asphalt and tarmacadam practice in Air Ministry work arose later in the war as a result of the requirement for surface carpeting of existing runways. Other early ones were tried with grouted concrete. This was a system of grouted stone and gravel in situ with colloidal cement grout. It was found that the system was neither quick nor as satisfactory as the normal concreting processes and after the initial trial on one or two airfields the process was discontinued.

By this time the bomber airfields were being equipped with flying control towers of very utilitarian design and almost all new bomber stations being constructed had three runways. Ideally, the main runway followed the direction of the prevailing wind with the two shorter runways laid at 60-degree angles; all the runways were 50 yds wide and they were linked by a perimeter track which encircled the airfield. There were many variations from this standard, usually necessitated by local geography, both on the wartime airfields and on the prewar bomber airfields to which runways were added in very many cases. From 1942 to 1945 the main type of airfield was constructed to class A standards, the main runway being 2,000 yds by 50 yds with the two subsidiaries being 1,400 yds by 50 yds with 100 yds cleared area at both ends as overshoot. Three emergency runways were constructed, each being 3,000 yds long by 250 yds wide with overshoots at each end of 500 yds long by 40 yds wide.

To give an example of an airfield, Lakenheath was built as a very heavy bomber airfield with three runways 3,000 yds by 100 yds and two 2,000 yds by 100 yds. The construction was 10 in and 12 in high grade concrete on consolidated and stabilised foundation; 50 per cent of surfacing was 12 in concrete. The total area in runways, perimeter tracks and hard standings was 1,035,000 sq yds plus 26,000 in road diversion. The total cost was £2,120,000 and it took 18 months to complete. Peak labour was 1,035 and peak surfacing output per day 1,820 cu yds. In one average bomber airfield some 18,000 tons of cement, 90,000 cu yds of aggregate and 50 miles of drainage pipes and cable conduits were absorbed.

The bomber airfields were built in the Eastern Counties and it became general policy that in the layout of a station the accommodation should be dispersed. The lesson of dispersal had at long last been learnt by the planners, so that the technical buildings were sub-divided to provide a main technical area containing two hangars, usually both 'T2's, and the principal workshop, stores, armouries, etc, and two sub-sites each usually containing one hangar and minor ancillary buildings. Each group was sited between the ends of runways and relative to the dispersed aircraft it served. On many of the stations constructed for Bomber Command the additional hangar was a 'B1'. This was a design also used by the Ministry of Aircraft Production and was another example of wartime corrugated iron architecture but it had a much more steeply pitched roof which gave a greater clear height within the hangar which was particularly useful for heavy repairs, engine changes, etc, where the services of a crane were needed. On the typical bomber airfield dating from 1942 onwards the bombers

Handley Page Hampdens in flight – the early raids.

spent almost all of their grounded life on concrete hardstandings which were dispersed around the perimeter track and only went under shelter when they required major repair or overhaul.

Scattered around the airfield were a number of domestic sites which provided living and messing facilities. The domestic accommodation was normally sited relative to the main technical area in groups housing either 250 personnel of all ranks or 400 personnel in certain less vulnerable areas as defined. A distance of 200 yds was maintained from the technical area and sites were separated one from the other by distances of approximately 200 yds. Within this scheme of siting either one, or in the case of later, larger stations, two communal sites containing the dining room, institute, sergeants' and officers' messes and bath houses were provided. The total number of sites, related to airfields under this policy, depended of course on the number of persons to be accommodated, but it was normal for 20 separate areas of land to be involved.

A Handley Page Hampden taking off.

Hampden and four-man crew. 10 October 1941, Syerston.

Requirements for the accommodation of WAAF on stations necessitated additional dispersed sites both for sleeping and communal buildings within the principles stated above, but it later became policy for RAF and WAAF to share the same dining room, institutes and messes and the WAAF communal site was then omitted.

The layout of building within each individual site was intentionally without symmetry or pattern as an aid to concealment and, so far as possible, sites were selected so that huts and buildings could be located to follow the lines of hedges or the perimeters of woods. This scheme of layout and siting, whilst inconvenient to personnel and difficult in station administration, was most effective in its purpose of providing substantial concealment from aerial observation.

The main hutting in general use and types known as temporary brick, 'X', 'Y', 'Z' and Lain were developed. Nissen hutting was used substantially for the larger communal and technical buildings as an alternative to brick construction. Briefly the Nissen consisted of light, approximately semi-circular steel ribs at 6 ft $0\frac{1}{2}$ in centres

Hampden Mk I, AE196 of 408 Squadron RCAF at Syerston, being made ready for ops.

covered externally with corrugated steel sheeting and lined internally with one of the types of wall boarding. Floors were concrete. Spans of 16 ft, 24 ft and 30 ft were available and whilst the former was standard provision for sleeping huts and quarters, it was possible by a combination of the three spans to plan buildings of practically any shape and purpose, either by locally-constructed connecting links or the provision of flat roofs over direct junctions. Ends of huts of these spans were constructed of brickwork or alternative material on site.

Huts on similar principles to Nissen were produced in asbestos,

83 Squadron Scampton – early days. Back safely from a big raid to be greeted by comrades who reached home a little ahead of them.

namely Turner's Everite and the Handcraft huts. Other types used were the Orlit Huts, which consisted of a concrete pier, beam and infilling construction. A few BCF Standard and Hall huts were also to be found on a few airfields. The main others were Ministry of Supply and Maycrete huts, having Maycrete walls and sectional timber and felted roofs; also Seco hutting. This form of construction was used extensively for the more complicated types of buildings from 1943. Marston Shedding, Romney huts and Iris huts were used to a limited extent from 1943.

Also around the perimeter, preferably as far away from the living sites as possible, were to be found the bomb dump where the assorted ordnance was stored, the petrol storage tanks (the usual provision for an operational bomber station was two 72,000 gallon installations), and the sewage works. Also situated where it was as harmless as possible was the range where the turret guns could be test fired into a large mound of sand, a brick-backing wall often

A squadron of Whitley heavy bombers being refuelled and bombed up in readiness for another attack on enemy targets.

bearing scars indicating the rounds that nearly got away! Dominating these wartime bomber airfields were the water towers, rectangular steel tanks perched up on steel legs, which provided headaches to those responsible for attempting to camouflage the airfields. At the end of 1939 the daily consumption of water from all sources was some $4\frac{1}{2}$ million gallons. By the end of the war period these quantities had increased to nearly 40 million gallons from all sources.

Several types of flying control tower had been introduced as the war progressed, most of them box-like structures with their rendered brickwork camouflaged with drab paint, each successive design being more utilitarian and austere than its predecessor. Each bomber station had a control tower, often situated near the perimeter track near to the technical site, and later in the war there were many local modifications to improve the view of the air traffic controllers by adding 'greenhouses' on the roof; sometimes even these were inadequate and it was not unknown for a second tower

A Wellington of No. 311 Squadron at East Wretham, Norfolk, beats up the airfield.

A Wellington of No. 149 Squadron, Mildenhall, gets airborne.

to be built superseding one that could not provide a suitable view of the airfield and its surrounding airspace. Near the tower were usually to be found several huts which served as accommodation for the duty crews and as garages for the crash tender and ambulance, and in front of the tower was the signals square in which could be displayed indication of the direction of landing or any restrictions temporarily in force at the airfield.

When the airfields were open to flying, a controller's caravan was usually located at the end of the duty runway, many of the airfields having a small loop of concrete laid adjacent to the ends of the runways for this purpose. By the final war years, most of the bomber bases in the United Kingdom were equipped with electric approach and runway lighting, a far cry from the flickering gooseneck flares that had been used to illuminate a landing path only a few years previously.

The manpower (should it be personpower in modern jargon to acknowledge the part played by the WAAF?) necessary to enable a bomber airfield to operate was enormous, somewhere in the region of 2,000 officers and other ranks on an average RAF station and up to around 3,000 officers and enlisted men on a base occupied by the US Army Air Forces.

Every station had a motor transport section responsible for a large fleet of motor vehicles of a very wide variety of types, from

Crews of 149 Squadron, Mildenhall, prepare for a raid.

A Wellington of 149 Squadron, Mildenhall, takes off during the early raids in 1941.

light pick-up trucks to massive aviation fuel tankers. Perhaps the most important form of transport, though, was the humble pushbike: essential for commuting between the domestic site and the other widely dispersed parts of the airfield and also very useful for getting to the local on the odd evening off duty! Driving or riding a bike at night on the roads around the camp was an interesting experience due to the black-out enforced throughout the country during the war, and particularly near airfields where there might be German intruders flying around ready to bomb or shoot-up anything that attracted their attention. All vehicle lights were masked to give the merest glimmer of light and the situation was not helped by the presence of vehicles driven by allied personnel who occasionally forgot our strange custom of driving on the left hand side of the road; fortunately the volume of traffic was minimal by present day standards.

Although the airfields built prior to the outbreak of war in 1939 had all the buildings grouped close together there must have been

A picture taken immediately after the Wellington bombers had returned from operations over Berlin.

Preparing a Stirling bomber for a mission.

an awareness of the targets offered to enemy bombers because 'scatter' airfields were designated, to which our aircraft could fly when war became imminent, thus making our bomber force less vulnerable to a surprise attack. Several squadrons did make use of these scatter fields for a short period but soon returned to their operational bases when the attacks did not occur. On their bases they were dispersed around the edges of the airfields, the Blenheims and Wellingtons being mainly on the East Anglian bases, the Whitleys in Yorkshire and the Hampdens in Lincolnshire, these operational squadrons being supported by the second-line squadrons in 6 Group. The early raids by home-based squadrons were carried out by these types of aircraft, those squadrons equipped with the single-engined Fairey Battle light bomber mostly being in France with the Advanced Air Striking Force. After the fall of France in 1940 the Battle was rarely used on operations but a new twin-engined bomber began to appear on the airfields – the Avro Manchester which started operating on the night of 24 February 1941 when 207 Squadron attacked a German warship at Brest. Three types of four engined heavy bombers were then brought into service, the Short Stirling (which actually preceded the Manchester onto operations by a fortnight), the Handley Page Halifax and the Avro Lancaster, the latter being virtually a four-engined improved version of the highly unpopular Manchester which it replaced. Various light bombers were used in small numbers to supplement these heavies but they were completely overshadowed by the Mosquito when bomber versions of that marvellous aircraft became available.

Stirling W7440 MG-W of No. 7 Squadron prepares for take-off. This was the first squadron to be equipped with these big four-engined 'heavies'.

The introduction of the heavy bombers was responsible for changes to the airfields. Grass surfaces which had been barely adequate for the Hampdens and Wellingtons were found to be totally unsuited for the much heavier machines and standards were laid down regarding the runways lengths, clearances, etc, necessary to operate these aircraft. The wind of change even hit the motor transport fleets, for example the new aircraft required such large quantities of fuel that the old tractor-hauled bowsers were inadequate and had to be replaced by large tankers.

When the European war ended in 1945 preparations went ahead to build up a bomber force to attack the Japanese islands but with the sudden end of hostilities in the Far East the familiar pattern of 1919 was repeated. The RAF was decimated as it contracted to a peacetime establishment and most of its airfields closed. Naturally the pre-war stations with their permanent buildings were retained in preference to the utilitarian wartime fields and gradually Bomber Command re-emerged as a peacetime force, initially with Lancasters and Mosquitoes from wartime stocks and then through new types until the V-bomber trio was brought into service, the Valiant, Victor and Vulcan. The former was withdrawn from service prematurely

Ground crew manhandling a Stirling bomber. Height of the Stirling is over 22 ft and its wing span under 100 ft.

with structural problems, the Victor was transformed into a tanker and the Vulcan survived until 1982 when it was scheduled to be withdrawn. However, when much of the Vulcan force had been disbanded, the Argentine invasion of the Falklands caused several of the surviving Vulcans to fly from Waddington *en route* for Ascension Island and the Falklands.

The ill-fated Avro Manchester.

Bombing up an Avro Manchester.

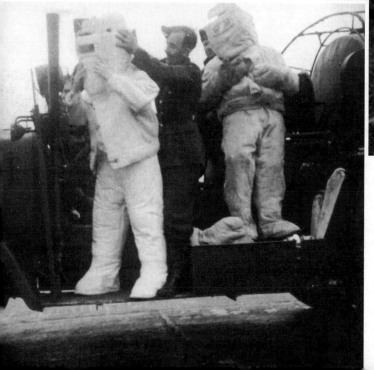

RAF firefighters.

The new four-engined 'heavies'. The aircraft, the men and the women needed to keep the RAF in the air. Front row, left to right – Flying Control Officer, WAAF parachute packer, Meteorological Officer. Air Crew: pilot and captain of aircraft, navigator and observer, air bomber, flight engineer, wireless operator/airgunner, 2 air gunners. Second row, left to right – NCO fitter, mechanic, NCO fitter. Flight Maintenance: 5 mechanics, electrical mechanic, instrument repairer, 2 radio mechanics. Third row, Bomb train, WAAF tractor driver and bombing up crew. Fourth row, left to right: Corporal mechanic, 4 aircraft mechanics, engineer officer, fitter armourer, 3 armourers, radio mechanic, 2 instrument repairers, 3 bomb handlers, machine-gunbelt fitter. Back row, Petrol bowser and crew, Avro Lancaster, mobile workshop and crew.

WAAFs on parade at Snaith.

The important side of any bomber airfield – the accounts section – Hemswell, summer 1944.

Three photographs showing maintenance being carried out on Lancasters in dispersal.

A mid-upper gunner does a pull-through of his machine-gun in a Canadian Lancaster bomber while his mascot 'Flak' looks on.

Riggers sitting on the nose of Halifax X-Terminator, *420 Squadron.*

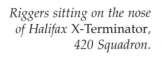

A ground crewman tries out the driving seat.

*Aircrews being briefed
prior to a raid.*

*The CO at briefing,
Snaith 1944.*

*The empty briefing
room. The tell-tale red
ribbon points to the
target on the wall map.*

*The crews get a helping
hand to put on their
cumbersome flying gear.*

With an aerial photograph before them, a crew go over the details of a raid with an intellligence officer.

A bowser and Lancaster.

A Lancaster getting bombed up ready for ops.

A Lancaster tanks-up.

Getting ready for ops.

The sting in the tail. The rear gunner of a Lancaster. The centre perspex panel has been removed for better vision.

The two gunners check over the ammunition.

Tea and wads – crew of 35 Squadron before night flying test. Linton-on-Ouse, 1942.

Aircrew ready for a raid, Holme-on-Spalding Moor.

A crew walks a little to help unwind before the mission ahead.

Aircraft LL939 – Skipper McKellar and crew about to board.

Preparing for a raid – Halifax bomber crew studying their map before taking part in an operational flight.

Crew of Easy Does It NN754 *pose before take-off Left to right: Flying Officer Timms (bomb-aimer); Flying Officer Graham (pilot); Sergeant ? (wireless operator); Sergeant Squires (flight engineer); Sergeant Dubois (midupper gunner); Flying Officer Valentine (navigator); Sergeant Giesel (rear gunner).*

No. 50 Squadron Swinderby – Lancaster crew joke before boarding.

Lancasters prepare to take off from Waddington on a daylight raid.

As darkness begins to fall, a familiar scene at all bomber stations just before the start of a raid. Here we see a Halifax at Tholthorpe about to take off.

The usual night scene at a bomber station. ED724 'M' Mother of No. 103 Squadron, Elsham Wolds, prepares for take-off, March 1943.

A bomber leaving for ops.

A Handley Page Halifax of 420 RCAF Squadron about to take off from Tholthorpe, Yorkshire. Note the mobile control and vehicles.

Flight-Lieutenant Raw-Rees and two WAAFs wave off the crews at Waddington.

Flight of a Halifax from No. 35 Squadron high above the clouds.

Lancaster JO-X of No 463 (RAAF) Squadron returns home to Waddington, 1944.

A bomber over the target area.

35 Squadron, Linton-on-Ouse, 1941. Return from ops.

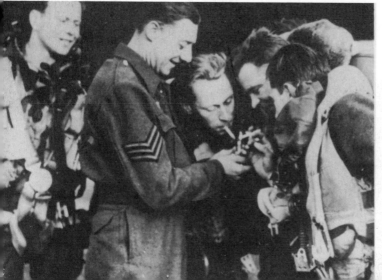

That welcome cigarette. The Sergeant has a light ready for the returning aircrews.

Middleton St George in January 1945. Ruhr Express *caught fire and was gutted after its 50th sortie.*

A mug of tea at the YMCA van for returning aircrews.

A bomber airfield in winter. Lancasters of 463 Squadron, snowed in at Waddington, January 1944.

The bomb-aimer of a Lancaster about to press the bomb-tit.

Returning crews awaiting interrogation.

Two of the crew of an aircraft examining a large piece of flak found in their aircraft after its return from ops over enemy occupied territory.

No. 103 Squadron at Elsham Wolds. Note one crew member with .38 revolver.

Lancaster crew pose for a photograph. Note the bomb-aimer in the nose.

LV937 'E'-Expensive Babe *after its 100th sortie – 7 December 1944 at
Snaith. From left: Flight-Lieutenant R. Kemp, Flight Sergeant A.
Townsend, Flight Sergeant J. Silberberg, wireless operator R. Williams,
Sergeant E, Hawkins, Flight Sergeant R. Jackson, Flight Sergeant F.
Thwaites.*

*Typical nose art
from one of many
bombers. The female
figure was about
the most popular,
the Daily Mirror's
'Jane' amongst
them. However,
Disney characters
were very firm
favourites such as
Mickey Mouse and
Pluto.*

Another sortie.

A bomber on dispersal.

A famous face – Cheshire (centre front) and crew.

Senior RAAF officers at RAF Waddington being presented to the Duke of Gloucester by the Station Commander, Group Captain Bonham-Carter. The Duke paid a visit to the Australian squadrons before he took up his appointment as Governor General in Australia in 1944.

Waddington, Lincolnshire, June 1944. Inspecting Lancaster 'S' Sugar after completing 100th bombing mission. Left to right: AVM Wrigley (RAAF), Group Captain Bonham-Carter, Station Commander, Duke of Gloucester, Wing Commander Brill, CO No. 467 Squadron (RAAF).

Winter scene at Waddington.

The station celebrates as the 100th bomb is painted on Lancaster B1 R5868 PO-S Sugar of 467 Squadron at Waddington. She went on to complete 137 sorties before retirement. For a time 'S' Sugar stood at the gates of RAF Scampton. She has now been removed to the RAF Museum.

Wing Commander R. Kingsford-Smith DSO, DFC, with members of his Lancaster crew of 463 Squadron at Waddington, June 1944. Flight Lieutenant Raw-Rees on right.

Crew of 'C' Charlie, No. 576 Squadron, Fiskerton. Left to right: Flight Sergeant Verhay, wireless operator; Flight Sergeant Andrews, navigator; Sergeant Wishart, bomb aimer; Flight-Lieutenant Campbell, pilot (Canadian); Sergeant Andrews, flight engineer; Sergeant Dicks, mid-upper gunner (Canadian); Flight Sergeant Scribner, rear gunner (Canadian). Four ground crew kneeling. After their last mission of the war to Berchtesgaden, 25 April 1945.

Skipton-on-Swale, May 1945 Victory Parade – a gaggle of WAAFs.

Award for crews who hit the target.

The end is near – salute of VE parade at skipton-on-Swale, May 1945.

Operational record of QR-N ED860.

CHAPTER TWO

The Bombs

Bombs assumed military importance with the rapid development of aircraft in World War I when they reached a size of 660 lb. At the outbreak of World War II, bombs normally ranged in weight from 500 to 1,000 lb. The standard 250 lb general purpose bomb was a ridiculous missile but during the early strategic bombing of German industries it was recommended that it was considered suitable for oil and fuel plants – to be followed by incendiaries. The 40 lb general purpose bombs could also be used for these targets and for billets used by troops, again, followed by incendiaries. Incendiary mixtures include white phosphorus, compounds of aluminium and iron oxide (thermite), aluminium and magnesium, aluminium soaps and a petroleum fraction (napalm), and others. Incendiary bombs were used in World War I and in vast quantity in World War II in the Allied bombing of Germany. By 1941 the Royal Air Force had the 4,000 lb high capacity blast bomb (nicknamed the 'cookie') and an ingenious device enabled it to be aimed without the huge tail that one normally associates with bombs.

Bombs of many shapes and sizes, ranging from 40 pounder to the 22,000 pounder.

Bombing up a Whitley of No. 58 Squadron at Linton-on-Ouse in 1940.

The early daylight raids proved that the Wellington bombers were easy to intercept and when hit were particularly susceptible to fire when their fuel tanks ruptured. This weakness led to the adoption of self-sealing fuel tanks and with the heavy bomber losses caused RAF Bomber Command to operate mainly at night for the duration of the war.

With the development of radio and radar navigation aids, culminating in such equipment as the H_2S radar, carried entirely on board the bombers, which could produce map-like pictures of the terrain beneath the aircraft through clouds and in all weather. With the new equipment came a new generation of four-engined bombers – the Stirling, Halifax and Lancaster – and ever larger bombs. The Lancaster was designed to carry bombs of up to 4,000 lb; it was adapted progressively to accommodate bombs weighing 8,000, 12,000 and finally 22,000 lb, the largest bombs dropped in World War II. The 22,000 and 12,000 lb medium capacity bombs were designed by Barnes Wallis. The 22,000 Grand Slam was

Bombs being loaded from the bomb dump.

Bomb load needed for 20 Lancasters.

first used operationally during an attack which wrecked the Bielefeld Viaduct on 14 March 1945.

By the spring of 1943 many bombers were equipped with the Mark XIV bomb sight and it gave the pilot more flexibility, for the bombs could be accurately aimed while the aircraft was climbing or making a correct bank turn. It was also better for the bomb-aimer who had to make fewer settings during flight.

On 22/23 April 1944 the 'J' bomb (30 lb liquid-filled incendiary) was first used operationally by Bomber Command during an attack on Brunswick. The incendiary cluster bombs caused a tight ring of fires immediately after impact. Brunswick was selected for this type of attack as a large proportion of its buildings were of timbered or half-timbered style and great damage was done in relation to the weight of attack. For this raid a force of 265 was dispatched with 741 tons of bombs, the bulk of which was incendiary cluster bombs.

In 1945, an enormous increase in explosive power was effected by development of the atomic bomb and in the 1960s and 1970s bombs were developed that could be released from the aircraft and guided to the target.

Ground staff loading parachute bombs into a Hampden aircraft.

Hampden P1333 being loaded with bombs ready for a raid.

Ground staff preparing a train of 1,000 lb bombs for loading up an Avro Lancaster which crouches in the background like a great bird.

Loading a Stirling bomber.

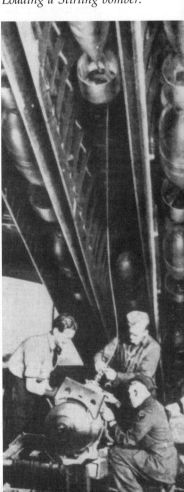

4,000 pounder being loaded into a Lancaster.

Top Loading a bomb into a Wellington bomber.

Bottom One of Bomber Command's Lancaster II aircraft being loaded for a raid.

A Halifax of No 6 Group (RCAF) being loaded for a raid.

4,000 lb bombs (cookies) waiting to be loaded on to Lancaster bombers.

Air Commodore A. Hesketh looking on as Lancaster B1, R5868 PO-S Sugar of No 467 (RAAF) Squadron is loaded with an 8,000 lb bomb. This was Sugar's 100th sortie and it was piloted by Pilot Officer T.N. Scholefield, RAAF, to Bourg Leopold on the night of 11/12 May 1944.

Bombing up No. 467 Squadron's veteran Lancaster B1 R5868 PO-S Sugar at Waddington on the eve of its 99th sortie.

A bomb-aimer peering out of his perch.

Inside the bomb-bay of 'S' Sugar after the bombs have been loaded. This was a typical tactical target load of one 4,000 pounder and 500 pounders. These were destined for a marshalling yard in France.

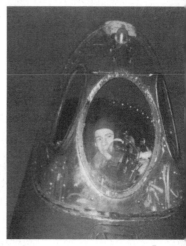

A Lancaster of No 467 Squadron with a typical bomb load – 4,000 lb 'cookie', three 1,000 pounders, 24 250 pounders and six incendiary canisters.

'Tallboy' being winched up – October 1944.

Two members of the crew of a Halifax discuss the load in the bay of their aircraft.

The first of the new 12,000 lb bombs which were being dropped on military targets in Germany and enemy occupied countries. An idea of its tremendous size is obtained by comparing it with the 500 lb and 1,000 lb bombs lying alongside.

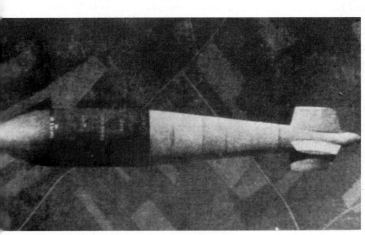

12, 000 lb of destruction on its way. This bomb, familiarly known as the 'Tallboy', was the first completely streamlined bomb used during the war and was the forerunner of the 22, 000 lb Grand Slam.

RAAF crew at Woodhall Spa pose in front of the 'Grand Slam' bomb slung beneath the Lancaster. This massive bomb is 35 ft 5 in long, with a diameter of 3 ft 10 in and is of the streamlined deep penetration type, being a scaled up version of the 6 tonner with a tail unit approximately 13 ft 6 in long. Its primary role was against underground structures and precision targets requiring deep penetration with maximum destruction and it was first used against the railway viaduct at Bielefeld on 14 March 1945.

CHAPTER THREE

Bomber Command War Theme

The Battle of the Ruhr

We were the devils of the night,
Our purpose – true – hell bent,
With fire and bombs we roared aloft,
Death to Ruhr our one intent,
    Winged chariots of death.

The game was up – all seasoned
    crews,
My God – we couldn't miss,
On a night like this,
Master bombers six,
    Winged chariots of death.

Dark night sky rent with Merlin roar,
The main force morons roll,
Brakes off! Full power!
We're on our way
    Winged chariots of death.

So climb, climb, climb, ye demons
    bright,
A thousand score,
That's the safety height
On deadly tack, there's no turning
    back,
Fight for the right every child might
    (ask)
    Winged chariots of death.

Doomed Rhineland cities each in
    turn
Smashed 'til their arteries severed,
Nothing was spared
All bone bared,
Newspaper headlines – who the hell
    cared!
    Winged chariots of death.

It's a point of aim!
We've done it again
My God – how the Hun must
    quiver!
Are there children down there?
None do we spare.
Laughter in hell, who the hell cared!
    Winged chariots of death.

Who can forgive them? Who can
    forget?
What fiendish monster's bidding,
There's a ransom to pay for this evil
    day
When it's all over – we'll never say
    Wild emissaries of death.

Written by Berny Kennedy, bomb-aimer, Lancaster 'V' Victor, 12 Squadron.
He was thinking of the emasculation of Hamburg when he wrote this poem
in August 1943.

Part Two

CHAPTER FOUR

Ops in a Wimpy

D uring the early days of the war the Vickers-Armstrong's Wellington was one of the main aircraft and was originally classed as a heavy bomber but, with the advent of four-engined aircraft (the Stirling was the first, followed by the Halifax and Lancaster), it became a medium bomber. With the coming of the four-engined bombers the Wellington was phased out of Bomber Command making their last bombing raid from England on 8 October 1943.

To start with the Wellington carried a crew of six: two pilots, navigator, wireless operator, bomb-aimer/front gunner and rear gunner. The navigator and second pilot were also trained to take over the gun turrets in an emergency. The pilot had a restricted field of vision and was very dependent on the way in which his crew carried out their respective duties. Leadership was as great a factor as mere flying ability. The pilot as captain of the aircraft was responsible for the safety of a valuable aircraft and the lives of his crew. This sense of unity knit together the tail gunner sitting isolated at the end of the long fuselage, the navigator in his screened cubicle poring over his maps, the wireless operator eternally

Wellington 'S' Sugar of No. 12 Squadron on dispersal at RAF Binbrook. This aircraft was used by Sergeant Richard Whiting and crew.

listening for instructions from base or by radio-loop bearings aiding the navigator, and the front gunner straining his eyes at the night sky ahead, above and below for the first sign of danger. Thus, although it was the pilot alone who had to make all the decisions, it was done on the information furnished by his crew. Often, indifferent pilots backed by efficient crews came safely through the worst dangers, while excellent pilots with inexperienced or unsettled crews failed to return from operational sorties during which far less opposition was experienced.

The Wellington remained front line equipment throughout World War II. At the outbreak of war, six squadrons of Bomber Command were fully equipped and operational with Wellington Mk Is. By May 1941, there were 21 Wellington Squadrons in Bomber Command. One squadron equipped with Wellingtons was No. 12 at Binbrook.

Sergeant Richard Whiting was a bomb-aimer/front gunner of a Wellington crew of No. 12 Squadron. The following is an account of his experiences. Sergeant Whiting mentions the dropping of 'leaves'. This was known as 'Razzle' and consisted of a celluloid folder about 6 in square, containing a piece of phosphorus embedded in damp cotton wool. The idea was that when dried out the phosphorus would smoulder, the celluloid burst into flames and hopefully set the wood on fire. They were dropped over the Black Forest area.

'The awareness of being up there sometimes overwhelmed you, not with fright, but with a sense of wonderment and amazement and it wasn't until it was all over you realised that the flak, etc, was real. It takes a lot of explaining and a lot of understanding. Still, my effort was only a small contribution to the war effort.

'I have heard many tales about different aircraft but my choice of them all was the Wellington or "Wimpy" as we called her. She was the apple of my heart. I've flown in "Wimpies" with Bristol Pegasus engines, Rolls-Royce Merlin engines, and American Pratt & Whitney Twin Wasp engines. No. 12 Squadron was equipped with Merlin – in line, Glycol-cooled engines which, apart from their vulnerability to the cooling system being punctured, were the best most of the time, and flame traps were fitted over the exhausts to stop the flames being seen at night. Pegasus engines were the safest being radial and air-cooled, but Wasp engines were the fastest and most powerful.

'The cold was a problem. Although the gunners were issued with electrically heated clothing, you had to keep switching it on and off. In 1941/42 it didn't seem consistent at one temperature. It wasn't always the cold but their size which was the big drawback of a lot of gunners, myself included. I was around 5 ft 11 ins and when seated in the turret my knees were tight against the metal which, being the most forward part of the kite, on occasions got really cold. This transmitted into the knee joints and after six or seven hours in the same position you can imagine what it was like when I got out of the turret. I used to crawl back to the bed and there was a heating tube with which I "defrosted" my knees.

'Icing up of the aircraft was definitely a menace more than a problem. Take, for instance, a trip we did to Berlin. I think the entire force came to around 90 aircraft. Of these only 45 to 50 returned and this was due to the abnormal icing conditions which were more or less all the way to the target. The cloud top was around 19,000 to 20,000 ft and the Stirlings, Wellington (Pegasus engines) and some others were unable to reach this height with a bomb load. Luckily, we managed to stagger up to 20-21,000 ft but the whole operation was a dead loss. The heavy flak was just bursting above the cloud top and that was the only guide to the target. So it was more or less blind bombing. The cloud was around 15,000 ft thick so there was no chance of sighting any landmark.

'From 1940 to 1942 Binbrook was the home of No. 12 squadron and during this period operated from grass runways. To me the life at Binbrook was the happiest I spent in the Royal Air Force. Although many lived on the camp, many others were billeted in manors, halls and other places in the vicinity of the camp. Discipline wasn't in any way strict, but I can say the effort was 100 per cent. There was a great camaraderie between officers, NCOs and men, a camaraderie which unfortunately seemed to deteriorate later on, when I was posted down to No. 3 Group, where the relationship between the locals and the Royal Air Force wasn't the same as in and around Grimsby and Cleethorpes. There were also the effects of "Butch" Harris's reorganisation of Bomber Command, and aircrews. One of these was that of reducing the number of men in aircraft. The Wellington was then manned by a pilot, navigator, wireless operator, bomb-aimer (front gunner), and rear gunner. This meant the second pilot was omitted and the front gunner was the bomb-aimer instead of second wireless operator. In my opinion this was a mistake because at the most vulnerable time from attack by night fighters over the target, the front of the aircraft was unprotected due to the bomb-aimer coming out of the turret to drop the bombs.

'I had many disturbing moments in my capacity as front gunner. On take-off my position was in the rear of the kite mostly looking through the astrodome and not until airborne did I enter the front turret. On entering the turret, the doors were closed and the bulkhead door locked from the inside of the plane and it was entirely impossible to open the bulkhead door from inside the turret, so once you were in, you were completely in the hands of someone inside the kite to release you, due to the air pressure which was caused by the speed you were travelling. And in a "bale out" you *had* to get back to the front entrance or escape hatch to hop out, otherwise the props would make mincemeat of you. So you can imagine the front gunner's predicament during an emergency. Anyhow, on the night of 5 August 1941, my second op in 12 Squadron, we were detailed to bomb Aachen in the Ruhr district. I was still nervous and a little scared to say the least. I was still pretty green at the game. Anyhow we were soon to see the intense flak barrage that protected the Ruhr. During the flight there we passed through a lot of cloud and an electric storm, with thousands of miniature flashes and sparks playing all around the metal and guns. To say it was cold was putting it mildly although I had my heated suit switched on. We found the target and bombed it with the usual jinking, etc, and turned for home, but scarcely five minutes after we had left Aachen, I spotted a fighter coming down from 12 o'clock high. I gave the alarm over the intercom and Pete started evasive action, but balls of fire were whipping past us. To me they seemed like dustbins and I didn't realise until afterwards that they were tracer cannon shells. I had him in my sight and waited until he was in range. I pressed the triggers – nothing happened. God, what was wrong? I whipped the "toggle" out to cock the guns again and found the cocking pin was only half-cocked. After cocking I pressed the triggers again. The guns fired once and stopped. I whipped my gloves off and lifted the loading latch, all the time waiting and watching out the corner of my eye for the fighter returning. The belt fell away from the gun so I had to reload it. I noticed during this operation the amount of ice on the breech block. My damned guns had iced up. Meanwhile Pete had managed to get amongst the clouds for a little cover. I slammed the loading latch down and started cocking and firing to get the breech warmed up and what a lovely sound when they fired normally. But I'd forgotten about my hands, and only realised how cold and numb they were when I tried to put the "toggle" away in its pouch. It was sheer hell getting them back into my gloves. I had just done so when we emerged from the clouds and there sitting above us was another fighter. He swept down to attack us on the port side but after one attack and a reply from front and rear guns he gave up. We had another half-hearted attack later on from another fighter but he too gave up. By now, I could feel my hands again and I was in some pain with them, especially on the joints of the fingers, so I switched the heating off. We set off for home, but being short of fuel we made an emergency landing at Wattisham and whilst taxiing to the dispersal area the engines cut. No fuel! That was when I realised that, apart from experience, you needed a hell of a lot of luck in the bombing game. On taking my gloves off I found the skin had stuck to the inside of the gloves, particularly the part of the joints and knuckles that were tight to the heating inside the gloves when I manipulated the turret controls. After having a session each day in front of the sun lamp for a fortnight my hands were back to normal. Even so, during that time it didn't stop me from visiting the Ruhr a couple more times. It's funny, the first half dozen or so operations you felt nervous and frightened but after that until the last half dozen of the first tour you became a little contemptuous, and the last few before you got "screened" (rested) were complete hell, wondering whether you'd make it. So the middle sorties could really have been the worst, but owing to your state of mind you were liable to take them in your stride.

'Fighters started being a problem early in 1942 but the intense flak barrages were certainly a deterrent. A box barrage was a frightening experience. We encountered one at Hanover. When you see a wall of red-hot steel on four sides closing on you, there's only one way to go. Put the nose down and pray. You may not believe this but, when Pete put the nose down at Hanover, the wings actually flapped. How the devil they kept on I'll never know. It was estimated we were moving in excess of 400 mph. You know, somebody up there certainly liked us. Once we were down low enough we straightened out and off like the devil with the searchlights and flak coned above us. But you were never safe until you got inside your bed.

'On 19 September 1941 we were called to the briefing room at Binbrook and told we were going to strike a blow for the Russians. We were to attack Stettin on the Baltic Sea. Our Wellington was bombed up but owing to the long distance we had to fly down to Mildenhall and take on 750 gallons of fuel (the maximum) and then fly from there direct to the target. We set off from Mildenhall at 22:55 in 'S' *Sugar* and crossed the North Sea over Denmark, veering south and coming over Stettin from the south. The visibility was clear with no cloud and no moon. When we arrived over the target, there was no enemy action – no ack-ack and no searchlights. The

Binbrook, 1941 – rear of Wellington W5574 of No. 12 Squadron. Left, Sergeant Freddie Lockwood, rear gunner and right, Sergeant Richard Whiting, front gunner. With new crew, W5574 ditched in May 1942.

navigator gave his instructions to the pilot, Pilot Officer Pete Oleinek, straight and level at 10,000 ft. We made our run and Flight Sergeant Bruce Croxton dropped the bombs dead on the docks. Still no ack-ack or searchlights. We made another run to take photographs and were just thanking our lucky stars for such an easy target when, as if at the flick of a switch, all hell let loose. Searchlights that must have been waiting patiently picked us up and ack-ack fire was all around. We waited for the impact of a bursting shell. It certainly came, blowing a hole 3 ft in diameter on the port side just behind the wing. The skipper continued violent evasive action whilst I, in the front turret, began to think this was it. I didn't know how much we were damaged but knew by the bank and the violent shudder of the kite that it was bad. Pete, the pilot, put the nose down and dived towards the ground. I heard him shout over the intercom "Get Dickie out of the front turret, Bruce, I don't know how much damage we've got". He was throwing the kite around something terrific whilst we were descending at a terrible rate. Next thing I heard Bruce reply "I can't move, Pete, with the evasive action!" Well, in my mind came the answer. This was the end. Bruce, the navigator, couldn't move for the force of "G" and I couldn't bale out, I would have gone straight into the props if I had. I saw the ground coming up towards us, then suddenly Pete pulled the nose up hardly 50 ft from the top of a tree. All this time small arms fire (tracers, etc) was whistling around and through the kite. How no one was hit was a miracle. Pete warned the gunners (front and rear) to hold our fire. The tracers would give away our position. We were now so low I could see streets and huts lit up by subdued lighting. But not until I saw the sea below us did I breathe a little easier and when we had passed the danger of offshore flak ships, the second pilot, Sergeant Junior Eliot, and Bruce checked the damage and the amount of petrol left. The damage was bad, Junior reported, the fuel was down to 250 gallons, and way over the sea to the right we could see the lights from Sweden. It had taken 500 gallons of fuel to get so far and we had the full distance to get back on 250 gallons or cross the Baltic and bale out over Sweden. Pete said we had an outside chance of getting back and we all agreed to take the chance. The plan was for me to come out of the turret and jettison all unnecessary articles to lighten the kite and Pete to fly low, so as not to wast fuel climbing. The rear gunner, Sergeant Freddie Lockwood, was to keep an extra keen lookout, the wireless operator, Sergeant Len Barham, was to keep ready to send out a distress signal if we hit any snags we hadn't noticed. With a will I started throwing belts of ammunition down the flare chute earthwards. Anything that moved was thrown out. Then I broke the oxygen bottles from the racks and threw them down the chute. Only one thing was left – the Elsan toilet which was a part and parcel of the Wellington. I got the axe and cut it away from its base. Junior opened the escape hatch and standing forward of the hatch I threw it out. Before Junior could close the hatch, the contents had come out of the container and caught in the back draught, whipped back into the kite, and I was in the way and covered from head to foot with Uno Wot. From then it was all laugh and jokes as I tried to rid myself of the smell of disinfectant-plus. We finally passed over the coastline and were soon going in to land at Mildenhall but not before Pete warned we weren't down yet. The bullets or shrapnel might have punctured a tyre. And he was right. We touched down on the runway and after about 50 yds spun over on to the grass. We spun round a couple of times and stopped, tilting over due to a flat tyre. But that didn't count, we were safe and down after $8\frac{1}{2}$ hours. After briefing we had a couple of hours' sleep on the floor of the sergeants' mess. A new wheel was put on the kite and we flew back to Binbrook where 85 holes were counted in poor old 'S' Sugar, plus the big hole in her side. For his part Pete Oleinek was awarded the Distinguished Flying Cross and may I add that the Elsan toilet was well used by the maintenance crew on dispersal area where facilities were at a minimum.

'The first 4,000 lb bomb from Binbrook and, I suppose, the beginning of the "cookies" took place on the night of 17 January

1942. There had been other attempts to drop these "Biguns" but there'd been snags and no photographs. The primary target was Hamburg, but if it was 10/10ths cloud, we had to move over to the Ruhr and find a target clear enough to drop the bomb on *and* take photographs. Failing this, the last resource was to drop it on Emden. The aircraft was Wellington *Z8709* and the floor inside the aircraft had been removed, that is at the rear of the wireless operators' and navigators' cabins or seats where the bed was. When hung up, the bomb protruded into the fuselage some 18 in and maybe 5 ft long, so that the modified bomb doors could close and therefore not impair the aerodynamics. During the briefing we were told the target, etc, and the news that only six aircraft would be out that night including ours and each carrying a 4,000 lb bomb. Stress was put on taking photographs for confirmation of its success and also, which I thought was a very demoralising piece of information, the shell of the bomb was extremely thin and could be penetrated by a minute piece of shrapnel. The aircraft was dispersed on the tarmac outside the hangars and I think everybody at Binbrook turned out to see us off. On take-off, usually, I stood looking out of the astrodome but this time I sat on the end of the bomb. If that went off I doubt whether it mattered whereabouts in the aircraft you were. On being airborne I entered the front turret and was locked away for the night. Hamburg, when we reached it, was 10/10ths cloud and so was the Ruhr but for 50 miles around Emden there wasn't a cloud. The ground was covered in snow and with the moon it was perfect for spotting anything. The flak and the searchlights were already on and we prepared to make our run-in

Bombing up a Wellington at Binbrook.

straight and level. The flak was terribly close and we were running through puffs of smoke. I could smell the cordite. It seemed ages before Bruce in his Canadian drawl said "Damn it, Pete, you'll have to go round again!" Oh no, I thought there's only us over the target and they were hellishly close with that flak and, worst of all, the thin shell of the bomb. We turned, did a little jinking and then straight and level. The smell of burning cordite was terrible. I bit my lip, banged on the guns and said to myself "Get rid of the damn thing, Bruce!" But Bruce was thorough, he went all the way, and when I felt the aircraft jump I gave a sigh of relief. "Bomb gone!" Next the photographs, and sitting there in the front turret looking ahead and all around what we had to face again for a few "pictures" it seemed hopeless. Straight in amongst it and it seemed years before the photoflash went off, but when it did, same old procedure, nose down and get the hell out of it. When I saw the reflection of the moon on the sea below I thanked my lucky stars once again and remembered what Freddie Lockwood used to say "I'm glad I'm not the front gunner. He always sees what he's going in to. I always see what I've gone out of". The raid was a complete success. All six aircraft bombed Emden, the only possible target, and all returned with good photographs to prove the 4,000 lb bomb's worth.

'Apart from that operation we had some strange tasks. There was the paper round, which consisted of leaflet dropping as well as the bombs, but the most ambitious was setting fire to the forests of Germany. I never heard of any results of this but the idea was that we took with us a 5-gallon drum of water and bundles and bundles of "leaves". I didn't know the chemical composition, but on the way to, I think it was Magdeburg, the navigator and second pilot had to dip these leaves in water and throw them out of the aircraft. They would land amongst the dry trees in the forests and when dried out burst into flames, thereby setting the forests on fire. I may add, we only took them once. They were about the size of a pound note, with an elastic band around a bundle. During their descent the elastic came off or broke and the "leaves" spread over the countryside. That, at least, was the theory.

'Usually, when 20 minutes or so from the coast on the way back from any "op", it was the duty of the wireless operator to switch on the IFF (Identification, Friend or Foe), which was a transmitter sending out a signal to the receivers based on land, to tell them we were friendly aircraft coming in. Unfortunately, on this occasion, after a long trip, which was boring for Len, the wireless operator, he nodded off and when we were over the mouth of the Humber we were greeted with bursts of small arms fire and light ack-ack, with a searchlight or two. Naturally the first query was whether the IFF had been switched on. Len had wakened up by now and switched it on but it took a few minutes to warm up. The firing came from the south bank of the Humber, so we turned north, but on doing so the sound of the barrage balloon warning came over the TR9 (radio aircraft to ground). This was a sound like a siren but very low in tone, and was picked up when heading towards a balloon barrage. No matter which way we turned the sound was still there and we were down to 1,000 ft with foggy visibility below. We turned back out to sea after firing the identification colours of the day, intending to come back over land north of Spurn and land at Driffield, but on arriving over Driffield, we learned the 'drome had been bombed heavily and the runways were u/s. Once more we headed south, over land this time, but the fog was persistent and visibility was very poor. It seemed like hours, but was only five minutes or so, as we strained our eyes to catch a glimpse of the flashing beacon which was attached to every 'drome. We couldn't go too low, because Binbrook aerodrome sits on a hill 600 ft high and we couldn't go too high in case the fog shut out the welcome beacon. Suddenly, out of the darkness, I spotted a dim light flashing out two letters of the alphabet. I told Bruce over the intercom, he consulted the list of beacon letters of the day and found it was the beacon at Elsham. Within ten minutes we were circling Binbrook ready for a landing in semi-fog, which we made without incident.

'The funny thing about this was that I was on the Doncaster-bound train going on leave later that day travelling with an old friend of mine from Carcroft, who was a sergeant in the RAs and stationed on the Humber coast, and during the conversation he was telling me about an incident earlier that morning (around 3 am) when some silly **** nearly got blown out of the sky because they hadn't received the "friend" signal and only because an officer of the RAs thought it was a British 'plane by the sound and delayed the order to fire, just long enough for the aircraft to get away. I explained the circumstances to him and even to this day, we hint about the day he nearly shot us down.

'The Germans visited Binbrook on several occasions. Once a crew were coming in to land when they were shot down and two of my friends who had been with me since joining up at Blackpool, Sergeant Alan Wakeford and Sergeant Ken Harrison, were killed. As the weeks went by my circle of friends got less and less, until when I left Binbrook in February 1942 I reckon they numbered no more than half a dozen. But it was a thing you had to live with.'

CHAPTER FIVE

Bale Out

I t was about 02:30 on the morning of 21 September 1941, that Wellington 1c, *L7886 PM-X* gently arched her back as the bombs left their slips at regular intervals. The pilot gave a sigh of relief when 'Bombs Gone' came through the intercom. All he had to do now was bring Wellington *PM-X* safely home, but that was easier said than done.

The crew of *PM-X* consisted of Pilot Officer Ken Wallis, captain and pilot; Pilot Officer J.E. Ward second pilot; Sergeant E.E. Fairhurst, front gunner; Sergeant N.F. Rouse, wireless operator/air gunner; Sergeant P.E. Walker navigator and Sergeant K.E. Clowes, rear gunner. They had been briefed to bomb a target at Frankfurt, but complete cloud cover over the Continent had prevented any identification of the target in spite of a long search. In those early days of the war there was no question of dropping bombs indiscriminately, so they carried them back to their secondary target, the invasion barge concentrations on the Dutch coast. This gave them problems, for the long flight with a full bomb load had left them very short of fuel and they knew they could not reach their base at Elsham Wolds in North Lincolnshire. Happily, East Anglia would be much nearer and they looked forward to touching down again on that friendly soil.

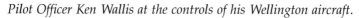

Pilot Officer Ken Wallis at the controls of his Wellington aircraft.

As they were half-way across the sea the wireless operator started to receive warnings that all southern England was in fog. Minutes later they were soon able to see the first woolly layers covering the dark sea. Increasingly frequent and anxious checks of the fuel gauges suggested a desperate situation. However, Pilot Officer Wallis had got down in fog before and he had confidence that he could get in from a timed circuit (there were no other aids) given some cooperation from an airfield.

The aircraft droned steadily on and they realised they had crossed the English coast when they saw searchlights under the fog, giving homing directions. This was done by moving the beam from vertical to horizontal, as a pointer. By then they had been advised that Linton-on-Ouse was still clear of fog but they knew that they had no hope of reaching that haven, north-west of York. Things were now getting critical and the captain had to advise of their desperate shortage of fuel. As he followed the searchlights to the north-west he continuously called 'Darkie' on their primitive TR9 radio-telephony set. 'Darkie' was for such emergency use, but there was no reply.

Suddenly the searchlights ahead of them started to point to the right, at right angles to their course. 'At least somebody cares, even if they wouldn't speak to us', joked Pilot Officer Wallis. After following the new course for a few minutes he received a call 'PM-X, this is Binbrook, what do you require?'. The captain quickly replied that the fuel gauges were showing empty and requested permission to attempt a landing. The reply was that the airfield was in fog and it was not possible to land. But for Pilot Officer Wallis anything was possible and he asked for the 'Chance' Light, the flarepath floodlight to be switched on and off and was able to see the flashes under the cloud. Keeping calm and collected, Pilot Officer Wallis set the aircraft along the known line of the flarepath for a timed circuit.

Soon he was on the heading for landing, with wheels and flaps down. Slowly PM-X lowered into the fog and the captain gripped the controls more firmly. Lower and lower sank the aircraft and as they passed below 200 ft the pilot searched desperately for the runway lights. Suddenly a red light, probably on a hangar, flashed by and instinctively the pilot pulled back the controls and opened the throttles for another try. After a few more attempts to land, with hair-raising last second avoidance of disaster, the captain felt it was pointless to continue to place the rest of the crew at risk. They seemed completely confident that their captain would get them down safely but, after each shaky pass the confidence of Pilot Officer Wallis was fading rapidly. Time was now running out and before making any further attempts to land the pilot called

Binbrook and asked permission to 'Bale out' his crew. However, instead of giving that permission Binbrook said they must fly to Linton-on-Ouse. Wallis quickly snapped back his reply, explaining that they had no fuel showing on the gauges when first over Binbrook. However, while replying both engines stopped and settled the discussion. After a few moments of silence Wallis advised Binbrook that they were all baling out.

Luckily, while talking to Binbrook, the lightened bomber had been climbing vigorously to nearly 4,000 ft. Also, although the engines had cut, they came on occasionally, in screaming fine pitch followed by backfires as the last intermittent gulps of fuel came through. Pilot Officer Wallis gave the order to bale out and held the aircraft against the bursts of assymetric power, prolonging the descent to give his crew a chance to get clear. Meanwhile he started to put on his own parachute. The parachutes they were then using had harness and lifejacket contained in one garment, which they likened to their girlfriends' camiknicks. A chest-type 'chute could be attached to hooks on the chest while a pilot's seat-type 'chute used hooks on either side of the buttocks. The ripcord for the seat 'chute had a handle in a pocket which fitted to turn-studs on the chest, operating by a longer inner and outer cable. Crews were in the habit of tucking this ripcord between the 'chute and its attached cushion, otherwise it dragged in the mud.

So, as the Wellington sank in bursts of noise and silence in the darkness, Wallis fitted first the two important hooks. Then he tried to get at the ripcord but it was completely trapped between the cushions and the 'chute, in spite of his heavings and struggles. Undoing hooks he got the ripcord out and managed to fasten it to two of the three turn-buttons – one was missing. The big hooks were reattached and he felt ready to go but he paused as he thought

The remains of Wellington lc L7886 PM-X, 103 Squadron, which crashed in a stubble field on Paradise Farm, Hutton-le-Moor on 21 September 1941. The captain was Pilot Officer Ken Wallis.

of his crew. Holding the roof handle Wallis leaned over to starboard and looked through the door down the fuselage. Someone had had the sense to turn the light on and he looked down an empty cathedral of geodetics. He was very thankful to be on his own. Heaving himself from the high seat down the steps to the forward hatch he reached down and opened it. According to the drill, the front gunner should have opened it and left it that way but Sergeant Fairhurst had been in the astrodome when the order to leave had been given. He had politely waited for the others to pass before coming to get his parachute from the forward stowage. He had given the captain a 'thumbs up' and gone aft again.

The altimeter showed 700 ft as Pilot Officer Wallis glanced at it as he prepared to tip himself through the hatch. But he had a strange feeling – he felt too comfortable, considering that he was wearing a seat-type 'chute. It normally pressed against the back of the legs. The cause of the pilot's 'comfort' was that the 'chute was still on the seat, attached to the pilot by lift webbing which had been released during his struggle to extricate the ripcord from between the cushion and the 'chute. Webbing was draped over the seat-raising handle and had Wallis jumped he would have been suspended under his doomed aircraft. As the seconds ticked away he gathered everything in his arms, then rolled himself into a ball as he tipped through the open hatch. He caught a glance of the black shape as it passed over, pulled the ripcord and a mighty blow in the wrong place suddenly had him swinging painfully beneath the beautiful sight of the opened canopy.

'I was filled with worries at the loss of my aircraft, where it might fall and the fate of my crew. I also had visions of church spires, weathercocks and lightning conductors in the fog beneath me. These thoughts faded as sounds of my abandoned bomber started to increase as it circled back towards me. It appeared out of the fog coming straight towards me, but banked. I had nerves to the tips of my parachute but my dear old aircraft missed me and the next moments were filled with a dreadful sound as she hit the ground. Immediately after, in the total silence, a steam-hammer blow went up my spine. I came to beside a hedge dripping in the fog, my parachute visible on the grass in the faint light.'

The tail section of Wellington PM-X – upright in the stubble field.

Pilot Officer Wallis shook his head and as he peered into the thick fog his first thought was that he could not have got down in such conditions. Then, for no good reason he tried to remember where he had been. He knew the name had two Fs. As the effects of the concussion wore off he recalled Frankfurt and was then driven to move to find out where the crew were and where the aircraft had fallen. As he stood up he felt a painful lump forming on his spine. In great pain he gathered up his parachute and started to walk – but which way? He paused and looked around and as he did so he remembered the Mauser pistol that he had in his sidcot pocket. He pulled out the pistol and fired two shots into the air. Voices answered from the fog and a short while later he was met by Mr George Hubbert who was one of the Home Guard that had been called out to join the search party. Carrying his parachute Wallis walked down Mount Lane towards a light which was at Mr Dawson's house. Mr Dawson was on fire-watching duty and the door was immediately opened in answer to their knock. It was now about 04:00 and the owner was making a cup of tea. Pilot Officer Wallis was pleased to join him, though something stronger would have been more welcome. While Wallis drank his tea a search was conducted by senior warden, Mr George Fawcett, in the surrounding area for the aircraft and other crew. After his tea and short rest Wallis went with the village policeman, PC Booth, to his house and telephoned his CO, Wing Commander Ryan, at Elsham Wolds. He was very pleased to hear that he was safe and would call for him in the morning.

At 08:00 the Wing Commander's shooting brake arrived and Pilot Officer Wallis eased his aching back into the front seat. Their first stop was at the wreck of *PM-X*. The aircraft had ploughed across a stubble field on Paradise Farm, Holton-le-Moor, killing one rabbit. The farm is now owned by Trevor Kent and to this day nothing grows on the site of the crash. The rest of the crew were collected from farm cottages. They were accompanied to the car by farm workers, all smelling strongly of alcohol.

After a visit to Nocton Hall, X-rays revealed that Pilot Officer Wallis had only a compressed spine. All the crew were then given a week's leave. Pilot Officer Johnnie Ward, the second pilot, decided to make the most of his time and married his girlfriend. However, his was a rather sad but typical tale. After his return from leave he did three more trips with Pilot Officer Wallis then he got his own crew. He had brought his wife up to Lincolnshire and they lived in a room at a near-by rectory.

One day Pilot Officer Ward told Pilot Officer Wallis of a nightmare he had had of his aircraft in flames but he had woken up in their bedsitting room to see the light of the flames of their coal fire flickering on the ceiling. A few nights later, as they were returning from an op Wallis saw the remains of a Wellington burning near Elsham, and the geodetics were clearly visible. Thinking of Ward as soon as he got out of their aircraft he asked whose aircraft had crashed. The reply was 'Mr Ward's'. Wallis thought the nightmare had come true. 'I didn't learn otherwise until I got to the debriefing, where I was assailed by a Johnnie Ward rather more than usually lively, helped by a generous tot of rum! They had nursed their aircraft back only to crash and burn short of the airfield, but they had all escaped.

'It was in March 1942 when I was returning from a short leave, I had arranged to meet my fiancée, Section Officer Peggy Stapley, in the Saracen's Head, Lincoln, that I learned that the nightmare had come true. Returning from the first raid against Lubeck, a medium-sized Baltic port, on 29 March they had been attacked by fighters over the Heligoland Bight and set on fire. They got a radio message out to the effect and advised, "fighters attacking again" '.

Wallis was first an operational 'Lysander' pilot in Army Co-operation Command on dawn anti-invasion patrols, etc. As a 'Wellington' bomber pilot he did 28 operations against Germany. After a period of instructing and running the Gunnery Training Flight at Enstone, a satellite of Moreton-in-the-Marsh, he took a crew to Italy where he did a further eight operations. In the latter part of 1944 he was posted back to the UK for the Specialist Armament Officer's Course. The war was coming to an end and he wanted to stay in the RAF but knew that his peculiar eyesight would be a bar to a permanent commission in the GD Branch. (He had been turned down twice before the war. In 1939, as a licensed pilot he was able to 'slip in' under the Civil Air Guard scheme!)

Wallis then held a number of very interesting armament posts and managed to get back flying, on pistons and jets, anything from a Meteor to a B-36. With the rank of Wing Commander, Wallis retired from the RAF, as head of the Tactical Weapons Group, at A&AEE, Boscombe Down, in 1964, at his own request. Armament was then in the doldrums and many projects were being cancelled. He decided he would like to concentrate on his own autogyro designs, which had already been with the Army Air Corps for two years or so.

Today Wing Commander Kenneth Wallis is well known for his autogyros, his most famous being *Little Nellie* (*G-ARZB/XR943*), which starred in the James Bond film *You Only Live Twice*, which was made in Japan. Reymerston Hall, Norfolk is the Wallis headquarters which houses a fleet of autogyros that do varied work. He also has many mementos from those far off wartime years.

CHAPTER SIX

That Special Breed of Men

Regardless of his family's views the strong determination shown by Jack Halstead finally won the day and he joined the ranks of 'That Special Breed of Men', the men of Royal Air Force, Bomber Command. This is his story.

'At the outbreak of war I was at school and as a schoolboy hoped that the war would last long enough for me to get in on it. My father was a pacifist and such were his narrow views that when it was discovered that I had joined the Boy Scouts I had to leave. The Air Cadets and Army Cadets followed on similar lines. At the age of 17 I was working on a tank production line and as such I was reserved from military service. I was told, volunteer for air crew and you can leave, go LMF and you can return. At 17 I needed parents' consent and in due course the form arrived for my father to sign. It went straight into the fire. I reported it accidentally destroyed and by intercepting the postman obtained another. This time the form was signed by a pal who had a good hand representing my father and it was witnessed by my former headmaster who accepted the signature as genuine. At 18 years 3 months I was called for service in the Royal Air Force.

'After initial training as a flight engineer at St Athan I was awarded my brevet, promoted to Sergeant on my 19th birthday and posted to 1654 Heavy Conversion Unit at Wigsley to commence in-flight training. With some 40 hours to my credit I joined my first

A Lancaster awaiting the order to take off for a raid on Germany.

crew under Flight Sergeant Landridge who had just arrived from a conversion unit. Familiarisation, circuits and bumps, bombing, fighter and searchlight affiliation on Stirlings and the crew were becoming accustomed to four-engined aircraft. Such was the pace that this was achieved in 50 hours' flying and we were away to No. 5 Lancaster Finishing School at Syerston. After ten hours on Lancasters we were classed as fit to join an operational squadron.

'September 1944 saw us posted to 467 Royal Australian Air Force Squadron at Waddington. As was the practice in many Squadrons, new crews were nursed somewhat and were sent initially on easy operations or Milk Runs as they were known, the aircraft used usually belonging to a crew on leave or resting. Operations to Kaiserslautern, Wilhelmshaven, Walcheren (two) and Brunswick saw our initiation complete. We were accepted.

'The incident I am about to relate took place many years ago. I have been careful to ensure that with the lapse of time the facts have not become distorted and the contents are true and factual to the best of my knowledge and belief.

'On 18 October we were allocated Lancaster *DV396* to be known as *PO-B Baker* or more commonly to be known as B for Bastard. This aircraft had previously flown with No. 9 Squadron at Bardney and had over 400 hours logged. How many of these were operational I do not know but it was certainly a veteran. We were eager to test *our* aircraft and did so that very afternoon. The test showed the plane to be sluggish, particularly on three engines, but ours was not to reason why and we accepted it.

'Nine days' leave followed and we returned ready once again for the fray. On 30 October there was another Milk Run to Walcheren and on 1 November a night operation to Homberg. And so to the operation in question.

'The crew consisted of Flight Sergeant Landridge (captain/pilot), and three other Australians (navigator, wireless operator and bomb-aimer). I was the flight engineer, Sergeant Derek Allen the mid-upper gunner and the remaining member of the crew the rear gunner, a small stolid Lancashire man. Now about this time, despite having completed eight operations without having been tested in combat, it was thought by the Australian crew members that the rear gunner would buckle under pressure. A vote was taken and it was agreed that a replacement should be found. I hope the rear gunner survived the war because he never let the side down. By coincidence (or was it?) an Australian gunner, whom I only knew as Len, had been released from hospital after having been wounded in an aerial fight over enemy territory and was willing to join our crew. I only met Len for a few minutes at the briefing on the night of 2 November. The very fact that he had been wounded on operations and returned for more, made him a brave man.

'We were briefed for a raid on Düsseldorf, it was to be an all-out effort on a difficult target in ideal weather. There was a full moon and little or no cloud was reported over the target. With a bomb load of 14 x 1,000 lb high explosives we were to bomb the Krupps Armament Works. A press release after the raid described it as having been carried out by 1,000 heavy bombers dropping more than 4,000 tons of high explosives in conditions which were favourable to the Germans, bright moonlight and no cloud cover. In fact 992 aircraft were dispatched and 946 attacked the target with 4,484 tons of bombs. Sixteen of our bombers were lost, one being from 467 Squadron, which was our aircraft.

'At the outset this was no different from any other operation but we knew the dangers of the target ahead. Gain height over Lincolnshire, rendezvous over Reading and set course for Germany. Certain doglegs were to be made and feints towards diversionary targets being marked by other Groups. It was a beautiful night but having been warned of the possibility of enemy activity nerves were somewhat on edge and once the enemy coast was crossed a continuous series of banking searches was made. From time to time brief glimpses of other aircraft were seen. As the target area was approached we could see the diversionary targets being marked in the hope that they would draw the enemy fighters and thus reduce the amount of time they could stay in the air.

'A good run in at 17,000 ft despite the medium to heavy flak, the moments of high tension when an aircraft is a sitting target, then it's left ... left ... steady ... and ... bombs away. If there was heavy flak there were seldom enemy fighters in the area, a time of relaxation for the inexperienced, head down and go for home. On leaving the target area we were coned for some minutes by a master searchlight which is probably one of the worst fears. In the beam of a searchlight you are seen by all, you dive, you corkscrew, you twist and turn and if you are lucky you escape or out-run the range. If you are unlucky you are passed from one light to another or picked up by a night fighter. We escaped – so far we were lucky.

'We were racing for home when the rear gunner reported a 'plane going down in flames on the port side. Sometimes they were dummies released by the Germans but there was no doubt about this one. Then we saw another 'plane going down a little nearer. A fighter flare to port illuminating the sky and seven pairs of eyes searching the skies looking for the shadowy streak of a fighter. Within seconds a report came from the rear gunner, understandably somewhat panicky "Do something, skipper, do something, dive port!" Not the drill as per the book but corkscrew we did. The attack had commenced and the 'plane was raked by a burst of machine-gun or cannon fire. Our gunners replied. Here he comes again, a second strike and the port engine goes up in flames. The fighter obviously realised that we had "bought it" because he never returned for the kill.

'We were unable to get the fire under control either by feathering the prop or using the built-in extinguisher. "Captain to crew, captain to crew", cool as a cucumber and according to the book. "Prepare to abandon aircraft." The intercom came alive with chatter, predominantly the rear gunner in a hell of a state reporting that he was trapped in the turret. The hydraulics had been damaged and he was unable to rotate the turret. The pilot then issued an order for the mid-upper gunner to leave his position and go to the rear to try to chop the rear gunner out. He was to report on intercom as soon as this had been done. With that Sergeant Allen, the mid-upper gunner, went off intercom into the darkness of the body of the 'plane. It was now well on fire and the pilot ordered the remainder of the crew to "abandon aircraft". Regardless of what a lot of people think, the aircrew I knew were not trained in parachuting. A drop from the nose of a Stirling into a canvas sheet was your lot. However, training or no training, the crew needed no second bidding.

'Bomb-aimer, engineer, wireless operator and navigator followed from the nose in that order. I later learned that two actually landed on the same football field. I landed in a forest and took to my heels not being aware of my whereabouts other than we had passed over Aachen sometime previously. In due course, the four made their way back to England where we met in the Kangaroo Club by chance, never to meet again.

'Meanwhile of course the drama was taking place in mid-air. It would appear that Sergeant Allen made his way to the rear and succeeded in chopping out the rear gunner. Flight Sergeant Landridge remained at the controls of the doomed aircraft awaiting the call that the rear was clear. The bomber was now burning fiercely. Suddenly the old Lancaster broke its back and split into two halves. Sergeant Allen fell out and was able to pull his 'chute. The plane fell to earth near the town of Spa in Belgium. The locals there told me that they had seen the wreckage and where one of the bodies fell. They thought the other, presumably the pilot, was in the wreck and they had no idea what happened after that.

'Sergeant Allen obviously made his way back to England because sometime later, after I had returned to operations, I was pleased to see an item in the *London Gazette* stating that for his part in the action Sergeant Allen had been given the Conspicuous Gallantry Medal. As far as I am aware the pilot, equally as brave, did not receive any recognition but then that was aircrew and Flight Sergeant Landridge RAAF served in the best traditions of the Royal Air Force, as did thousands of other Australians.'

CHAPTER SEVEN

Learning the Trade

M ost operational aircrew during 1939-45 were in their early 20s, quite a number of them still in their late teens. Nightly they witnessed death of friends and companions and it made them into men almost overnight. This is the story of Sergeant Tom Wardle (later Flight-Lieutenant) who was already in his late 20s at the time he joined the Royal Air Force:

'I was accepted into the Royal Air Force for training as a pilot. Our status then was known in the "trade" as U/T Pilot, Navigator, Wop, A/G. I went first to ACRC at St John's Wood – our first get-together in the force was at Lords Cricket Ground, where we were split into flights and billeted in blocks of flats overlooking Regent's Park. Our meals were taken in the restaurant at the zoo and I well remember how the baboons in the monkey house, which was quite nearby, used to make fun of us as we queued for meals every day.

Instrument panel of a Lancaster.

From London I was posted to No 6 ITW at Newquay, then to Shellingford in Berkshire for EFTS. It was while we were there that the purge came for the new aircrew duty of bomb-aimer, brought into being by the new four-engined bombers – Lancs, Halifaxes and Stirlings – coming into service.

'Flying training was temporarily suspended, but we were all given a CFI's test (Chief Flying Instructor) and I came out of it with far from flying colours. U/T pilots were urged to volunteer for the new job, but very few did so, and a week later we were all posted to Heaton Park in Manchester, where we waited for the chop. It came for me, and I was posted to Jurby in the IoM for training as a bomb-aimer. Our disappointment was tempered somewhat by the fact that we were told that as we had done training as pilots, we would be looked upon as second pilots in case of emergency. In point of fact this never was really followed up, and the only time I tried flying an aircraft was on a cross-country exercise in a Wellington from OTU at Hixon, where I was sent from Jurby and where I crewed up with Charlie and the rest of the lads with the exception of Bill Whitehouse, mid-upper, and George Taylor, flight engineer, who only joined us when the crew was increased from five to seven as we converted to four engines. On that occasion we had been doing some simulation bombing at St Tudwals, a tiny island off the North Wales peninsula, and Charlie asked me to take over after we had completed the exercise. I hadn't been in the pilot's seat five minutes when the starboard engine suddenly spluttered and then packed up. Charlie hurriedly resumed his seat, feathered the prop and we made an emergency landing at Llandwrog near Caernarvon. That was the one and only time I flew a bomber!

'I had my first flying clothing issue at ITW in Newquay. This consisted of an inner suit, one-piece boiler-suit fashion, of brown silk or nylon (I'm not sure which) quilted with kapok, and an outer suit made of a sort of very close weave cotton gaberdine material which was referred to as a "sidcot". It was a one-piece garment with zips and I wore it as an outer suit for practically the whole of my service. We also had those ugly brown sheepskin-lined flying boots with soles that looked like galoshes made from crepe rubber. I hated them – when we had to stay overnight at Llandwrog we went into Caernarvon and I had to walk about in them all night, and ended up with blisters on my heels. Later on I swapped them for a pair of second-hand boots with black leather uppers and khaki canvas legs which were much more comfortable, but unfortunately when we were later issued with electrically heated clothing I couldn't get the socks on inside them. At this particular clothing store I remember there was also a pair of the super flying boots all in black leather such as were issued to the fighter boys. They were just my size, but the sheepskin lining of one of the boots was matted with dried blood, and I just couldn't bring myself to take them. Dead man's boots? Who knows. Anyway, in the meantime we had also been issued with Irvin suits, the sheepskin jacket and trouser suits. These were beautifully made, but I only wore mine once on ops (although I often wore them on training flights). This was on my third full op with Flight Sergeant Cook, the Australian, whose bomb-aimer, Bluey Freeman, was down in Scunthorpe trying to sort out his policeman bashing problems. When I was put with their crew the gunners told me that they had put Bluey's guns into the turret for me. So they had, but unfortunately they had omitted to arm them, and I only noticed this as we were taxiing to the end of the runway for take-off and I had to get up into the turret to do it myself.

'The turret had a fold-away seat which was awkward at the best of times, and I was wearing, on top of my battle dress, my full Irving suit, my Mae West, and, of course, my parachute harness. As I tried to struggle up into the turret, the trigger for the compressed air bottle on my Mae West caught on something, and the damn thing blew up. I was stuck halfway in and halfway out of the turret, jammed tight like a cork in the neck of a bottle. It was ages, or so it seemed, before I was able to get at the release valve and deflate my Mae West, feed the belts of ammo into the two Brownings, and get back to my position down below. By this time we had taken off and were climbing. I was absolutely bathed in sweat, but as we climbed higher and higher the cold air got up between the gap in the trousers and I began to get cold. It felt as though all the perspiration was freezing in a clammy cold blanket inside my flying clothes, and I've never felt colder or more miserable in my life. I never wore that suit on ops again.

'Later on, of course, we had the heated clothing. This, as I remember it, consisted of three parts – a sort of hip-length jerkin with elements sewn into it something like an electric blanket, slipper socks and gloves, again incorporating heating elements, and with press-stud connections, and with leads from the bottom of the jacket to the socks. These I never wore because, as I've said, I couldn't get my boots on over them, and I can honestly say I suffered from "cold feet" every time I went on ops! The whole outfit could be plugged into a socket in the bomb-aimer's compartment.

'This compartment formed the nose of the aeroplane. On top was the gun turret, ring-mounted for lateral movement, and armed with two Browning .303 machine-guns which could be elevated and depressed. Each gunner was responsible for his own guns, and would take them out of the turret on landing and take them back to the gun room for cleaning next day. I don't recall ever firing my guns whilst on ops but I always had to clean them well as, being in a forward-facing turret, the bores got filthy and would very soon have rusted. The front of the compartment was a large perspex dome with a flat clear-view panel fitted into the lower half and a glycol spray pipe in the upper rim for anti-icing use. The bomb-sight was positioned above this, and immediately behind it was an upholstered body rest for the bomb-aimer, who would kneel behind it on the upholstered cover of the escape hatch. The switch and pre-selector panel was at the side of the compartment to the right, with the bomb-tit in its housing. It was the bomb-aimer's first duty to check the switches as soon as he got into the aircraft. To the left was the camera control, and behind it the F.24 camera with its 5 in focal lens projecting through the floor. This was loaded with a magazine of film and the control was set to expose eight frames, computed so that the fifth frame was the bombing photograph, which meant that if all the correct settings had been used and the 'plane kept absolutely straight and level and on the same course during the 10 seconds or so after pressing the bomb-tit, it would show the point of impact of the bombs. This was all a bit hit and miss but was the only way of assessing the success of the mission. One of the prime settings was based on the terminal velocity of the bombs used, but usually a mixed load was carried, which didn't help.

'Behind the bomb-aimer on the right, and serving as a step up into the cockpit was a square tank containing the glycol. Above this was a small opening panel through which the bomb-aimer could look into the bomb bay in order to check if all bombs had been released or if there were any hang-ups. If there were it was probably due more to icing rather than any malfunction in the circuit, which could be a bit dicy when the 'plane descended to warmer air. In this event the pilot would usually open the bomb doors over the sea and throw his aircraft about as much as possible to try and dislodge the hang-up because nobody liked landing with them still aboard, and the release hooks could not be reset after the circuit had been broken.

'The small inspection lamp was the only means of illumination in the bomb-aimer's compartment. It was very tiny – about 3 in long with a small bulb shining through a white translucent perspex panel which gave just enough light to check any switches or controls but not enough to be seen outside the aircraft. It was on a long lead attached, I think, to the bomb panel. On the right hand side, between the bomb switch panel and the glycol tank, was the stowage for the bomb-aimer's parachute.

'The bomb-sight I used on my first tour was the old CSBS (course setting bomb-sight). On my second we had the Mk XIV. The compartment was the coldest part of the aeroplane, I think, but I would always have lived there rather than in the rear turret – at least we were only just in front of the pilot's and engineer's positions, and we could see where we were going! Talking of the front turrets – I really don't think they served a very useful purpose. I know, I stayed in the bomb-aimer's compartment for most of the flight on every op. The turret was difficult to get into – the seat I have spoken of swung in an arc up into the rear, leaving very little space to manoeuvre oneself into position when wearing full flying kit and Mae West, and to the best of my recollection I don't think there was any connection for the heated clothing. I remember on one occasion seeing what I took to be an enemy fighter coming straight at us from the opposite direction – it passed directly over us, in fact we were damn lucky it didn't hit us – and the closing speed was such that I wasn't even able to identify it, much less climb into the turret and have a go! It could even have been one of our own PFF Mosquitoes on its way home.

'We were very lucky in our tour in that we never really ran into any serious trouble. On reflection, and thinking how ropey some of the navigators were, I suppose it could also have been that we were a good crew! Certainly on my very first operation I had some evidence of this. As you know, I was flying as spare with another crew and when we were returning over the English coast we were suddenly engaged by some very accurate flak from our own anti-aircraft batteries. This was discovered to be because the wireless operator had forgotten to switch on the VHF recognition signal and also the navigator was so far off course that we were thought to be an unidentified aircraft. We finally landed at base about half-an-hour after everyone else, and when I finally got back to my billet I found Whit, our own wireless operator, waiting up in a minor panic as he really thought I'd bought it on my first op! I don't think any of those crews which completed a tour and went on to do a second, and sometimes a third, ever made that sort of mistake. In any case, I regret to say that on the very next op after I finished flying with them (I flew three times altogether, one abortive) they failed to return and I never found out what happened to them.

'One of the things that I, personally, disliked most about night ops was the presence of thick cloud over the target area. There is something, I think, unique as experiences go in making a bombing run over a heavily defended target in the Ruhr or on Berlin. On a clear night, kneeling in the front nacelle of a Lanc with 20,000 ft of nothing between you and the holocaust below, and aiming your aircraft straight and level with your eye glued to the sights – steady, steady, left, left, steady ri-i-ight, steady, bombs gone! I think the bomb-aimer at this time was the luckiest member of the crew. For those few seconds he was virtually in command of the aircraft and needed all his concentration for the job in hand – after all, this was the culmination of everything that had gone before – "the name of the game", to use a current cliché. He had no time to worry about flak or fighters – just the run-in, the actual bombing, and the few seconds straight and level on the exact same heading until the light on the camera control went out telling him that his photograph had been taken. The rest of the crew just had to sit there and sweat it out at a time when the kite was most vulnerable. The babble of conversation over the intercom, as soon as I spoke those magic words – "Okay, Charlie, get weaving" – revealed the pent-up tension they had suffered. But when the target was obscured by cloud it was different. The tension was there, all right, even more so sometimes. When you are silhouetted, no matter how dimly, against a blanket of thick cloud there is a feeling of nakedness that is hard to describe, and when the target is all but invisible, you begin to wonder what the hell you're doing there, anyway!

'This was how conditions were on the night of 8 April 1943. At briefing we had been given the target, Duisberg, and warned to expect up to 10/10ths cloud over the target. We were to bomb at 21,000 ft using the Wanganui technique, which meant that the Pathfinders would drop sky markers – white, green, then red – which would be used as an aiming point for our bombs. The success of this method depended on very precise settings on the bomb-sight, course, height and speed. I never liked it, and much preferred to see what I was aiming at. The bomb load was one 4,000 lb "cookie" and 12 SBCs (small bomb containers, each containing 90 incendiary bombs).

'It was a dull, moonless night when we took off at 21:10 and started to climb to the pre-arranged height for our rendezvous with the main force over Sheringham. I was then a sergeant bomb-aimer with No. 103 Squadron based at Elsham Wolds in Lincolnshire. It was my 23rd op, but our 20th as a crew, as I had done three ops with other crews before we started our tour together. The crew were Pilot Officer Charlie Blumenauer, pilot and skipper, Sergeant Leslie Proud, navigator, Sergeant George "Buck" Taylor, flight engineer, Pilot Officer "Willie" Whitehouse, mid-upper gunner, Sergeant Alan "Whit" Whitaker, wireless operator, Sergeant Bob Griffiths, rear gunner and myself, Sergeant Tom Wardle, bomb-aimer/front gunner.

'Charlie Blumenauer was a Canadian from the Okanagan Valley in British Columbia. He was a very stolid sort of guy with a not very well developed sense of humour, but as reliable as the Lanc he drove. He married a girl from Stafford whom he met whilst we were doing our OTU at Hixon. Les Proud was tall and lanky with a long rather sad-looking face decorated by a rather Mexican-looking moustache, but he had a very keen, dry sense of humour which had us in stitches many a time. He came from the Stockton-on-Tees area. George Taylor, nicknamed "Buck" came from Alfreton in Derbyshire, and was the quiet one of the crew. I don't know much about his background, but after we split up at the end of our tour I heard later that he had been killed on a second tour. Bill Whitehouse was an American "Brummie". He had gone to America with his family at the age of two and stayed there until his father returned to Birmingham about 12 years later, I think. He had transferred from the RAF Regiment to aircrew, and only met up with me when we were posted to conversion unit after leaving Hixon. He lives in Solihull. We were great friends, and still keep in touch. Alan Whitaker had also lived in either America or Canada, I'm not sure now which, and at this time lived in St Annes on Sea with his mother – I think his father was dead – who had a furrier's business in Blackpool. He was married halfway through our tour and we all went to the wedding with the exception of Charlie, who was getting himself engaged on that same leave down in Stafford. I was Whit's best man.

'Bob Griffiths – "Griff" – was the character of the crew. I think its safe to say, however, that he was born in Canada but had spent most of his life in the States, in Georgia, in a small town called Social Circle. He certainly had that sort of outlook – to him anyone who was coloured was a nigger – and it was Griff who nicknamed Charlie "Massa Blumenauer" because he maintained he was a slave-driver! All in good fun of course – "Put away dat whip, Massa Blumenauer, I'se a-coming, boss" was one of his favourite quips.

He always spoke of English money in "bobs" (shillings) and pennies, and instead of saying a pound would say twenty bobs – "twen'y Bahbs" it sounded like.

'I was the oldest member of the crew at thirty-one, and for some reason they all called me Joe. I was a failed UT pilot, which was how I came to be remustered as a bomb-aimer, and looking back on it now I guess it was the luckiest thing that happened to me, because I became part of one of the best crews anyone could wish for.

'Griff always reminded me of Bob Hope. He had the same wise-cracking sense of humour and even looked a bit like him, with the same "shovel" nose, though our Bob sported a small moustache. His relief every time we returned safely from an op would manifest itself in typical Hope-like boastfulness – "Gee, fellers, I'm a hero", he'd say. But he was a great guy and we had lots of fun with him. I often wonder what happened to him.

'Our aircraft was Lancaster *ED751*, and it was our third op in her. Our route from Sheringham was over the North Sea to the Loch Ness monster shaped island of Overflakee – so easy to identify on a clear night, but lost beneath the cloud tonight. It was up to Les to get us there, and I couldn't help him. All the rest of us could do was keep a constant lookout for fighters as we stooged along above the cloud.

'When we crossed the coast Charlie started "weaving" – a sort of corkscrew manoeuvre up and down and to each side of our course which was adopted by all aircraft in those days to try and confuse the enemy radar defences. We also used to carry "window" – metalised strips of material which were jettisoned down the flare shute and also created havoc on the radar screens. Our course was now towards Duisberg in the Ruhr, and conditions, apart from the weather, were pretty easy. There was very little flak, and we saw no fighters, the last leg of our course to the target area being fairly uneventful. As we neared our destination the cloud layer got thicker and more dense, and the tops were right up to our operational height of 21,000 ft. Eventually Les, the navigator, came over the intercom to me and asked if I could see anything. "We should be coming up to target now", he said. There was no moon, but in the light of the stars the layer of cloud below me looked like a carpet of dirty grey cotton wool, thick and impenetrable, and never a glimmer of a flare or sky marker to relieve the gloom.

'"Can't see a thing", I replied. "Keep going for a bit." We seemed to be completely alone in the sky. I remember thinking it strange that I could see no other aircraft and wondering if Willie and Griff in their more advantageous positions in the gun turrets could see any.

'Then, ahead of me, and who knows how many thousand feet below, I saw a faint glow beneath the cloud, just as I was beginning to think we were too late on target and had missed all the markers. Whether it was indeed a PFF flare or the glow from fires on the ground I couldn't determine, but it was the only thing to be seen, so I guided Charlie towards it and when I had it properly in my sights, pressed the bomb-tit.

'"Bombs gone", I said, and although it seemed rather superfluous, held the course steady for the photograph to be taken. Then suddenly, all hell was let loose around us. Heavy flak bursting on our starboard beam lit up the sky, and we could hear the rattle of small fragments of shrapnel on the wings and fuselage. Charlie closed the bomb doors and threw the Lanc into violent evasive action. We twisted and turned like a firefly, but couldn't shake off the flak. I think we must have been late, and the ack-ack crews down below had isolated us and got a real good fix before they let us have it. Charlie Blumenauer was a damn good pilot and completely unflappable as a rule, but this time he had been taken by surprise and I think that just for a moment he panicked. His aerobatics became more and more violent, and still the flak was bursting all around us, then suddenly we were in the cloud and out of control. I had been flung backwards and found myself sitting on the glycol tank which forms a step down from the pilots cockpit to the bomb-aimer's compartment. I was plastered to it as though by some huge invisible hand, and felt the flesh of my cheeks being drawn tight in that curious way one feels when affected by "G" force. I remember watching with a sort of detached curiosity the small, shrouded inspection lamp which I used for all my bombing settings waving gently about in mid-air at the end of its flex, and wondering how it managed to defy the force of gravity. And I felt like death. I have never been able to completely overcome air sickness, and even now, in the comfort of a modern jet-liner any pronounced turbulence makes me feel grotty. But I don't think I've ever felt worse than I did that night. My stomach had been left somewhere back above the cloud, and I was plunging down at God knows what speed and wondering if I'd ever get it back. There was a babble of voices over the intercom asking Charlie what the hell he was doing, and Charlie shouting back that he didn't know, but the aircraft was out of control and he was trying to get it back on an even keel.

'Afterwards Les and George, the flight engineer, tried to reconstruct what happened. Apparently Charlie, in trying to avoid the flak, slipped into the cloud in a steep banked turn and it was so thick that, with nothing to orientate himself by, turned it over on its back and the aircraft fell like a stone 10,000 ft, from 21,000 to 11,000 in a few seconds. He managed to regain control using the artificial horizon and coaxed it back to 18,000, still in thick cloud, when he stalled the aircraft and plummeted back to 10,000 before bringing it under control again. George says the airspeed indicator passed 380 mph on the way down, but trying to get back up was a different kettle of fish. Les gave Charlie a course to fly and slowly we staggered back to a safer height. Fortunately, we seemed to have lost the flak – there were still bursts in the vicinity of the kite, but I think they probably thought we had been shot down when we went into our first dive, and had switched their attention to some other unfortunate.

'By this time I was flat on my back on the padded cover of the escape hatch in my compartment, using the padded armrest behind the bomb-sight as a pillow. Advice and comments were still crackling back and forth between the rest of the crew. I suppose my silence began to be noticed, and someone, I forget who, shouted "Are you all right, Joe?" I said I was, although I felt far from it, and the conversation resumed, rather subdued now, as everyone realised that the skipper was gradually winning the battle. His main worry was the cloud which was still as thick as ever, and he kept saying, if only he could break cloud he'd feel a lot happier, as then he'd know if we were still the right way up. I suppose all this took only a very few minutes, but it seemed like a lifetime, and I was feeling so ill I honestly couldn't have cared less if we'd been hit or not. At last we were back up to about 20,000 ft and, after a period of silence Charlie said, "I think we'll break cloud in a minute".

'Another short silence, and then Les, in his dry, north country voice, "Does anybody mind if I break wind?" The tension was broken, and everybody laughed, even me, bad as I felt. Sure enough, in a few moments the cloud began to thin, we could see the stars again and then we were once more in a clear sky. What a relief! And as Les worked out a new course for home I began to think that perhaps I wasn't going to die after all – in fact with each moment I began to feel better, and soon I was able to sit up and attend to my normal duties. When we got back above the cloud Les found we had not been very far off course, and although we were all a bit shaken up, the aircraft didn't appear to have sustained any serious damage.

'We got back to Elsham without further incident and I was feeling more or less back to normal when we landed. Looking back on it now, it doesn't sound very exciting, but it was enough for me. It's the ones you get back from that you're able to remember, isn't it?'

CHAPTER EIGHT

Devotion to Duty

They called them 'Press-on types' in the Royal Air Force; crews who pressed on to target. Call it determination or sheer bloody-mindedness if you like but these men carried out their duties, sometimes against impossible odds.

This is the story of a mission carried out by the crew of Lancaster *'O' Orange VN5733* of No. 50 Squadron, Bomber Command at RAF Skellingthorpe, Lincolnshire: Flying Officer W. Abercrombie, pilot; Flight Sergeant T.A.W. Morris (RCAF), navigator; Flight Sergeant A.G. McKenzie (RCAF), bomb-aimer; Sergeant R.G. Hutton, flight engineer; Sergeant T.L. Burr, wireless operator; Pilot Officer Murray (RCAF), mid-upper gunner; and Sergeant McDonald, rear gunner.

Following the successful daylight raid by Lancasters against Le Creusot on 17 October another surprise daylight raid was mounted by No. 5 Group a week later. This was against Milan by a force of 88 Lancasters and meant a round trip of 1,700 miles. Deeper penetration into enemy-occupied territory was only possible by using routes ill-defended by the enemy. Sergeant Hutton, the flight engineer on *'O' Orange* tells the story:

'We were called to briefing early in the morning of 25 October 1942 for a daylight attack on Milan, Italy. With a full load of 2,154 gallons of fuel we took off at mid-day. Our bomb load was approximately 8,000 lb. The route was low level (250 ft-300 ft) over the Channel to avoid enemy radar and fighters; the first rendezvous being Lyons and to fly in gaggle formation to our second rendezvous over Bodensee (Lake Constance) flying over the Alps and attacking Milan at 9,000 ft. Unfortunately, owing to adverse weather conditions, we were nearly ten minutes late at Bodensee and the skipper asked the crew whether we should go on. It was agreed that we should go on for we had not brought our load of incendiary bombs all that way for nothing.

'As we descended towards Milan in brilliant sunshine, having crossed Mont Blanc we ran into thin cloud and saw several Lancasters returning. Then we found ourselves to be a single aircraft being shelled, it seemed, by every gun defending Milan. Our height was then about 8,000 ft – the skipper decided there was no future there and put the aircraft into an almost vertical dive (I guess many people in Milan would think we were crashing) and found ourselves over the centre of the city, less than 500 ft, identifying the Cathedral quite clearly. We circled Milan in comparative safety, observing many fires and actually seeing fire brigades working. Flight Sergeant McKenzie, the bomb-aimer, located our target which was the railway goods yard and sidings. The skipper brought the aircraft round and we did a low level (100 ft-200 ft) run up with bomb doors open dropping the bombs on target.

'At this stage there was a terrific rat-tat-tat of machine gun bullets hitting the aircraft and we heard a gurgling on the intercom and knew some member of the crew had been hit. We cleared off into the countryside to sort ourselves out, still at low level. Imagine being in a sealed greenhouse, with the sun pouring in, over the Plain of Milan, kitted up with full flying gear – was it hot! I clambered down the fuselage to find the green cushion for sliding down into the rear turret which looked as if a huge rake had ploughed through it, and I dragged the tail gunner, Sergeant McDonald, out of the turret and up to the rest-bed between the two spars, sliding on hydraulic oil and blood. On examination I found Mac had what appeared to be a .5 machine gun bullet in his neck which I suspected was lodged across his tongue and another bullet had shattered his left arm just below the shoulder.

'At this stage the skipper called me up saying he wanted my help. I went forward and found the starboard outer engine with the temperature off the clock and no oil pressure. I told the skipper I was shutting down and feathering and he made the necessary adjustments on the trim. I lifted his earphone and shouted to him "Mac is badly hurt and he cannot take oxygen. If we are to get him home we can't exceed 9-10,000 ft." The skipper nodded and said he would try to find a way through the Alps.

'I went back to Mac with Sergeant Burr, the wireless operator, taking with me a sheet out of his log-book and a pencil. At the rest-bed I dressed the wounds as best I could, putting Mac's arm in a sling. Knowing that Mac could not speak I put the pencil in his right hand and he scribbled the words "I guess I have had it – when you get home write to River Plate House". (He was actually a Chilean subject having volunteered for the Royal Air Force.) In my own state of mind I started to write a message back but then realised Mac could still hear and I shouted in his ear "Don't be a bloody fool". We wrapped him up in our Irvins and went back to our stations to find the skipper just lifting the Lanc clear of the peaks. Flying over France we decided to break WT silence and requested medical assistance and permission to land at Boscombe Down.

'Having crossed the Channel at low level to avoid enemy fighters we made a safe landing after being in the air for nine hours and had just 154 gallons of fuel left. We were instructed to taxi to flying control where an ambulance met us. A doctor and two ambulancemen arrived between the spars and the fuselage and were having a debate as to how to get Mac out. Mac, overhearing this, swung his legs over the rest-bed and walked down the fuselage, was put into the ambulance and I went with him to the medical centre. The rest of the crew were taken to debriefing. The sergeant medical orderly required Mac's rank, name and next of kin but by this time I was very irritable and told him to go to hell. I felt a tug on my leg and it was Mac asking for a pencil again. I gave him the sergeant's pad and pencil and Mac supplied the required information including his next of kin. Mac was taken by ambulance to hospital and I returned to the rest of the crew.

'We were awakened at 6 am to be told that Mac had died. We were all so upset, we got up; the aircraft was refuelled and we were about to take off on three motors when a civilian engineer arrived to say the aircraft was completely un-airworthy and he was grounding it. There were about 70 bullet holes in the aircraft. We slammed the door, took off on three motors and returned to Skellingthorpe. When we arrived I was handed travel warrant, etc, taken to my billet for a cleaning up and sent home within the hour.

'Strange to say, the bomb-aimer/front gunner was called Flight Sergeant McKenzie so both were called Mac but never in the aircraft was there any difficulty in identifying which Mac was being called. Because McKenzie was so disturbed I took him home with me where we received telegrams from Air Marshall Harris and our station commander congratulating us on the immediate awards of the Distinguished Flying Medal. In an earlier sortie (31 July 1942) our third op, Düsseldorf, Sergeant McDonald was credited with the shooting down of an Me 109 and he never knew he had been awarded the Distinguished Flying Medal. Milan was our 28th op. All the crew were decorated following this attack on Milan with the exception of the mid-upper gunner who was only a temporary member of the crew.'

Sergeant Hutton completed his first tour of ops with No. 50 Squadron. He was commissioned in 1943, having started his second tour, and was Flight Engineer Leader of No. 619 Squadron at Woodhall Spa. He completed his second tour in December 1944, eventually being demobbed in 1946. Flying Officer Abercrombie became Wing Commander, DFC and Bar (for one week Commanding Officer of No 83 Pathfinder Force) reported missing over Berlin, Christmas 1943. This story is dedicated to his memory.

CHAPTER NINE

Mission to Geissen

RAF Skellingthorpe was situated three miles west of Lincoln just outside the city boundary. From October 1942 to June 1945 it was the home of No. 50 Squadron. Also, during this period from April 1944 to June 1945 it was the home of No. 61 Squadron of No 5 Group, Bomber Command. One crew flying with 61 Squadron was Flying Officer Laurence A. Pearse, an Australian, pilot; Flight Sergeant Robert Pettigrew, also an Australian, navigator; Flight Sergeant Alan Barker, mid-upper gunner; Flight Sergeant John Murray, engineer Flight Sergeant Arthur Edward Perry, wireless operator (air); Flight Sergeant Alan Baker, bomb-aimer; and Flight Sergeant Robert Gillanders, Scottish, the rear gunner. They remained throughout as a crew and completed their tour of ops together. This is the story of one of their ops on the night of 6 December 1944 as told by Flight Sergeant Perry, the wireless operator.

'I awoke about 8 o'clock on a bitterly cold morning and walked the 50 yards to the ablutions for a wash and shave (our quarters

Crew of Lancaster 'N' Nan in front of their earlier aircraft QR-X. *Left to right – Alan Baker (bomb-aimer); Bob Gillanders (rear gunner); Alan Barker (mid-upper gunner); Laurie Pearse (pilot); Bill Perry (wireless operator); John Murray (engineer) and Bob Pettigrew (navigator).*

were worse than any of the training stations we had served on) and then down to the mess for breakfast. After this we made our way down to the flying section either on foot or by bicycle (most of which had been acquired by devious means) to attend the morning parade which was held at 9 o'clock. This was a very informal affair and was held to verify the availability of each crew. This formality over, we made our way out to our aircraft 'N' Nan (2nd) at a dispersal pan about a quarter way round the 'drome. Once out there each member of the crew carried out an inspection of his own equipment. In my case it meant first plugging in the trolley accumulator and shorting out the switch with a penny (the latter was in fact a chargeable offence) I was then able to check all the W/T and R/T equipment without draining the aircraft battery. After all checks had been carried out we made our way back to the squadron office. The terse message on the blackboard inside announced "War Tonite, Briefing 14:30". We were then off duty till that time. The navigators would then pump Peggy the map clerk to find what charts were being issued. The engineers would find out the petrol load and the bomb-aimers the type of bombs being loaded. From the information thus gained we would then attempt to work out the possible targets.

'We were, of course, confined to camp and the telephone was disconnected so there was nothing to do but go to the billet and rest. An hour before briefing we went down to the mess for our meal of bacon and eggs, after which we collected our flying rations (sandwiches, boiled sweets and bars of plain chocolate plus a flask of coffee if you had a flask) and then we made our way to the briefing room. We were told that the target was to be Geissen, a town north of Frankfurt, and were given a brief description of the target (marshalling yards), defences over the target and *en route*, and weather. The crews then dispersed to their various sections, in my case to the signals section where a detailed briefing was given on such things as call signs, W/T frequencies, colours of the day (these had to be written on rice paper to be swallowed rather than fall into enemy hands). After this we collected flying gear, parachutes, etc, from the locker room and were taken out by crew bus to our aircraft dispersal pan. Everyone carried out a further equipment check, engines were run up and mags checked and then shut down. We then stood outside in the cold air and smoked and talked and half hoped to see the two white Very lights fired from the control tower which would indicate the operation had been scrubbed. There was still plenty of time to get into town and enjoy ourselves. No such luck this time, so at the agreed time we boarded the aircraft, stowed the ladder and locked the door. Engines were started and we taxied out to join the queue of Lancs on the perimeter track. Aircraft were converging onto the end of the runway in use from both sides, 61 Squadron from one side and 50 Squadron from the other and were allowed onto the runway singly from alternate sides. My first duty was to load the Very pistol with a red cartridge in case of emergency. Finally it was our turn, a green light from the Aldis lamp in the control van at the end of the runway and we turned onto the runway. I usually stood in the astrodome at this point to acknowledge the waves and good wishes of the station personnel who lined both sides of the runway for the first 50 yds or so. This was the time when your feelings were at the lowest point and these demonstrations worked wonders (who could quit in front of all those people anyway?). Brakes on, engines up to zero boost, a second green light, brakes off and we were rolling. Nothing to do now except sit down and brace myself against the bulkhead (no seatbelts). The only sounds were from the engines and the navigator calling out the speeds from the ASI repeater. The build-up of speed seemed desperately slow and with a full bomb and petrol load on, the runway seemed woefully short. We became airborne and gained height over the 'drome. I tuned in to the squadron transmitter and then changed the Very cartridge for the colours of the period. We set course at about 17:00. About 20 minutes later I tuned in the group transmitter and kept a listening watch on this frequency. If no messages were to be passed, the group transmitter would send a time check and a number every half hour at 20 minutes and 50 minutes past the hour. The number was to enable the signals leader to check that the wireless op had not fallen asleep (not unknown). At about 17:50 we crossed the English coast and I reeled out the trailing aerial. All distress frequencies were on the medium wave and these were worked on the trailing aerial. An uneventful sea crossing and the French coast was crossed about 45 minutes later. I reeled the Trailing aerial back in and we continued across France in a series of doglegs. No sign of life on the ground or in the air except for the odd Lanc which would suddenly appear from nowhere. Fifteen minutes before H hour, target indicators were observed going down dead ahead. It was now time to go over to the master bomber's W/T frequency and my job at this time was to receive instructions given by the controller. These were a repeat of instructions given on VHF set and received direct by pilot and action on these messages became necessary only if the VHF set did not function satisfactorily. The controller confirmed that the TIs were accurately placed and we were able to fly straight in on our bombing run at 10,000 ft. We were the second wave in and the German gunners now had the track and height of the stream. At this height they were able to reach us with heavy, medium and light flak. The sky above the target was filled with bursting shells, a lot of which were "Flaming Onions" – tracer shells fired from a rapid firing gun. These seemed to climb very slowly into the air and every one seemed to be coming direct at our aircraft (illusion). As they climbed higher they appeared to increase speed and would streak past (hopefully) like a streak of lightning. The aircraft commenced to buck violently, some of which was due to bursting shells but most was due to slipstream of bombers in front of us. The bomb-aimer was now giving instructions to the pilot and the bombing run seemed to go on and on and on. Suddenly a clicking beneath our feet and a sudden lifting of the aircraft made it unnecessary for the bomb-aimer to shout "Bombs away!" followed by "Let's get the hell out of here!" He was not a man subject to dramatics and his outburst was indicative of the ferocity of the German gunfire. However it was still necessary to fly straight and level for about one minute to obtain a photograph (failure to do so could result in the operation not being counted towards a tour). During this period I spent as much time as possible in the astrodome helping the gunners search the sky for enemy fighters, a large number of which were in evidence over and around the target area. We finally turned for home and about 10 minutes later the controller sent the "operations over go home" signal. I then reverted to the group transmitter frequency. A few minutes later the skipper asked me to go aft and check that the photoflash had cleared the chute OK. After this I settled down to a period of listening out and looking out and changing the colours of the period at the due times and the return trip was accomplished without further incident. After landing, just before midnight, we taxied round to dispersal and proceeded to the debriefing room via a crew bus. On entering we were given a mug of coffee with the option of a shot of rum (thick treacle-like stuff). We were then questioned by an interrogation officer about all the aspects of the operation. After this we walked to the mess (transport was available but the walk helped you to unwind) for our post-op meal. It was during the meal that we heard that *Sugar* and *George* were missing and others damaged. Finally back to the billet and asleep within minutes of climbing into bed.'

CHAPTER TEN

Flying as a 'Spare'

In April 1944, Warrant Officer Alan Cuthbertson, a Canadian from Winnipeg, Manitoba, Canada was posted to No. 1661 Heavy Conversion Unit at Winthorpe, near Newark. He was training to be a bomb-aimer and during a night training flight met with an accident. While landing at Waddington a tyre burst on their Sterling bomber and the undercarriage collapsed. Cuthbertson ended up in a body cast. The rest of the crew were all right and continued their training. They served at Skellingthorpe, near Lincoln. However, on 12/13 August 1944, on a raid against Russelheim in Germany, they failed to return from their 23rd operation and with the exception of his replacement bomb-aimer, they were all killed.

After a period of rest and further training Cuthbertson was posted to No. 227 Squadron at Balderton where, on the night of 26/27 November 1944 he made his first operational sortie, as a 'spare' bomb-aimer. As it was during the winter season, foul weather frequently intervened with air operations which would be cancelled at the last minute, or even after becoming airborne.

Alan Cuthbertson (centre back) with other crew members of No. 57 Squadron at East Kirkby, April 1945.

'A few days earlier I had attended briefing for a raid – to be my first – on a deep penetration to Breslau in eastern Germany which had been "scrubbed" because of poor weather. Now the target was to be Munich, a city said to be well defended, and a long flight for my initial operational sortie. I wasn't apprehensive since by this time I had had a long intensive training, including some minor accidents which had delayed my posting to an operational squadron.

'Early in the day – departure was to be nearly midnight – there was assembly of those aircrews taking part for general briefing of the planned route, weather conditions, target markings and enemy's defences. We then had to draw maps, escape kit and a most important item, a parachute. Supper was eaten – perhaps some mutton, beans-on-toast or Welsh rarebit. Reading, cards and letter writing, perhaps some snoozing, occupied the evening. Around about 23:00 we were transported to our aircraft which were widely dispersed around the airfield. Engine run-ups and other pre-flight checks by each crew member were then performed. Control tower signalled take-off time with a bright pyrotechnic (radio silence was absolute) fired into the air and all aircraft began their slow taxi out onto the perimeter track leading to the runway for take-off. There was usually a number of station personnel at the take-off point to wave to the departing aircraft. With engines roaring the Lancaster rumbled off down the runway at 23:45 and became airborne in the darkness of night. Course was set, engines synchronised and climb to altitude began. Within a short time the coast was crossed and we droned on, seemingly alone but for the occasional bump to remind us that we had encountered the slipstream of other aircraft of which there were several hundred heading for the same target.

'The enemy seemed oblivious to our presence on this occasion although their radar would have signalled an impending raid while we were still over the British Isles. There was not yet any sign of anti-aircraft barrage or searchlights probing the sky. It was a cloudless and moonlight night but no hostile aircraft made their presence known along the route which took us in a south-easterly direction. My vivid recollection is that we crossed over the Alps which were ruggedly beautiful in the full moonlight. One or two of the larger Swiss cities were also visible since they were not "blacked out", indicating the status of a neutral country surrounded by nations at war. We approached Munich on track, on time, at the approximate hour of 04:00. Other aircraft became visible in the strong light of moonlight above and fires below. The Pathfinders had preceded us to drop their target indicators and our bombing

Alan Cuthbertson in Lancaster 'J' bound for Lutzkendorf.

approach run of several minutes was made under good conditions. We dropped our bomb load of 18 x 'J' type clusters at 18,250 ft and on leaving the target we increased our speed with a steep dive to evade the defences which, although expected at the "cradle of Nazism", that night were caught napping and I for one was thankful indeed. The return route was again over Switzerland and without incident for the following several hours before landing at base in full daylight, tired, but glad to be back. The duration of flight was 9 hours 5 minutes and the debriefing by the Intelligence Section for details of the trip was a necessary prelude to a meal of bacon and eggs followed by a few hours of sleep.

'Subsequent intelligence provided the information of success of the raid without loss of any of our aircraft. I had been flying "spare" on this occasion during the absence on leave of the regular bomb-aimer. The crew members were strangers except for that one time when the Air Force placed us together as a crew. It was my good fortune not to be with them again on the following trip to Heilbron from which they did not return. My own next operational trip – again as a "spare" – proved that a Lancaster could absorb flak damage and remain airborne with three engines on which to get back to base, and that, too, for me is a story with a happy ending.'

Cuthbertson continued to fly as a 'spare' but it was unnerving not knowing the crew. At long last he was posted to No. 57 Squadron at East Kirkby in Lincolnshire where he became part of Squadron Leader Hodgkinson's crew.

His first operational sortie with Squadron Leader Hodgkinson and his crew of veterans of previous operational tours (several 'gonged' members amongst them), was on 8 April 1945. At 17:50 they took off from East Kirkby in Lancaster DX-J bound for Lutzkendorf. Their target was the twin crude-oil refining and synthetic production plants. These were to be some of the last battles and were made on oil objectives. Lutzkendorf had in fact been bombed four nights earlier but the bombing had been hampered by black smoke which rose early during the attack. They had been sent to finish the job and their bomb load was 1 x 4,000 lb 'cookie' and 14 x 500 lb bombs. On return to base, landing was not permitted because of fog cover and they were diverted to Wellesbourne Mountford where they were debriefed and spent the remainder of the night before returning to base. The log-book of Warrant Officer Cuthbertson states that the mission took 9 hours 20 minutes and passed without particular incident. The target was 'well pranged'.

Warrant Officer Cuthbertson took part in 'Operation Exodus' and brought back from Lille in France 24 very excited and grateful forces personnel who only a short while earlier had been prisoners. He made a second trip to Brussels for the same purpose but for reasons unknown they returned empty. These were his last missions before returning home to Canada.

CHAPTER ELEVEN

Four Years in Service

Thisis the story of Bruce Douglas Bancroft who was born in
Rochdale, New South Wales, Australia on 29 October 1916.
Known as Doug Bancroft, he enlisted in the Royal Australian
Air Force on 28 February 1942, service number AUS 421635. He
gained his 'Wings' as Sergeant Pilot in Canada in March 1943 and
arrived in the United Kingdom the following month.

*Air crew and four of the ground crew of Halifax III LV792 NP-E, 158
Squadron, Lissett, Yorkshire, April 1944. Air crew: Standing, back row,
left to right—Sergeant Len Dwan (without Mae West or harness),
wireless operator; Sergeant Ken Leheup, mid-upper gunner; Sergeant
David ('Jock') Arundel, rear gunner; Sergeant Len ('Spike') Cottrell,
engineer; Flying Officer Eric Tansley, bomb-aimer; Pilot Officer Doug
Bancroft, pilot; Pilot Officer Alwyn Fripp, navigator. Names of four
ground crew in front row are not known.*

'On arrival in the United Kingdom I was eventually posted to an Operational Training Unit at Abingdon, Berkshire on Armstrong-Whitworth Whitley aircraft and it was here that I teamed up with my first crew members:- Pilot Officer Eric Tansley, bomb-aimer; Sergeant Alwyn Fripp, navigator; Sergeant David Arundel, rear gunner; and a Sergeant wireless operator who was transferred to 101 Special Duties Squadron after a few weeks and was replaced by Sergeant Leonard Dwan, wireless operator. From Abingdon we flew on one "Nickel" (Newspaper dropping raid) over France.

'From Abingdon, my crew and myself were posted on 8 November 1943 to Driffield airfield (which was non-operational at that time, having been rendered unserviceable by enemy attack in 1943) to undergo a commando-type battle course. On reporting at Driffield, we were placed under the instruction of a section of the King's Own Yorkshire Light Infantry (KOYLIs) and advised by the NCO in charge of our group that all rank was to be disregarded for the duration of the course. This action was willingly accepted by all, but imagine our feelings, as aircrew, when we received an issue each of rifle, bayonet, webbing, backpack, ammunition, boots, etc, and were advised that one must always move at the double and that, in any case, the marching rate was 140 to the minute. The weather was exceedingly cold with snow and ice in abundance as we ran miles and miles around the countryside. We climbed over high brick walls and back again, over barricades by ropes, jumped great ditches full of icy water and mud, crawled on our bellies under low bridges through streams which were about to freeze up, scaled rope ladders, ran across fallen trees, fixed bayonets and charged madly at straw dummies and screamed like banshees and then ran the several miles back to camp at Driffield in pouring rain where the hot showers were always most welcome to soothe the aching, bruised bodies and thaw out our veritably frozen bloodstreams. At the conclusion of several weeks of this training we had learnt what would be required if we were involved in a joint exercise such as a combined effort to secure an airfield, etc, and we were all certainly more fit than when we arrived at Driffield.

'My crew and I were posted from Driffield to the Halifax Conversion Unit at Rufforth, Yorkshire at the end of November 1943 and here we were joined by Sergeant Kenneth Leheup, mid-upper gunner, and Sergeant Robert Stacey, flight engineer. Rufforth had been the base for 158 Squadron from 6 November 1942 to 28 February 1943. The weather was still holding very cold, wet and foggy. Rufforth Conversion Unit was equipped mainly with ex-operational Halifax II aircraft fitted with Rolls-Royce Merlin XX motors, many of which had done a considerable number of flying hours and the ground crews were kept very busy maintaining a degree of serviceability under the prevailing difficult weather conditions. Although the morale of my crew was of a very high standard, as was the case with all the aircrews, the frustration grew as the weather continued to stop flying operations for long periods and personnel moved about in the rain, the mud and the snow day after day.

'My crew did get one break when a lone rabbit was seen near our Nissen hut. There was a long chase across the muddy fields, over ditches and through hedges until it was eventually caught and triumphantly brought back to the hut where it was beheaded with a fire-axe, skinned and nicely baked in front of the coke fire. Of course, the drying out and cleaning of clothes and boots was rather a lengthy process but all enjoyed the tasty meal.

'On 21 January 1944 I was sent from Rufforth across to 10 Halifax Squadron, Melbourne, Yorkshire, to fly as second pilot (2nd "dickie") with a crew from there in an attack on Magdeburg. The bomber force consisted of 749 aircraft of which 55 failed to return. We were attacked by three enemy night fighter aircraft and ran into very heavy anti-aircraft fire over Wilhelmshaven.

'On 7 February 1944 we were detailed for three-engine daylight landing exercises, using Lissett as the airfield with a Halifax II (*EB195*) from our unit at Rufforth. Following several successful three-engine landings, we were making another left-hand circuit with the starboard outer engine shut down. In the final turn to the landing approach at some 600 ft altitude with undercarriage down and flaps at 30–40 degrees down, there was a violent explosion in the starboard inner engine which sent pieces of engine cowling and carburettor air-intake flying into the air. The engine stopped, leaving only the two port engines running. The aircraft swung to starboard in a diving turn and, as there was insufficient power available in the port engines, all that could be done was to endeavour to fight the controls down to the ground. The aircraft hit the ground in more or less a landing attitude, wiped off the undercarriage in a ditch, cut through several hedgerows, knocked down several circuit light poles and came to rest about 30 yards from the back door of a farmhouse. The farmer rushed out from the farmhouse and called out, "Is anyone hurt?" On being advised that the crew were shaken up but unharmed, his next words were "What about my bloody turnips? – seven of you b......s in the last week!"

And sure enough, when I looked over his fields, there were six more aircraft scattered about, either with their tails in the air or on their bellies with broken backs, as was ours. A few weeks later, when we were posted to 158 Squadron, Lissett, our sleeping quarters were just outside this farmer's entrance gateway but he would always drive past us on his way to the mess area for his pig scraps and leave us to walk the mile or so – rain, snow, or sunshine.

'As the cold, bleak days and weeks passed, we were gradually able to build up sufficient hours of experience on the Halifax II and we were able to do a few hours on night landings during the odd nights which were free of fog. On the night of 16 February 1944 we were detailed for night circuits and landings in Halifax *DK173* and after completing several such exercises we made a landing approach and touch-down. As the wheels touched the runway the aircraft began to sway from side to side and no amount of rudder or braking control or even engine power seemed to be able to control the erratic swaying. As the aircraft's speed dropped off, the swinging about became worse and although my early thoughts had been of a blown-out starboard tyre, I erased this thought because of the violence of the side-to-side swaying motion and the failure of the aircraft to answer to applied controls. Eventually the aircraft dropped to the runway on the starboard side, the starboard wing hit the ground, the aircraft swung violently in a semi-circle and came to a halt. On a full investigation the following morning it was found that the main holding shaft attaching the starboard undercarriage to the wing had simply fallen out of the old aircraft in the circuit area and left that undercarriage to be loosely held only by auxiliary attachments such as hydraulic lines and struts. It was found that the aircraft was not economically repairable and it was written off.

'A few days after this incident, Sergeant Robert Stacey, flight engineer, received a posting to another unit and Sergeant Leonard Cottrell joined the crew as flight engineer. Sergeant Cottrell, incidentally, had such a crop of fuzzy hair that he had permission to carry his field-service cap tucked into his tunic belt as it was impossible to keep it on his head. He had also been with us as a passenger when we crashed at Lissett on 7 February.

'We were posted to 158 Squadron, Lissett, on 29 February 1944 and on 1 March 1944 I was detailed to fly as a second pilot (2nd "dickie") with one of the squadron crews captained by Flying Officer Doug Cameron (I think) in a Halifax III *LV792-E* to attack Stuttgart. The attack was carried out without incident and I and my crew were to attack that same target twice more during our tour with 158 Squadron. Whilst I was on this detail, the remainder of my crew was called out of bed at about 2 am to assist in the clearing of snow from the runway and the spreading of salt to prevent icing up of the surface in preparation for the landing of the returning aircraft early in the morning.

'158 Squadron had just recently been re-equipped with the Halifax III, having commenced using this aircraft on operations on 20 January 1944. As my navigator, Flight Sergeant Fripp, had been trained in the use of H$_2$S we were detailed to use various squadron aircraft as available fitted with this equipment until, after several weeks on the squadron, we were allocated *LV792 NP-E (Easy)*. It was my contention that this aircraft had the smoothest running and best engines on the squadron as the previous captain had really "nursed" them along.

'Whilst many of the aircrew carried what they claimed to be were lucky charms, possibly the most notable one during out stay at Lissett was that of the Pilot Officer (later Flying Officer) C.E. Smith who sported a real Air Force type moustache. He always carried with him, when flying, a large white toy elephant some 18 in tall which was known as "Dumbo". "Dumbo's" flying position was in the cockpit beside Smith at all times and Smith himself got the nickname of "Dumbo" Smith. His aircraft was *LV907 NP-F Friday the 13th* from early April 1944 until the beginning of August 1944. For myself, I always insisted on having my cap hanging on the emergency hydraulic pump lever – for what reason, I still fail to understand.

'As the weather began to improve in March, operations were stepped up, including the last massed bombing attack on Berlin on the night of 24/25 March 1944 when we were detailed as one of the wind-finder aircraft in the bomber stream. For the attack 158 Squadron dispatched 15 aircraft to join the second and third of five waves. Zero hour on the target was set at 22:30 on 24 March with each wave being allocated three minutes over the target. I and my crew were flying in Halifax III *NP-C* fitted with H$_2$S radar (I think the serial number was *HX344*). We were to attack in wave three due over the target between 22:36 and 22:39. We were logged as airborne at 18:59 and landed back at base at 01:44 (6 hours 45 minutes). The meteorological report advised good weather all the way with very slight and variable winds. We were detailed to fly below 1,000 ft to keep below the enemy radar screen until about 100 miles from the enemy coast at which point we were to climb to our bombing height of 20,000 ft to cross the coast and to continue at that altitude. On reaching the enemy coast, my navigator, Flight Sergeant Alwyn Fripp, advised that we had drifted some 50 odd miles south of track and that he had calculated the wind velocity as 100 mph from the north and that his new ETA target was about 22:52 (some 15 minutes late). I instructed him to have the wireless operator, Sergeant Leonard Dwan, immediately to advise Group of this wind velocity and direction and for him (Flight Sergeant Fripp) to give me a new course directly to the northern side of the target area in order to pick up some of the time. We arrived in the target area still some ten minutes late and noted that the bomber stream was widely scattered. Anti-aircraft fire was very concentrated but we were able to make a good bombing run up to the target and get our load of incendiaries and high explosives onto the target. Enemy fighter aircraft were very active in the searchlight area and even in the flak area but as several searchlights converged to form a cone I pushed the control column forward and we dived through the space which they had left clear.

'Still using the wind velocity and direction as calculated by Flight Sergeant Fripp we were able to maintain the original flight plan tracks back to base without incident although whilst north of Osnabruck we could see well to the south, over the Ruhr Valley area, that many aircraft had drifted down there and were caught in the heavy defences of that area and many were being shot down there. Of the 73 aircraft from the Command which failed to return from this operation, 158 Squadron lost two.

'Essen was our next target for 26/27 March and we attacked above 10/10ths cloud using H_2S. Before crossing the Dutch coast on the homeward leg, the starboard inner engine main drive shaft snapped. This allowed oil from the constant speed propeller control to escape, which feathered the propeller blades. The engine was shut down and a smooth homeward run and landing were completed.

'Attacking the marshalling yards at Villeneuve St George on the night of 9 April 1944 close bursts of heavy predicted flak jammed the bomb-bay doors in the closed position and we were unable to open the doors to release our bomb load onto the target although we made seven runs over the target, each time endeavouring to get the bombs away. Eventually, I decided to leave the area and try to jettison the load over the sea. The bomb-bay doors were opened by emergency procedures over the English Channel and the bomb load safely jettisoned although an amount of damage was done to the

'E' Easy of No 158 Squadron, Lissett, 1944. Halifax bomber used by Pilot Officer Doug Bancroft.

fuselage bomb-bay doors in the effort. We landed back at Lissett some considerable time after all the other aircraft.

'On the night of 2/3 June 1944 we were involved in an attack on the marshalling yards at Trappes in the outskirts of south-west Paris. A total of 128 bombers were dispatched and 124 bombed the target under clear skies. With nearly a full moon it was perfect for the enemy night fighter pilots and 16 aircraft failed to return, five being from our squadron.

'Our aircraft was attacked at 7,500 ft by a Ju 88 and raked by cannon fire. Fire broke out in the bomb-bay and the starboard inner engine burst into flames. With the hydraulics shot away both turrets were out of action. With the loss of the hydraulic fluid the wing-flaps and bomb-doors fell down. The exploding shells blasted a hole 3 ft in width across the floor. The crew fought the flames and having used all the fire extinguishers beat the dying flames with their hands and feet until all was extinguished.

'While all this was going on I set course for home, steering a course by the North Star and crossed the English Channel at 2,000 ft and landed my badly damaged bomber at Hurn near Bournemouth with two blown-out tyres – tail wheel and port undercarriage tyres. On approaching Hurn we were down to 900 ft and losing height continually. Once the undercarriage up-locks were released on the down wind leg of the circuit and the undercarriage dropped and locked under its own weight we were committed to the landing as it would not have been possible to go round again. Here I learned that Sergeant Dwan, who had been severely wounded in the legs, had either fallen or baled out through the large hole in the fuselage floor. Sergeant Cottrell and Sergeant Leheup were also missing.

'I would add further to this account by advising that my flight engineer, Sergeant Leonard Cottrell was picked up by French

Resistance forces and eventually returned to England; whilst Sergeant Kenneth Leheup, mid-upper gunner, was taken PoW. He landed safely by parachute and advises that, after wandering about for some time, he stepped into some bushes to relieve himself and found that he had walked into an anti-aircraft gun position where he was very quickly apprehended. Sadly, my wireless operator, Sergeant Leonard Dwan was very severely wounded in the attack and his body was never found. His name may be found in the Books of Remembrance at the Royal Air Force Memorial at Runnymede.

'For this action an award of an immediate Distinguished Flying Cross was made to Flying Officer Tansley, Pilot Officer Fripp and myself (now Pilot Officer) and an immediate Distinguished Flying Medal to Sergeant Arundel. Unfortunately, also, during my temporary absence from Lissett, Sergeant David ("Jock") Arundel after having completed 22 operational missions and one "nickel" raid with us, was detailed to fly as replacement air gunner for one attack on Amiens with another crew on 12 June 1944. The aircraft was shot down by an enemy night fighter and Sergeant Arundel lost the sight of one eye through being hit by a piece of shrapnel. The crew baled out and Sergeant Arundel was assisted by French Resistance forces and later returned to England.

'A new crew was formed with myself, pilot; Flying Officer Tansley, bomb-aimer; Pilot Officer Fripp, navigator; Pilot Officer Thompson, rear gunner; Flight Sergeant Proctor, wireless operator; Sergeant W. McLean, mid-upper gunner and Sergeant Tiltman, flight engineer. We were allocated another H_2S equipped aircraft, Halifax III *HX356 NP-G Goofy's Gift* and the ground crew under Sergeant Fitzpatrick, fitter, proudly emblazoned the insignia of the DFC and DFM on the fuselage in our honour. This aircraft carried us through until we were screened from further operations on 1 September 1944. During the homeward run from Stuttgart on the night of 24/25 July 1944 we were attacked on six different occasions by enemy night fighters before crossing the enemy coast and owing to the amount of evasive action taken were compelled to land at Hemswell airfield before reaching base in order to refuel.

'On the night of 16/17 August 1944 we were detailed to target mark as a backup force to PFF on the dock area of Kiel and were loaded up with target indicators together with 16 x 500 lb bombs. Cloud cover over the target area necessitated bombing blind from 18,000 ft using H_2S, and the bombing photographs showed direct hits with bombs and target indicators in the target area. Although flak was very concentrated and enemy fighters were very active, the attack was successful. Sadly, though, as we were making our cross-wind leg in the circuit area preparatory to landing I saw *LK839 NP-S* captained by Flying Officer Rosen, RCAF flying parallel on our starboard side suddenly dive to starboard and crash into a field at Foston-on-the-Wolds, Yorkshire. Some of the crew died instantly in the crash and the remainder died a short time later.

'The night of 18/19 August 1944 saw us detailed for an attack on Sterkrade, north-west of Essen. The target area was very heavily defended with anti-aircraft gunfire and searchlights with little cloud cover. At the end of the bombing run at 20,000 ft a heavy explosion just under the tail sent *Goofy's Gift* into a vertical dive. I remember for a moment thinking about being on a parallel line to the searchlight beams. The dive was so steep that I was unable to pull back the control column to get the aircraft flying level again. On glancing at the air speed indicator I noted that it was well above 360 mph and rising fast. Winding back steadily on the elevator-trimming tab control, the nose of the aircraft came up, at first very slowly and then more quickly, and old *Goofy's Gift* levelled out at 1,500 ft still doing a high air speed from the impetus of the long dive. Some short time later a voice over the intercom called, "Navigator to skipper! What are we doing down here and at this air speed?" The crew in the nose section had not felt any unusual sensation, apparently. Gradually the air speed reduced from the impetus gained and we flew the remainder of the homeward leg across Holland and the North Sea at 1,500 ft to land at base without further incident.

'We were detailed for several more attacks on various enemy targets, by daylight and night, until reporting as usual to 'A' Flight office on 1 September 1944 I was informed by the flight commander that Flying Officer Tansley, Flying Officer Fripp and myself had completed our tour and were screened from further operations. We were also informed by the squadron intelligence officer that our bombing record showed 22 direct hits and 9 target area aiming points from a total of 34 operations flown together as a crew, a result which could only have been achieved by complete co-operation between each and every crew member, strict discipline and high morale.

'Flying Officer Tansley and I were seconded to the Ministry of Supply for a liaison lecture tour of munitions factories for several months whilst Flying Officer Fripp was posted to Marston Moor, Yorkshire as a navigation instructor. After completion of the assignment with the Ministry of Supply, I was posted as an instructor to Lichfield OTU and from there in (either January or February) 1945 I received a posting to 96 Transport Command Squadron being formed at Leconfield, Yorkshire. There I met again some of my friends from 158 Squadron, Lissett including my good friend Flying Officer "Dumbo" Smith, still with his white elephant "Dumbo". As the squadron was forming, our aircraft began to arrive – 25 brand new Halifax VIIs. The ground crews were set to work on these new aircraft, setting them up to carry troops and stretcher cases and polishing the fuselages and wings to a silver colour. We were advised that we would be flying troops and materials to India and bringing wounded personnel back to England, using Cairo as a staging post. Some weeks later we were advised that the squadron would be operating from a base in the south of England and all aircrew were given two weeks' leave. Less than a week after commencing leave we all received telegrams cancelling our leave and recalling us immediately to our unit at Leconfield. Arriving back at the unit we were advised to prepare to fly the aircraft to Cairo where we would be based. On flight testing one of the aircraft, Flying Officer Max Hubbard, RAAF, was killed together with his crew and several ground crew who were in the aircraft when it crashed into a hill near Leconfield whilst descending through cloud.

'Within a few days of being detailed to prepare to go to Cairo several crews began to ferry the new aircraft back to the Handley-Page works to be scrapped, much to the complete disgust of the whole squadron. Several of the squadron aircrews, as advance party, were then flown out to Cairo West whilst the remainder entrained for Ganrock on the Clyde and embarked on a troopship for Egypt. Thus ended 96 Squadron's formation and stay at Leconfield, Yorkshire.

'With the war now over I was demobilised from the Royal Australian Air Force on 8 February 1946 at Sydney, New South Wales. During my four years of service I was awarded the Distinguished Flying Cross and George Medal.'

CHAPTER TWELVE

The Routine Flight

February 1944 and Sergeant Payne was just 19 years of age and had already completed 13 operational missions which included nine devastating raids over Berlin. He was a wireless operator of a seven men crew in Lancaster *VN-B Baker* with No. 50 Squadron at RAF Skellingthorpe on the outskirts of Lincoln.

At this stage of the war every effort was being made to step up the offensive against Germany. Air Chief Marshall Harris was still against any interference with the existing combined bombing offensive against German industry. He believed that bombing, if on a sufficiently large and sustained scale, could be the weapon to bring Germany to its knees and end the war. Bomber crews were given extra flying training on every available day when they were not required for operational duties. Sergeant Payne was on such training duties during February 1944.

'I remember clearly it being a cold but sunny Saturday afternoon on 12 February as we climbed aboard the crew bus which

Taken at Skellingthorpe, No. 50 Squadron. Left to right (last two)
Sergeant Moore, engineer; Sergeant Higgins, mid-upper gunner; Mike
Beetham's original crew, left to right Sergeant Ball, rear gunner;
Sergeant Bartlett, bomb-aimer; Flying Officer Beetham, pilot; Flying
Officer Swinyard, navigator; Sergeant Payne, wireless operator.

transported us to the far side of the aerodrome where the aircraft were dispersed. As this was to be only a training exercise an old Lancaster W4119 with many hours to its credit was used for this purpose, as all the operational aircraft were kept fully maintained for instant use. To save time on landing and taking off in a fighter attack exercise such as this, our full crew of seven and part of another crew (pilot and two gunners), ten men in all, were taking part.

'We took off and in a few moments were heading for the coast of Lincolnshire, where we were detailed to contact a Spitfire to commence fighter interception. The Spitfire was soon located and as cloud base was 3,000 ft it was decided for safety to start the exercise above it. At 6,000 ft and well above cloud our pilot called up the Spitfire and instructed him to make his first attack.

'For half an hour both planes circled and corkscrewed above the peaceful Lincolnshire countryside and the first part of the exercise was completed successfully. At this stage the Spitfire was holding off to allow pilot and gunners to change places and, this completed, the Spitfire spiralled down once more to attack. At the word "go" the Lancaster started its corkscrew but during its first dive to port a sudden explosion came from the port outer engine and in seconds was a mass of flames. Our own pilot, being senior and more experienced, took control of the aircraft and immediately gave the order "Prepare to abandon aircraft". Fire extinguishers were set off in the engine causing steam to eject but it was fruitless as the fire soon had a firm hold. The scene inside the aircraft was one of great activity, gunners leaving their turrets and all crew members adjusting parachutes and harness. I was the wireless operator in the crew and my parachute was always stowed on the seat beside me and I could not help thinking as I clipped it on of our flight engineer who had boarded the plane without his. I remember him saying in the crew room that as it was only a training flight he wouldn't bother to bring his. I noticed that smoke was entering the aircraft and glancing out of the window I could see the flames spreading rapidly. By this time our pilot had realised the position was hopeless and gave the order to "abandon aircraft". 'As I left the wireless operator's compartment I knew the forward hatch was open by the oncoming rush of air and saw our navigator making towards it. As my exit was at the rear, with my parachute firmly clipped into the chest position I made my way to the rear door which was by now fully opened and fastened back. Several members of both crews were clustered round there, all hesitating as to who should go first.

I didn't know at that moment that the bomb-aimer had successfully left from that exit. The mid-upper took the plunge next but contrary to the drill laid down he stood upright in the doorway and jumped. He didn't get very far, as our next view of him was spread-eagled over the tail plane. When he recovered his senses he pulled his release handle and was snatched away as his 'chute opened. After that no one seemed eager to jump but knowing the extent of the fire now raging in the wing I gladly accepted the opportunity and, sitting in the appropriate position, eg, crouched with back to the slipstream, I made an effort to roll out sidewards but was blown back in by the slipstream. My second attempt was more successful and I found myself rapidly falling towards a cloud layer 3,000 ft below the aircraft. By this time I was frantically tugging at my parachute release, which had no effect, and added to this a white mist was swirling around me so I knew I had reached the cloud layer only 3,000 ft from the fields below. Terrified, and with tears filling my eyes, I prayed desperately to God to help me as I felt sure I had only a few seconds to live. Some instinct told me to examine my parachute pack and to my intense relief I saw it was one of the four carrying handles I was gripping and not the release ring. Immediately I pulled at the release ring and was overjoyed to see the white silk passing over my head as the parachute opened with a "crack". I was amazed at the silence around me, which was shattered by the Lancaster crashing into the ground somewhere below me. A black rainbow of smoke showed clearly the descent of the Lancaster, which was now a raging ball of fire, and above it part of the port wing was falling like an autumn leaf. Owing to my swift descent, although I was the last to leave the aircraft alive, I was the only member to see it crash. I continued to drift slowly, losing little height, with the 'chute swinging lazily sidewards. I noticed I was being followed as I saw a 'chute not far above me. My efforts in shouting brought no reply but my attention was taken up with the ground which was coming up fast. I seemed to be drifting towards a huge lake or sandpit and I began wondering whether I should take my boots off, and was about to do so when I saw the danger was passed. It was a ploughed field that I finally crashed into and rolling over in the mud I was very relieved to find I was down and in one piece.

'The crew member following me down wasn't quite so lucky, drifting just that bit further down in to a small pine wood. I heard the snapping and cracking of branches as his 'chute vanished among the trees. I ran quickly to his aid but a local farmer was there before me, and was already helping him out of the wood, carrying his parachute for him. It turned out to be the pilot of the other crew in the aircraft (a young Australian) but I could tell by the way he was mumbling and the silly questions he was asking that he was not in his right state of mind.

'It didn't take long for a van from the RAF Aerodrome East Kirkby to come and pick us up to take us back to their camp. It was there we found out that four men had perished in the bomber, the rear gunner and flight engineer from my own crew and both gunners from the second crew. Incidentally, when the medical officer saw the state of the Australian pilot and listened to his wandering mind, he was taken away in an ambulance and I never set eyes on him again.

'The Lancaster, as it happened, crashed on RAF East Kirkby Aerodrome narrowly missing two other aircraft. We were each in turn asked if we would care to help identify the four bodies in the burned out wreck, one of which was our flight engineer who flew without his parachute, but no one cared to oblige.

'After a check-up and a large capsule from the MO we were allowed to go to our respective messes for tea, and as the three remaining NCOs from our crew entered the Sergeants' mess, someone who knew our mid-upper gunner shouted, "Hello Jock, what are you doing here?" Jock replied "We came in that Lanc that crashed here this afternoon". This caused a great deal of laughter from all the onlookers but I'm afraid we didn't feel like joining in. We hung about in the mess for what seemed like ages, feeling very miserable and speaking very little to each other. I couldn't get my mind off the thought of those crumpled bodies that must be somewhere out there on the aerodrome, who only a few hours before I had been laughing and joking with.

'It was approximately 11 pm when we arrived back by road to Skellingthorpe and one of the first to greet us was the MO who examined us and found that Jock, our mid-upper gunner, had sustained a number of broken ribs, obtained during his collision with the tail-plane. These had to be strapped up and we were all given sleeping tablets, which had the necessary effect. Our rear gunner who was killed in the aircraft had never flown before without his "good luck" charm – a brass Lincoln Imp – but on this occasion it had been left behind on his other tunic and waking at noon the next day it was the first thing that caught my eye as the sun shone on it. It was vital to Bomber Command that this incident should not unnerve us and we were made to report to the Flight

Offices where a waiting Lancaster was ready to take us on a routine flight to see if any of us showed any excessive fear. For a few moments during take-off we exchanged one or two weak smiles to hide the feelings we had deep down in our stomachs, but our youth and recklessness soon overcame our feelings and after 48 hours' leave to attend the funerals of our crew members, we were ready to get back to the job in hand. I must add that I could never agree with the findings of the court of enquiry held soon after, that the cause of death and crash was "panic in the aircraft".'

Just seven days after the crash Sergeant Payne was back in action with 50 Squadron. With two new crew members, Flight-Lieutenant J. Blott, rear gunner and Flight-Lieutenant Ted Anderson as flight engineer, they were again a seven man crew and in Lancaster *LL744* took part in a raid against Leipzig. This crew went on to complete their tour (30 operations), the last one being a quiet one against Toulouse repair and assembly factories in *LL744* on 1 May 1944. Only 72 Lancasters took part in the raid. They were airborne at 21:35 on 1 May and landed at 03:10 on 2 May – a flight of 5 hours 35 minutes.

Sergeant Payne left the Royal Air Force in July 1946 with the rank of Warrant Officer and to this day cannot understand why they carried out violent evasive manoeuvres in an aircraft designed only for training and considered unfit for operational duties.

CHAPTER THIRTEEN

The Last Letter

The following is an edited version of the last letter that was sent to the sister of Sergeant Henry Conrad.

'Dear Sis,

A couple of days ago I received a card from you saying: "Good luck to you and your crew" – thanks for those few kind words. I couldn't have received it at a more appropriate time. So to prove what a good type I am I'm going to try and give you *all* the gen on a trip to Leipzig I did on Wednesday night. All set? Here goes then.

'About 10 o'clock Wed. morning we were told we were "on" tonight. That's all we get to know, so between that time and briefing time we get things checked up. Such things as testing helmets, and oxygen attachments etc. We went back to the mess, had "very little" lunch (stomachs are inclined to feel a bit queer about that time) and sat reading or writing in the mess until briefing times were announced. Briefing times were put up about 13:30, Pilots at 14:00, Navs at 14:15, Wops at 14:15 etc. and main briefing at 15:00. We then collected all our flying clothing, and went along to our respective briefings. I was told the various things to do and expect. Any questions?

1295094 Sergeant Henry Conrad, RAF (VR) 49 Squadron.

None of us had any so it was just "Good luck boys, see you tomorrow!" We then went along to the main briefing, and there in a large room with maps and what not on the walls, each crew sat at a table and discussed with the rest of the crew what we had been told individually. It was then that I first saw the route. I obviously can't tell you that but it ended at Leipzig. I couldn't help laughing inwardly when I thought of Uncle Bill's home being paid a visit. It wasn't a personal feeling, it was just as if I knew the place.

'At briefing then, the whole crew discusses and decides on a plan and everyone is ready. The Wing Commander of the Squadron and the CO of the camp are there and they say a few final words. On the way out – briefing having finished – you give all personal belongings on you to the intelligence officer, who keeps it until you return, the idea being you have nothing at all on you if you land over there. The last words I heard when I left the briefing room was "Good luck, Sergeant" from the CO to which I replied, "Thanks, Sir".

'From briefing we went straight to crew room and got fully dressed, Mae West, harness, parachute, etc, pile in a bus, and away to our respective kites. I was in 'P' Peter. We were in the kite about an hour before take-off – that gave us bags of time to check every part of equipment thoroughly. At the precise minute Johnny yelled out "All set to taxi out", we answered "OK". Next thing Johnny yelled out to the ground crew: "OK, here we go", or words to that effect. Feeling very queer, but not actually scared, we taxied round to the runway. At the runway were dozens of people, from the CO down. They stood and cheered, and waved as each kite took off. It may sound strange but it was a very touching sight and I got quite a lump in my throat. Then, from Johnny, "OK boys, here we go." One big Lancaster with seven chaps and a most terrific "cookie" (or bomb to you) and hundreds of incendiaries, went roaring down the runway and after what seemed ages, lifted into the air. From then on, I was doing my job, the nav and pilot discussed the course to steer, the engineer checked the instruments and the gunners just sat.

'About 60 miles from the enemy coast, Johnny told the gunners, "Keep your eyes open, boys". Then I heard someone say that we'd crossed the coast. Once again I had that strange feeling. My cabin was all blacked out, so I couldn't see a thing unless I switched off all lights and pulled the blackout from the window. This I did every so often, but all I could see were searchlights, light flak and darkness. About a quarter of an hour to Berlin I heard the most horrible thing I've ever heard. Instead of the usual roar of engines, there was lots of spluttering and unevenness. We were then at about 20,000 ft. What I heard next really and truly gave me the worst feeling I've ever had in my life. I heard Johnny say, "Stand by to abandon aircraft!" I can remember myself saying, "Oh, my God", someone else said "Prison, here we come". Johnny said "Here goes my 21st birthday party" (Johnny was 21 that day). We all put on our 'chutes and the gunners got out of their turrets. I wasn't really scared, I don't quite know what it was. I thought of all sorts of strange things. Maybe I was scared – I don't know. George said "Try and make for Denmark, it's only 200 miles away". We all laughed but it wasn't funny. The idea you see is not to be captured, but to get out of Germany and back to England.

'All this time the engines were making terrible noises. What actually happened was that the two outboard motors had failed completely and the two inners were just about to do the same. From 20,000 ft we came down to 10,000 in a few minutes which seemed like years. Johnny said: "OK boys, I'm afraid this is it, when we get to 7,000 ft JUMP!" We all acknowledged half-heartedly. At about 9,000 ft the miraculous happened. The engines kicked and spluttered and, as suddenly as they'd stopped, that roar of four engines started again. Believe me, it was the sweetest sound I'd ever heard. Someone said: "Is the panic over?" Johnny said "Yes" and then we laughed and cheered, and swore, in fact did all sorts of balmy and unairman like things. In no time at all we were back up at 22,000 ft, heading for home as fast as possible. The bombs had been dropped as soon as the "fun and games" began. From then on it was up to George (our navigator) to get us home. We started back, weaving about the sky keeping a look-out for night fighters.

'Then we had more panic. Every few minutes Johnny called the gunners on the intercom to ask if they were OK. This particular time there was no answer from Derek, our mid-upper gunner. After a few tries Johnny said, "Mickey (that's me), go and see what's wrong with Derek." I put on my emergency oxygen bottle which lasts 10 mins. I went back but couldn't budge Derek – he was unconscious. Having a gunner unconscious over enemy territory is no joke so I tried like hell to get him from the turret. I couldn't manage it, so Lofty our engineer came back as well and together we struggled like mad to drag him out. By that time I was beginning to suffer from lack of oxygen myself and I struggled back to the nearest oxygen container and tried to plug in. Lack of oxygen makes you dull and stupid after a while and that's how I was. After a few breaths of oxygen I tried to get back to my seat and I realised my oxygen tube was broken. The next I knew, George was holding my oxygen tube on for me and I was awake and normal again. I couldn't move from my seat though because of the oxygen. All this time Lofty had been trying to bring Derek round. This he eventually did, although Lofty himself was just about on the point of collapse. We were still about 300 miles from home, but once again we were all set. Derek got back in his turret and full speed ahead we went. It was then just a question of luck. We came upon very little flak and no fighters. But we were over the sea, and then at the English coast. What a relief it was and what a trip!! We landed, got interrogated, had egg and bacon and so to bed. I slept like a log.

'And that was our little trip to Leipzig. Everyone had trouble, all through the weather. It was ice that made our engines cut, that was why at 10,000 ft they started again. We lost none from our squadron.

'That was that, but last night our bombers went to Leipzig for the first time since 1940 – 18 of our planes are missing.

'Well, kid, that's it, now for God's sake don't say I don't tell you anything. I'm still quite happy and well and in a way looking forward to tomorrow – I expect we're "on" again.

'My love to all at home and I hope you are all quite well. I've no intention of writing this all again, so you can show it to Min if she wants. My regards to you both, Min and Lou.

'Love, Henry.

'PS: Incidentally this letter is not intended to make me a hero and it's not intended to be melodramatic. It's just what happened on that particular raid. Cheers for now kid, and don't let the London air raids bother you – think of Hamburg, Hanover, etc.'

On the night of 2/3 January 1944, a total of 383 aircraft were dispatched against Berlin. A total of 311 attacked the target. Icing conditions forced many crews to jettison all or part of their bomb load before reaching Berlin. There were gale conditions over Germany and Berlin was covered by cloud. Bombing was wide of target and a total of 27 aircraft were lost. The crew of 1295094 Sergeant Henry Conrad, RAF (VR) of 49 Squadron, RAF Fiskerton, Lincolnshire was one of those 27 missing on the raid. Sergeant Conrad is recorded on plaque 227 at the Air Forces Memorial at Runnymede. He was born 16 April 1921 and was married only two months before going missing.

CHAPTER FOURTEEN

A Rhodesian's Adventure Over Stettin

During World War II there must have been very few Rhodesians (now Zimbabwe) who could equal the wide and meritorious experience of Wing Commander Reginald Melville Stidolph who, for a period in 1944 commanded No. 61 Squadron of Bomber Command.

Since the outbreak of war Wing Commander Stidolph had served in all the main theatres from England to the Far East and he had flown in a great many operations against the enemy. He came to England in 1935 and joined the Royal Air Force, receiving a short-service commission and serving in a bomber squadron. He trained in navigation for a year and at the end of 1937 he went to the Fleet Air Arm, specialising in torpedo work with seaplanes until early in 1939. As Flying Officer he was given command of a detached flight in an ack-ack co-operation unit. Wing Commander Stidolph

Wing Commander Stidolph (with microphone) gives Gaumont News *interview after Berlin raid.*

Wing Commander Reg Stidolph (flat cap) with some of his crew of No. 61 Squadron, Skellingthorpe. His two flight commanders are either side of him.

explained that he was whipped away at 24 hours notice from the ack-ack co-operation unit and put aboard an RAF depot ship for servicing flying boats going to the Mediterranean. He saw service in Malta, Alexandria and Gibralter until Italy declared war.

In November 1940, he was controller of flying boats at Suda Bay, Crete, and in March 1941 he found himself in Egypt as flight commander in a squadron of Blenheim fighter bombers and carried out eleven operations in the Western Desert. The following August he took command of the squadron with the rank of Wing Commander. In December 1941, after being severely beaten up by German bombers and ground strafing, the squadron was sent back to the Delta to re-equip. Within a week it set out for Burma, arrived in Rangoon on 5 January 1942, and began operations against the Japanese. After the evacuation of Burma Wing Commander Stidolph returned to India, where he commanded a very advanced RAF base. Then back to England, but not before a flight to China. His worst experience was being bombed at Jarabub Oasis, where they were

Wing Commander Reg Stidolph.

living among gullies and wadis. Though most of the aircrews escaped injury, 35 ground crew were killed. After being in command of No. 61 Squadron at Skellingthorpe for three months he had by this time completed more than 50 operations, which included 19 in Blenheims in the Western Desert and 17 in Burma.

In January 1944 Stettin was again on the target lists after having been left undisturbed for over eight months. On the night of 5/6 January, 358 aircraft were dispatched to bomb Stettin and 348 attacked the target. Fifteen aircraft failed to return. Despite the weather being clear and the target markers well placed, the attack undershot to the west of the town and only about 20 per cent of all bombs actually hit the town. The raid also highlighted the hazards of a densely-packed bomber stream as the planned time over targets was cut to a minimum and many Lancasters had to dodge bombs falling from aircraft flying overhead.

Wing Commander Stidolph piloted a Lancaster bomber during the raid on Stettin and brought it back on two engines, landing with only three minutes' supply of petrol left. Stidolph gave this account of that night's experiences:

'We had trouble with icing but we got to the target and dropped our bombs. Soon after we left Stettin a Messerschmitt 210 attacked us from astern. I saw tracers coming at us and heard the mid-upper gunner calling "fighter" over the intercommunication. As I did a quick dive and turned away, both gunners reported strikes on the fighter. We last saw it diving away with smoke coming from one of its engines. Both the gunners were sure it had been destroyed, but it had hit us badly and set the port outer engine on fire. We stopped the engine and put out the fire. The mid-upper gunner reported that we had lost half the tailplane. I could not control the aircraft on three engines, so I throttled back the starboard outer, and opened my two inner engines to full power, and came home mainly on those two engines. It took us six hours instead of four. Ninety miles from the English coast we were worried because our petrol was getting low, and I made for the nearest airfield. We crossed the coast with under 20 gallons in our tank, and had only 10 gallons when we got down safely on a small grass landing field.'

For the confirmed destruction of an enemy night fighter south of Stettin at 03:57 hours and for bringing his aircraft back to England in spite of extensive damage sustained in the encounter and extreme difficulty in controlling it, Wing Commander Stidolph was awarded the Distinguished Flying Cross. His uncle, Major R.C. Nesbitt won the Victoria Cross in the Mashone rising in 1893, when he was in the Rhodesian Pioneer Column.

CHAPTER FIFTEEN

Unkindly Light

Searchlights, as a means of detecting night flying aircraft, were widely used by the Germans from the very day that World War II started. They were not too effective in the early period and if the wandering beams did manage to fall on an aircraft then the average pilot considered that he had a good chance of shaking them off by carrying out certain abrupt manoeuvres. If, and when, a bomber became well and truly trapped in the cone formed by three or four searchlights then it provided a much coveted and easy visual target for all the anti-aircraft guns in the vicinity. Determined to make the most of such an opportunity the gunners would put up a concentrated hail of fire and could frequently ensure that the aircraft was doomed. More often than not, the target exploded or descended steeply in flames.

When the gunners were successful, the searchlight operators used to take a boyish delight in holding their beams on the falling wreck as long as it was practicable to do so and this habit encouraged members of the attacking force to hope for a little immunity by the use of a simple stratagem. It became the practice for bomber crews to strive for a position about one mile to the rear of any comrade who had the misfortune to be held in a cone, availing themselves of the fact that the full attention of the defence forces was closely occupied.

Alas, this loophole disappeared, because the Germans learned to be far more ruthless and businesslike. As soon as it became quite clear that a stricken aircraft was *hors de combat*, they promptly resumed the hunt for more victims. Eventually, the introduction of radar took the guesswork out of the whole situation. From that very moment it became quite impossible for a pilot to shake himself free from a searchlight cone. Searchlights assumed an infinitely more relentless and pitiless role in the German defence organisation, and became a very positive menace. At about this same period, a pilot passed the remark that searchlights provided enough light at an altitude of 18,000 ft to enable a person to read a newspaper quite easily. This observation was generally regarded with scepticism and derision.

On the night of 29/30 March 1943 Lancaster *EO586* of No. 207 Squadron took off from Langar, Nottinghamshire on a raid against Berlin. It was one of 329 dispatched but owing to severe icing conditions only 213 bombed the target. A total of 21 aircraft was lost on the mission. Lancaster *EO586* survived; Squadron Leader Gilbert Haworth was the navigator and takes up the story:

'We did not suspect that we were due for a unique and very trying ordeal. The moment that the nose of our aircraft entered the Berlin defence zone the dreaded bluish tinted beam of a radar controlled master searchlight fastened upon us fairly and squarely without any preliminary faltering or wavering. Within another two seconds, three supporting searchlights fixed their beams on us and we were well and truly coned. We had no illusions about our probable fate, nor did we even think about trying to shake off the cone. The aircraft cabin was as bright as day and nothing could be seen outside. We knew what to expect. A large number of 88 mm heavy flak guns would engage us as a visual target and would not cease firing until they had destroyed us. On the other hand, it might well be that our bomber would be allocated to the night fighter force, in which case the guns would leave us alone, keeping the airspace clear for a highly trained and competent pilot to close with us and by the gentle pressure of his thumb, cause his cannons to rake us from stem to stern.

'Which was it to be? It hardly mattered, the result would be the same, our aircraft would end in an almost vertical descent, streaming flames and shedding pieces as it fell. Within a matter of a few seconds we had jettisoned our bomb load as there was absolutely no possibility of carrying out a bombing run on our allotted aiming point. Our airgunners strained their eyes in a rather forlorn hope that they might forestall and outshoot any approaching fighter. Squadron Leader F. J. Woodward DFC dropped his pilot's seat to its fullest extent and manfully fixed his gaze inside the cockpit so that he could concentrate on instrument flying and doggedly hold the allotted course to steer. He knew full well that many aircraft had been lost in such circumstances for no other reason than that the dazzled pilots had lost control. At least the Germans were going to have to shoot us down.

'We all waited, not a word was said but we were all thinking the same things. Nothing seemed to be happening; true there was plenty of flak bursting in the sky and the flashes were in the areas all around us but, mystery of mysteries, there was no gunfire being directed especially towards us. We knew this because we could not hear the explosions of any shells. Months before, I had heard some wag on the squadron remark that there was no need to fear the flak unduly if you only saw it, as that was merely a waste of good panic, you should at least wait until you could actually hear the bursting of the shells. Easier said than done, in my opinion. However, our conclusion was that the ground defence organisation had decided that the target which we provided was to be for the sole attention of the night fighter patrols. The guns, doubtless, had other fish to fry.

'We settled down to wait, to wait as patiently as we could, to wait for the crash of cannon fire from an unseen opponent. Turning back was quite out of the question, we therefore flew steadily onwards and, as we did so, we found that we were skilfully handed over from one group of searchlights to another. There was nothing we could do in that nightmare situation, it was impossible to see outside our aircraft to any worthwhile degree because of the dazzle, and all sensation of speed seemed to vanish. The world had disappeared and we felt as if we were hanging motionless in space.

'The Berlin defence zone extended for about 30 nautical miles, our ground speed was 180 knots and it would take 10 minutes to fly clear of the zone. We could increase our speed by diving but to what avail? We could never outstrip a fighter and by losing valuable height we would provide the murderous light flak defences with a target that would be laughably easy to deal with. The seconds ticked by with agonising slowness, the suspense was a terrific strain on the mind and I, for one, began to wish they would start the shooting and get it over with. Five minutes elapsed and still we had no sign of either flak or fighters. Were the Germans having a little game and just toying around with us?

'I felt myself getting seriously alarmed, I was enduring an overdose of something I didn't want, a combination of an inability to act or to do anything useful and an excess of time to think – time to think of a burning aircraft, of dead and wounded men, of futile efforts to escape by parachute and an unpleasant reception from an aggrieved populace for anyone who managed to reach the ground alive. There was no conversation in our aircraft, none of us had anything useful to say and therefore nobody uttered a word. We all thought the same thing. The minutes which seemed so endless did eventually pass away and, quite unbelievably, the interval of time needed to fly clear of the defence zone expired. The long fingers of the last group of searchlights lost us and once more we were in the blackness of the night, heading for home and completely unscathed.

'How on earth had we got away with that little lot? What had gone wrong with the Berlin defence organisation? I found myself trying to imagine the angry recriminations going on between various German staff officers as they argued and bitterly complained about why a good target, so efficiently spotlighted, had been allowed to escape. It seemed to me that the theory of saturation bombing was vindicated, that hundreds of attacking aircraft had disrupted the ground liaison facilities, and vital equipment and key personnel being destroyed at the crucial moment, the enemy's defences had been swamped. We had been endowed with a remarkable anecdote that listeners would be disinclined to believe and I could now vouch that it was indeed possible to read a newspaper in the light of the searchlights at 18,000 ft. Nevertheless, methinks one would have to be in the right mood.'

CHAPTER SIXTEEN

Nuremberg Raid, 30/31 March 1944

I n the last heavy raid of the winter against Nuremberg on 30/31 March 1944, Bomber Command suffered its worst single loss of the entire war, when 95 aircraft failed to return and another 11 were damaged beyond repair. This was the high price Harris paid. The total casualties as furnished by the Stadtarchiv Nurnberg were: Germans killed – 28 men, 24 women, 8 children. Foreigners killed – 14 men, 1 woman. 139 dwelling houses totally destroyed, 238 badly damaged, 956 slightly damaged; 23 factories totally destroyed, 26 badly damaged, 26 slightly damaged; 6 public buildings totally destroyed, 19 badly damaged, 26 slightly damaged. The main areas bombed were the Konigstrasse and the Kesslerstrasse. Also damaged was the Reichsparteitaggelandes (the Nazi meeting area).

On the night in question 795 bombers were despatched, the force being made up of Halifaxes and Lancasters. Only 608 aircraft attacked what they thought to be the target and very few of the 2,148 tons of bombs fell anywhere near Nuremberg. Many aircraft, those without H$_2$S (airborne radar aid to navigation and target location device) bombed places as far distant as Schweinfurt, about 25 miles from the target, thus the

Warrant Officer Ron Buck. Decorations are: 1939–45 Star, Aircrew Europe, Italy Star, War Service Medal, Defence Medal, and below the exclusive Pathfinder Force badge.

attack was widely scattered. The cause of this dismal failure is quite clear and made up of many factors.

First, the German controllers ignored the 50 Halifaxes sent on a diversionary raid in Heligoland Bight and concentrated their night fighters around Bonn and Frankfurt-on-Main; as they guessed the probable target correctly, they easily intercepted the bomber stream. Incorrect wind forecast and the March winds led to serious errors in navigation, thus the bomber stream was soon well spread out. The high cloud, that was to give cover, dispersed over Belgium and left the aircraft exposed and severe icing conditions gave many problems. From Aachen a running battle was fought with more and more night fighters joining in. Vapour trails gave the skilful German night fighters a lead and they soon latched onto the bomber stream. The Pathfinders were 47 minutes late, and Nuremberg was covered in cloud. Even when target indicators were dropped, they could not be seen through the clouds and markers were as far as ten miles apart.

These, then, were the reasons why the mission was a total failure. To this day no one has yet given a reason why the tactics of Bomber Command changed to the direct approach for this raid. The track skirted two well known fighter beacons but no diversionary attacks were planned to occupy the fighters. It now looks as if the world will never know the reason.

We will relive that fateful night in Lancaster 'B' Baker No. 97 (Straits Settlements) Squadron of 8 (Pathfinder) Group at RAF Bourn, Cambs with Warrant Officer Ron Buck, an experienced rear gunner who recorded his impressions at the time, and even today, the raid is still clear in his mind.

'The whole aircraft vibrated as the four Merlins savagely roared into life, injecting confidence into the crew for the mission ahead. Suddenly, the green Aldis flashed and the four-engined monster thundered down the runway on its mission of death and, slowly but sedately, the heavily loaded Lancaster climbed into the night sky. For the rear gunner it was a great relief to look down and see the flare path going away and away. The rear gunner was far from the rest of the crew, shut off behind the revolving turret's door.'

Ron's only contact with the rest of the crew was via the intercom, on which pilot Peter Drane's voice now crackled briefly, 'Wheels up, flaps up, OK lads – 1,000 ft, settle down.' Ron centralised the rear turret and looked down at the dark countryside as he bade farewell to Mother Earth. He then switched on the gun sight and put the safety catches on the four Browning machine-guns to fire and settled down to the task ahead of him. At 22, Ron was a quiet, stocky fellow, a boxer up to international standard by the time he enlisted on 17 December 1940. He was turned down for aircrew, but in 1941 he was sent to Calgary in Canada to open up the Empire Training Scheme and it was there that he remustered as U/T air gunner and completed the training. Back to the UK in January 1943, he married Betty Marsh, his childhood sweetheart at Trinity Church, West Ham on 15 May 1943. The four Merlins beat out a rhythmic drone as Ron scanned the night sky. 'Enemy coast two minutes, skipper', came the voice of Trot the navigator.

Rear gunner Ron Buck takes up the narrative again:

'I take up a standing position in the turret, that's one of the advantages of only being 5 ft 6 in tall, for most attacks on Lancasters by night fighter come from dead astern and below, that's the blind spot. By standing up I can see down and astern through the clear vision panel cut out of the perspex of the turret. As I glance back through the dark sky I see we are giving off con trails from the engine exhausts. "Skipper, what height are we?" "18,000 ft Ron," came back the reply, "Why?" "We are leaving con trails behind". I was interrupted as the navigator broke into the conversation, "Not surprised, it's bloody minus 57 degrees outside". I unclipped my oxygen mask and spat on the barrel of the nearest gun, it was solid as soon as it landed.'

The aircraft droned on at a height of 19,000 ft, their bombing height, for they are briefed to bomb at between 18,000 and 20,000 ft. The tell-tale vapour trails gave Ron a very uneasy feeling, and the only consolation was that there were a few hundred other four-engined bombers all leaving vapour trails. It was certainly a very cold night with stars everywhere and everything was clear and fresh. 'One and a half hours to target', crackled the navigator's voice over the intercom. Ron continued standing, revolving the turret through 180 degrees searching the clear dark sky when suddenly to the port quarter a burst of cannon fire, tracers shoot through the darkness – an explosion – a big flash and burning metal falling out of the sky, cascading down like red hot rain – one bomber that will never reach the target or get home. In that split second seven men died, leaving no trace, and the only grave they will have is in the sky. They will be one of the many posted as missing who will have died without trace before the target is reached.

Ron carried on searching the sky, his eyes more vigilant than ever before, and within a short space of time he counted 12 blazing aircraft falling from the sky behind him, all spiralling down into

German soil below. In all his missions he has never seen 12 aircraft going down together before, and the thought crossed his mind that with only two more missions to complete a tour he was so near, yet so far. His brief thoughts flashed for survival for his crew and aircraft and for his wife Betty.

Running battles were now breaking out all over the sky. 'Flamers' were falling out of the sky by the dozen, Ron must have seen 60 or more go down behind him and he gave up reporting them to the navigator who usually logged them down and concentrated hard on watching the dark sky in front and below him. Suddenly he picked up the black ominous shape on the port quarter and slightly below. At first it was hard to identify at 400 yds or so but instinct told him it was hostile; he'd met them before on several occasions and he bristled as he gripped the four Brownings. 'Fighter, fighter port quarter. Prepare to corkscrew port', shouted Ron over the intercom, 'Got him Johnny?' 'Not yet', came Johnny Henderson's reply from the mid-upper turret. 'Standing by', came the quiet voice of Flying Officer Drane.

As the fighter came in on his curve of pursuit, Ron takes up the story in his own words: ' "Corkscrew! Go!" The nose of the Lancaster dropped so sharply that for a few brief seconds the fighter was lost but as we pulled out of the dive I picked him up again and closed in. Then, Johnny called "I've got him, Ron". "Good", I replied "Let's go together. Ready, Ready, Fire!" The fighter was now well in range of our .303 Brownings and I squeezed the triggers. I expected to see the tracers streaking into the Me 410, which I had now identified, but instead nothing happened. I froze, my mouth went dry and I waited for death, expecting a burst from the night fighter. Over the intercom Johnny's voice screamed, "My guns won't fire". The fighter held off not more than 100 yds away. As he did so, I checked the safety catches, which were all on "fire". Why didn't the guns fire? During all this time the aircraft carried on corkscrewing and I gave out a running commentary as the fighter followed us casually through our evasive action. He seemed to be biding his time. I called to Jock Donald, the wireless operator, to bring me a Very pistol. At least I could have a go at the fighter, and it might put him off if a Very cartridge burst in his nose. I kept up the running commentary, mainly to take my mind off dying. I expect the rest of the crew would have preferred not to have heard, for five of them could not see what was happening.

'The fighter closed in for the kill and I took a deep breath. Closer, so close I could now see the outline of the pilot's head in the cockpit, for he was within 20 feet of my turret and as Jock had not reached me with the Very pistol, I shut my eyes and waited for a quick death. After what seemed an age I opened them and, as I did, I was just in time to see his nose drop and he was gone. As the Me 410 vanished into the darkness below I offered up a short prayer – "Thank you, God. Thank you". I then called to the mid-upper, "He's gone, Johnny" and also the skipper, "All clear behind Skip". I felt the sweat cooling under my flying clothing and I felt cold and clammy all over. I could find no satisfaction from the outcome, only relief. I had wanted to see the tracers steaming from my guns and the German night fighter disintegrate as the bullets smashed home. It was both frightening and disappointing at the same time.

'As 'B' Baker pressed on to the target the crew were happy at being alive but very apprehensive in the knowledge they were unarmed should they be attacked again. Aircraft were still going down behind them and there appeared to be very little opposition. "Target five minutes, Skip", came Trot's voice over the intercom. "OK Trot", came the pilot's reply. "Going down into the nose Skip". "OK Wag", replied the pilot. "Ready when you are". There was silence as "Wag", the bomb-aimer, made his way down into the nose of the aircraft. The gunners continue searching the dark night sky. "Selecting bomb switches Skip". "OK Wag". "Two minutes to target", came the navigator. "In position Skip", announced the bomb-aimer. From this point on, the navigator took over as their mission that night was blind backing-up and they were to bomb on instruments. As they ran up to the target the navigator relayed the course heading to the pilot. "Bomb doors open", came the voice over the intercom. "Bomb doors open", came the reply from the pilot.'

This was the climax of the mission, the culmination, but as they ran in, it was very quiet. No flak, no fighters, no fires underneath the 10/10ths layer of white cloud, nothing to be seen on the ground. In fact it was very eerie and quite an anti-climax after what had gone before. Suddenly the aircraft gave a jerk. 'Bombs gone Skip, bomb doors closed. Get weaving.' For this crew it was normal procedure to weave out of a target and the term 'Get weaving' was a sign of relief that the explosive load had gone and it was time to head for home. Peter Drane placed a gold-braided naval hat on top of his helmet, switched on the intercom and, as he started to weave the aircraft from side to side, broke out into a well-known sea shanty 'A life on the Ocean Wave'. This ritual had taken place ever since the hat was acquired from the White Hart in Boston, Lincolnshire, after a night on the town. However, on this night the ritual was half-hearted for there was very little to celebrate. Ron called to the pilot as they turned for home and explained the situation about the guns being iced-up, for they faced a long trip home without any armament and the thought was not a happy one.

They decided to go for height and get out of the main stream and any night fighters. So, with its nose to the stars, *'B' Baker* climbed and, on reaching 27,000 ft, levelled off. For Ron in the rear turret it was very, very cold, colder than he could ever remember and he longed to get back to taste the steaming hot cup of rum and coffee at debriefing. As he swung the turret through its 180 degrees, taking the slipstream through the clear vision panel, his eyes above the oxygen mask felt like hot coals as the cold air hit them and they watered and felt raw, making the searching very hard. The journey home was uneventful and soon over the intercom crackled the navigator's voice 'Crossing enemy coast'. Ron was almost overcome with cold, then click, the intercom spluttered to life again. 'I'm going to start letting her down lads. Watch your ears', came the pilot's soft voice. Ron felt the nose drop and the tail lift and the wind noise increased as his ears started to sing. Soon they reached the English coast and picked up the friendly searchlight that was a navigational aid to all returning bombers. The navigator took a fix from the light and set course for Bourn. 'What height are we now Skip?' enquired Ron. '4,000 feet', came the reply. 'Thanks'. Ron removed his oxygen mask and rubbed his face. It was much warmer and more comfortable now, time to relax a little but necessary to keep searching for there was always the possibility of intruders, and also the danger from one's own aircraft. Mid-air collisions often happen to tired crews, too relaxed and not alert. He reached into his battle dress pocket and took out some cigarettes and matches. He cupped his hand as he lit his first cigarette and worked the turret with one hand. As he inhaled the smoke, his thoughts turned to home and Betty. Soon they were in the circuit and calling up, and in next to no time taxied into dispersal.

In the back of the garry, the crew exchanged opinions and talked about the raid and the attack by the fighter who never fired. Had his guns also frozen up in those extreme temperatures as theirs had? They were still all

Ron Buck at No. 3 B & G School, McDonald, Manitoba, Canada.

keyed up and would be for some hours yet. They were one of the
first crews back and, apart from the staff waiting to debrief them,
the room was quiet and empty. As they stood around drinking rum
and coffee, the Commanding Officer came over. 'How did it go,
Drane?' he enquired of the pilot. But before he could answer Ron
spoke up, 'It was a disaster, sir, from start to finish. I think we lost
a hundred aircraft tonight and whoever was responsible for
sending us ought to be shot. It was murder'. The CO was a bit taken
aback by this outburst, and, turning to the pilot, said 'Your rear
gunner's a bit over-wrought, Drane. Get debriefed and have a good
night's sleep'. As they sat down at the interrogation table, other
crews were now coming in, talking and gesturing excitedly, and one
was left in no doubt that it had been an exceptional night. They
each gave their information and Ron reported in no uncertain terms
what he had seen and their close escape. The intelligence officer
looked a little doubtful when he put the shot-down figure at 100,
for such a heavy loss had never happened before.

Ron made his way to the mess and silently ate his meal. In a short
time he was in bed, but not asleep. He lay staring at the ceiling and
his thoughts went back to a few hours ago – it seemed like a lifetime.
Over and over in his mind he retraced the drama that was played
out in the night sky over Germany. It was some time before sleep
finally came. Four decades later Ron Buck can still see in his mind
that German night fighter pilot on the fateful Nuremberg raid.

During the Nuremberg raid, Halifaxes suffered most heavily,
losing 30 out of a total of 93 dispatched. The Victoria Cross was
posthumously awarded to Pilot Officer C.J. Barton, RAFVR, Pilot
of Halifax III *LK797 'E'* of No. 578 Squadron 4 Group, for his
outstanding resourcefulness and bravery during the Nuremberg
Raid (see page 213).

That fateful Nuremberg raid is now part of history, and I wonder
if the spirits of those brave young men, killed that catastrophic night
and destined to ride the skies for ever, looked on at the Nuremberg
trials – it's a thought.

Aged 22, Flight-Lieutenant Peter Drane, DFC, RAFVR
(Pathfinders), was killed on 15 January 1945 while on his 67th
mission over enemy territory. To Ron Buck he was more than a
wartime friend and the eldest of his three sons was named Peter
after him. This true wartime story is dedicated to the memory of
that very dear friend.

CHAPTER SEVENTEEN

Failed to Return

One of the 95 that failed to return from the Nuremberg Raid on the night of 30/31 March 1944 was Lancaster *VN 'A' Able EE174* of No. 50 Squadron. The crew were Flight Sergeant G.A. (Jimmy) Waugh, from New Zealand, pilot; Sergeant Dennis (Chas) Chaston from Warwickshire, navigator; Sergeant D.C. (Jerry) Lynch from Buckinghamshire, bomb-aimer; Sergeant G. Prince from Surrey, flight engineer; Sergeant R.J. Dunn from Truro, Cornwall, the wireless operator (Air); Sergeant D. Sehlin, RCAF from Alberta, Canada, mid-upper gunner; and Sergeant R. Thibedeau, RCAF from Ontario, rear gunner.

On the night in question, No. 50 Squadron sent 19 aircraft to Nuremberg, one crashed on take-off, three went missing and one was damaged on landing. There were 15 men killed and 7 taken prisoner. Lancaster *'A' Able* was shot down at approximately 01:20 by Major Martin Drewes, Kommandeur 111 /NJG 1 of the Luftwaffe about 20 km north of Bamberg and was the 70th bomber to be shot down. The navigator, mid-upper gunner and rear gunner were killed.

'A' Able took off over Lincoln Cathedral from RAF Skellingthorpe, bound for Nuremberg. On reaching 21,000 ft the flight engineer found the starboard outer engine to be overheating. The crew had experienced similar trouble on two previous trips but had completed each operation successfully. This was their 13th operation and they didn't want to spoil their record with a 'boomerang', so the crew agreed with their skipper's decision to press on. Their route was via the North Sea, crossing the enemy coast near Antwerp, then Brussels and Namur, keeping south of Aachen to Bonn, and direct to Fulda where they changed course, heading south towards Nuremberg, with approximately 75 miles to target area. They were all well aware of the enemy searchlights

sweeping the sky and German night fighters were in evidence. They saw many of their bombers go down in flames and each time prayed it would not be theirs. At 01:15 they sighted the target ahead and Sergeant Dunn switched himself from the intercom to take a broadcast message from base. Suddenly the aircraft gave a sickening lurch and he looked up to see Chas, the navigator, standing up with his parachute on his chest, silhouetted against a mass of flames which were blazing past the starboard portholes from the outer engine, and waving frantically to him.

'I switched back on to the intercom in time to hear the two gunners acknowledge the order to "bale out", and the bomb-aimer shouting "I can't get this bloody hatch open". Not waiting to hear any more, I tore off my helmet, and clipped on my 'chute. I scrambled to the rear of the fuselage following the navigator, but the next moment a violent explosion threw me off my feet, and I was trapped, pinned to the inside of the fuselage of a blazing aircraft at 21,000 ft with nearly 12,000 lb of incendiary and high explosive bombs. My limbs were weighted, I seemed too heavy to move even a finger, and the whole world was gyrating madly. Suddenly, I saw a gaping jagged hole, through which the moon shone – the aircraft had broken its back at exactly the point at which I was pinned – and gave its last dying lurch. But in that instant, and before I knew what was happening, I was catapulted into the clean, cool night air above the Bavarian slopes.

'My parachute responded as soon as I pulled the rip-cord and, as I fell, everything seemed strangely silent and still – even the sound of aircraft had disappeared. It was like being in another world, for only a short while previously I had been trapped in a doomed aircraft, heading for the hereafter, and now by an amazing twist of fate that had saved me from certain death I found myself floating down on my parachute. I could see the landscape below me bathed in moonlight, and it appeared that I was heading towards the centre of a large lake. This made me take a grip of myself. I was alive and my thoughts were now for survival. It looked as if I was heading for some water and not being a swimmer, I reached for the lines as I had been instructed, to spill air from the 'chute and attempted to direct the drop towards the shore. I afterwards realised that I was spilling air from the 'chute in the wrong direction, but fortunately it wasn't a lake but merely a large clearance among a pine tree forest. Had I correctly handled my 'chute, I should have undoubtedly landed in the pine trees. As it was, I landed in the clearing close to its edge.

'The landing was perfect, and I even kept my feet. Within seconds I heard the aircraft explode nearby, and realising it was still fully laden, I hastily hid my parachute under a pile of dead branches, and found my escape compass. I recall laughing to myself as I thought of the breakfast I was going to miss, but no doubt the laughter was a trifle hysterical. As I set course for the south west, I heard the sound of small arms fire, and at first thought I had been seen, but soon realised that it was the ammunition from the aircraft exploding. It wasn't very long before I realised I was heading in the opposite direction to the one I wanted, having taken a reciprocal bearing. I circled back in a wide sweep to avoid the burning aircraft and headed, optimistically, towards Switzerland (which I thought to be about 200 to 250 miles to the south west.)

'It was very cold, bringing home to me the need for my Irvin jacket, which I had left in the aircraft in my haste to get out. The wireless operator position is the warmest in a Lancaster, so I had used my Irvin as a cushion. The water in the ditches was frozen, and I had difficulty in filling my water bag. It was then that I noticed my watch was missing, and my hands were bleeding from numerous cuts – the worst of these being a deep cut which appeared to have almost severed my little finger on my right hand. I later found that I had also a deep scratch down the side of my face. It was dark and several times I fell from one level to another, where the fields were separated by ditches, so I decided to lay up until daylight. This proved impossible because of the intense cold, so I plodded on, keeping away from roads and paths.

'As dawn broke I had been on the move for several hours, and the rough way across country was proving too tiring. I joined a track which led down through a fold in the hills, eventually joining a country-type road leading through a very small hamlet. By this time, I had removed all RAF insignia, but the small knife had slipped from its pocket inside my flying boots, so I pulled my trousers out over the boots to cover all except the black shoes which I hoped would pass inspection.

'I turned to my left to pass through the village, and saw several men leaving their homes for work, the women folk standing at the doors. I muttered the only German I knew, "Guten Morgen", and received replies without raising suspicion. With the intense cold, my water bag had frozen to my belt, to which I had tied the cord, and its contents had turned into a slush. It was bitterly cold, and in some parts there was snow lying on the ground.

'Once clear of the village I saw that a railway line on a low embankment ran parallel to the road on my right. Thinking that I would be hidden by the embankment, I crossed the line and saw the River Main running parallel to both road and railway line. It was broad and fast flowing. I decided to continue towards the east to find a way across the River Main, and thought that this would lead me towards Bamberg, having estimated that my position was between Bamberg and Schweinfurt.

'In about four miles I saw signs of the outskirts of a small town on the far bank, and then saw a bridge across the river. As I reached the bridge and commenced to cross, a boy overtook me on a pedal cycle and was obviously viewing me with some suspicion. I continued across the bridge doing my best to look like a vagrant, but was horrified to see the boy stop at the far end of the bridge and, looking back, seemed to be drawing the attention of a group of men who were standing idly there. There was no turning back however, for this would have drawn attention to me even more.

'As I slouched past I had my hands in my pockets, hiding both the water bag on my belt and my injured hands, and scowling at the ground. To my surprise I passed unchallenged, and hastily took the turning immediately on my right which would lead me down the south bank of the river, in the general direction from which I had come, but in a direction I knew the town extended only a short distance. To my consternation I was heading straight towards a small platoon of German soldiers, who were marching towards me. I just carried on walking and staring at the ground, and yet again, I passed unchallenged. As soon as I was out of sight of the town, I climbed the steep slope away from the river, intent on keeping away from all paths or roads. Later in the morning, I almost stumbled into a small group of huts which seemed like a military base, but I didn't stop to find out.

'I continued on across country in a south westerly direction and wondered about the fate of the other members of the crew. As far as I knew, both the front hatch and the rear exit had jammed, and I was the only survivor – the thought saddened me. I ate part of my escape pack chocolate as I walked, it was still very cold in spite of a watery sun and my thoughts turned to what it would be like again at night. I dreaded the thought and I knew I could not continue without some rest. During my travels I saw a group of children, but hid in the undergrowth until they had passed, and I later passed an old woman gathering sticks. I came upon her before I realised she was there, but she ignored my presence completely.

'Late in the afternoon I was climbing a steep slope out of a wooded valley, and was crossing a path at an angle, when I saw a group of men and women further up the path to my left. My direction would obviously give rise to some suspicion, but so would any immediate change in direction, so I continued and as I did, I heard a shout. I glanced up to see one of the men brandishing what I thought was a rifle of some sort, I continued without increasing my pace, but there came another shout, and I decided that discretion was the better part of valour, so I stopped, and the men of the group approached me cautiously. As they drew near I saw that what I thought was a rifle was a long-handled felling axe, and this was being used towards me in a threatening manner. He shouted something at me, but I was unable to understand and I replied, "RAF". He looked more scared than I was, and his friends stood well back. He said "Kamerad" and pointed into the sky, making a buzzing sound. He insisted I walked ahead of the group with my hands over my head, and he kept prodding me in the back with the axe. After some distance, one of the women of the group remonstrated with the men, and I was allowed to put my hands down.

'I was taken to a small hamlet where there was a small schoolhouse, and the local school master was consulted, who immediately took full command of the situation. We continued under his instructions along a rough lane, followed by most of the inhabitants of the village, the mothers keeping their children from getting too close to me, and the schoolmaster, wearing a little pork pie hat with a dust brush in the band, pushing his old pedal cycle with an air of great authority. We continued until we reached another village, this one much larger and I was taken to the house of the local mayor, and he telephoned, presumably, to the military. There was a nun in the house and she gave me a cup of coffee and a piece of Kummel cake.

'In due course, an SS Feldwebel came to the house and took me into custody. We left in a small car with a driver in civilian clothes, and after about 40 minutes arrived back in the small town I had passed through earlier in the day. The Feldwebel could speak a little English, and I told him I had crossed the bridge into the town, but this he refused to believe as he told me the bridge was always guarded. The SS Headquarters was the large house near the bridge, which I had passed earlier, and was opposite the garage bearing the Shell sign.

'I was searched, but was able to conceal all my escape kit. The elderly officer on duty telephoned Frankfurt, but I was unable to tell what his conversation was. After some considerable time, a lorry arrived with a number of Royal Air Force and Royal Canadian Air Force aircrew in the back, and I was put into the open back of the lorry. There was a guard with a rifle sitting on a chair or box with his back to the driver's cab. Several of the others were injured, but the conversation was brief, each of us being careful not to give away any information. I recall that *en route* to Schweinfurt we went through a snow storm, but we were all too tired and despondent to care very much. At Schweinfurt we were taken to a large room where there were a number of British and Commonwealth aircrew, and whilst they were kept to one end of the room, we were searched and allowed to join them one by one. At this time, I managed to place my escape kit (compass, maps, etc) on a narrow ledge, and later, after the guards had left the room I retrieved it.

'It was while waiting to be searched that I first noticed some of my other crew who were amongst those who were already in the room. They looked relieved and surprised at seeing me, for they thought that I had been killed in the aircraft, as I thought they had been. Words were not needed to exchange our relief to each other. We now totalled about 23 and were held in that same room at Schweinfurt aerodrome for the rest of that night and the whole of the next day. This gave me time to rest up a little and talk with the three other crew members.

'I learned of the events leading up to our having to abandon the aircraft, whilst I was engaged in receiving a wireless message, and not connected to the intercom system. It appears that we were hit in the starboard wing, most certainly by a German night fighter, and the wing was soon ablaze. The skipper gave the order for an emergency "bale out", and the bomb-aimer was attempting to get the front hatch open just as I became aware of the situation which was developing.

'The navigator, probably feeling that his best chances lay in escaping via the rear exit, was ahead of me clambering towards the rear. I noted that both gunners were struggling with the rear exit, but appeared to be having difficulty. The aircraft suddenly went into a steep dive which followed an explosion. I was told by the other three survivors that the hatch had opened at the front, and they had baled out. They saw the explosion which had blown the starboard wing off, and then the aircraft went down in the steep dive. They saw no other 'chutes emerge. It seemed to them that, just prior to striking the ground, the aircraft pulled out of its dive, and broke in two before finally plunging into the ground. It was obviously at this point that I found myself flung out of the aircraft, being lucky enough to have been pinned to the inside of the fuselage near the mid-upper turret, at the precise point the aircraft broke in half. I was in the air only a very short time before landing, perfectly on my feet, and it was only several seconds before the explosion of the aircraft and its load showered me with debris.

'The skipper was unfortunate to land on a cottage roof and was soon captured before he was able to recover from his ensuing fall. The bomb-aimer landed in pine trees, and found himself swinging some distance from the ground. His release knob had jammed and he was some time in getting free. At daylight his position was given away by some small boys who were on their way to school, and were over curious. The flight engineer was very unfortunate as his 'chute caught in a projection as he jumped and the fabric was badly torn, which resulted in a descent much faster than was safe. As a result he was badly bruised about his face and body and was unable to make much progress so he was caught fairly quickly.

'At 06:30 the following morning we were moved out to a waiting motor coach that took us to Schweinfurt railway station. The journey was difficult, made so because of our bombing, and this made us feel good, to think that our efforts had not been in vain. Rubble blocked many of the streets and the driver had parked a short distance from the station. We were ordered from the motor coach to a train standing at the platform in the station. There were a number of German people watching us as we made our way from the motor coach to the railway carriage and suddenly a man stepped forward. As I moved to go around him, he kicked me on the ankle and spat in my face. A guard later told me that this man had been a prisoner in England during World War I and had been kicked and spat upon so he was getting his revenge.

'At Frankfurt-on-Main we were alighting from the carriage when we saw a seething crowd of women on the platform, and they were crowding forward shouting "Anglo-American *Terrorfliegers*" – someone had told them who we were, and these women were clutching their pathetic bundles as they had been waiting for a train to take them away from the constant air attacks on the city. We were herded back into the carriage for our own safety, and while we were waiting to be shunted out of the platform, we could see the devastating damage caused by air raids. We could see the obvious results of Bomber Command's tactics. It was the German people who were suffering. Their morale was at breaking point and in a grim sort of way it was pleasing to see it, for many a brave young flyer had lost his life trying to reduce it to dust. They had been rewarded, for only the odd wall was standing as far as the eye could see, and it was apparent that the actual platform had been repaired to allow the trains to be used.

'Eventually we were taken to a suburb of Frankfurt to the emergency Dulag Luft, travelling by tram car. On arrival we were placed in small stone cells, three in each, with only a stool each to sit on. The following morning we were thoroughly searched, and this time my escape kit was discovered. I was placed in a solitary cell, which contained a bed, a stool, and one small window. There was a small radiator which was fully on during the day and switched off at night. While there someone in the next cell tapped on the wall and attempted to get into conversation with me, but I decided not to be drawn. Late in the afternoon I was taken to a small office and questioned, but I told the officer only those things he was entitled to know, name, rank and number. He got angry and told me he could have me shot as a spy. I was returned to my cell, my boots were removed and the lights went out, and the windows were shuttered from the outside.

'The next day I remained in my cell, and the following day, Wednesday 5 April at about midday, I was again taken to be interrogated, and when I still refused to answer any further questions I was told I would get no mail or food parcels if I continued to refuse to answer. I was returned to my cell and as I was waiting for the ritual of lights out, etc, the guards burst in and fetched me out again. I was marched down the corridor between four armed guards. We stopped outside another cell, and a fair-haired chap was brought out and we were marched away together. He was Jock McPhee, and he said he had been told he would be shot. Imagine our shock when we were marched into a courtyard with a high wall at one end, but we were marched across the yard and into a small compound where we were to await transport to a Prisoner of War camp in Lithuania (Heydekrug, near Memel).

'Whilst I saw Jock McPhee occasionally during the time we were prisoners together, I lost sight of him when we were repatriated, until a meeting in 1963, when a particularly vicious murder occurred at Nanjarrow Farm, Constantine near Helston where I was serving as the Inspector-in-Charge, and Jock McPhee, a Detective Sergeant in the Murder Squad of Scotland Yard arrived with his Detective Superintendent to carry out the investigation which resulted in two men being convicted for the murder, and they were the last two men in Cornwall to be hanged. Jock and I had joined the Police service on leaving the RAF – he in London and myself in Cornwall. We had a lot to chat about.'

CHAPTER EIGHTEEN

The Shuttle Raids, 1943

By a spectacular 'shuttle' raid, involving a round flight of something like 3,000 miles, RAF bombers demonstrated the might of Bomber Command and by so doing proved that not a single industrial target in southern Germany was immune from summer bombing. It was a brilliantly conceived and executed operation which beat all Nazi air defences. At this stage of the war there was ample evidence that the Germans had concentrated their night fighters in Western Europe to combat the intensive blasting of the Ruhr. They thought that in the short summer nights Bomber Command would have to concentrate on short-range targets.

On Sunday 20 June, 60 Lancasters of No. 5 Group under the leadership of Wing Commander Gomm of No. 467 Squadron were dispatched to attack Friedrichshafen in southern Germany. Gomm acted as 'Master of Ceremonies' and when the Pathfinder target indicators fell wide of the target he computed a 'false' wind which he instructed bomb-aimers to use. This closely controlled raid was a huge success and serious damage was done to the radio and radar workshops housed in the Zeppelin sheds. All the main buildings of the Luftschiffbau Radio Works had been hit. Friedrichshafen is on the shores of Lake Constance which separates Germany from Switzerland. It was the birthplace of the

Second Lieutenant Jack Russell and fitter 'Wally' with their Lancaster X, July 1943.

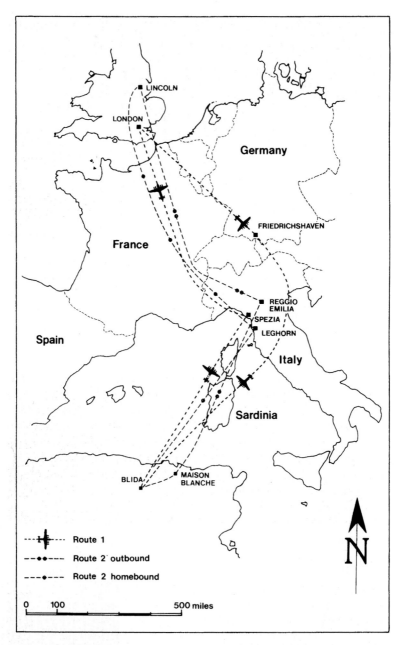

Map showing routes taken on 'shuttle' raids.

Crew of Lancaster ED655 'X' X-Ray of No. 57 Squadron who took part in the shuttle raids, July 1943. The two Americans, pilot Jack Russell from Long Island, New York, and navigator Richard Wright from Chicago, have just been commissioned Second Lieutenants in the US Army Air Corps.

Blida airfield, July 1943.

Lancasters on Blida airfield, July 1943.

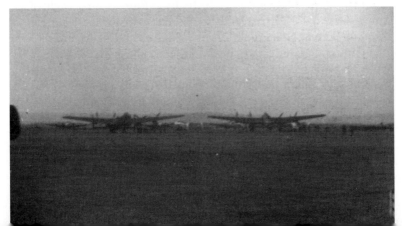

The boys from the first shuttle raid in Algeria making the most of the sudden holiday and a lifetime away from Hitler's war.

Zeppelin dirigibles and its virtual immunity from air attack hitherto is probably one reason why it was chosen for the manufacture of radio-location plant.

Shortly after the first explosions a fire reddened the horizon, gradually spreading and remaining visible until dawn. The detonations were so strong that even along the Swiss lake shore the houses shook. The lake is seven miles wide. After the raid the bomber force flew on to Blida in North Africa, thus outwitting the German night fighters which were sent to intercept on the assumed homeward route to England. This raid successfully proved that Allied gains in the Mediterranean could give valuable tactical freedom to Bomber Command. It clearly demonstrated that industrial targets in southern Germany like Mannheim, Stuttgart, Augsburg, Karlsruhe and Munich could be attacked even on short nights on the 'shuttle' service operation.

On the return to Britain three nights later on Wednesday 23 June, 53 Lancasters were dispatched and 49 bombed Spezia in Italy. Other 'shuttle' raids followed. On 15/16 July, four groups each of six Lancasters were dispatched to bomb transformer stations at Arquata Scrivia, San Polo d'Enza, Bologna and Reggio Emilia. One of the aircraft taking part in the latter raid was Lancaster *EE193* from 57 Squadron at Scampton. It was piloted by an American, Second Lieutenant Jack Russell from Long Island, New York. The other crew members were Second Lieutenant Richard Wright, also

The boys resting in AIgeria after taking in the sights and getting a few souvenirs for the return journey home on 23 June 1943, bombing Spezia on the way.

an American; Sergeant Nick Golden, navigator/bomb-aimer; Sergeant John Dow, wireless operator; Sergeant Jack Lazenby, flight engineer; Sergeant Ron Marston, rear gunner; and Sergeant Wally Bark, the mid-upper gunner. At the start of the tour both the Americans held the rank of RAF Sergeants and were commissioned as Second Lieutenants in the US Army Air Corps after 17 operational sorties. They both went on to complete the tour of 30 operations with 57 Squadron and each were awarded the DFC.

The small force took off at 21:30 in the fading light of the long summer evening and swept across France at 100 ft, rising to cross the Alps at 01:00. In deteriorating conditions they dropped down again to identify and bomb Reggio Emilio. However, they had great difficulty in identifying their precise target. They circled the target area for $1\frac{3}{4}$ hours during which time they suffered several attacks from Italian night fighters, but eventually they bombed the power station after three bombing runs from 1,500 ft. The bombers then went in at 400 ft to machine-gun the target area. The small force left Italy in daylight, crossing the coast south of Genoa and headed southwards across Corsica and the Mediterranean to North Africa, landing at Maison Blanche after being in the air for 10 hours 50 minutes. The following day they flew to Blida. Finally, to complete the 'shuttle', 33 Lancasters left North Africa on 24/25 July and made individual attacks against Leghorn in Italy from altitudes between 17,000 and 24,000 ft with very little opposition and then made an uneventful return to their parent stations in England. Lieutenant Russell in Lancaster *EE193* left Blida at 20:55 and touched down at Scampton eight hours later. The crew well remember the 'shuttle' raids for they brought back parcels of fruit, citrons, grapes, etc.

These shuttle raids against Italy were extremely successful, both in causing material damage and in finally destroying what little inclination remained among the civil population to continue a futile war.

Base Camp in North Africa for the RAF crews who took part in the first shuttle raid on 20 June 1943 – a chance to get the Bermudas on.

Dick Wright having a shoeshine in Algeria.

CHAPTER NINETEEN

Targets after D-Day

A fter the D-Day landings on 6 June 1944 the Allied air forces were still responsible for disrupting the German lines of supply as well as for protecting their own. By this period of the war the whole transport system along the original Seine-Loire line of interdiction had been thrown into such confusion by accumulated damage that all non-military traffic had all but ceased, while only a minimum of military movement was possible. It was now intended to widen the area of disruption by striking at traffic centres in eastern France, untouched or repaired since the pre-invasion campaign against communications. Thus between 13 and 30 June, RAF Bomber Command carried out 16 raids against key rail centres during which 1,774 aircraft were dispatched, 1,614 bombed their targets and 5,620 tons of bombs were dropped. The main targets were Aulnoye, Lens (15/16), Mondidier (17/18), Reims (22/23), Laon (22/23), Limoges (23/24), Vaires (27/28), Vitry-le-Francois (27/28), Metz (28/29), Blainville sur l'Eau (28/29), and Vierzon (30 June/1 July). Over the whole series of raids 65 aircraft (3.6 per cent) were lost, the worst casualties being sustained during the deep penetration to Vierzon when 14 out of 118 Lancasters were shot down (11.8 per cent).

Lancaster 'M' *Mike* LM619 from 100 Squadron at Waltham took part in the Vierzon raid. The crew, Pilot Officer Jack David Rees, pilot; Pilot Officer Jack Martin, navigator; Flying Officer Edgar Jackson, bomb-aimer; Sergeant Michael Dunphy, flight engineer; Sergeant Arthur Palmer, wireless operator; Sergeant Peter Daly, mid-upper gunner and Sergeant Victor Locke, rear gunner. Sergeant Palmer, the wireless operator, gives his account of the Vierzon raid:

'I had calculated that this trip would represent exactly 60 per cent of our tour: 18 out of 30 ops. There had been talk that raids on France would only count as one third of an operation but after the attack on the German barracks at Mailly Le Camp in France on 3 May when Bomber Command lost 40 odd aircraft out of a relatively small force, we had been advised not to worry too much about this threat.

'We had dropped our high explosives and were rapidly leaving the target area when the rear gunner reported an enemy aircraft dead astern and said, "Corkscrew Starboard, Go" and I heard our .303 Browning guns firing. We went into a steep dive and a few moments later Vic (the rear gunner) rapped out, "Make it tighter – tighter Dave" (Dave "Jack" Rees was the captain/pilot) and it seemed only seconds later that the aircraft was rolling over – we were plummeting rapidly from our 18,000 ft towards the ground and I was unceremoniously deposited on to the floor of the aircraft among a pile of Verry cartridges which had broken out of their racks; I then saw that Jack Martin had left his navigator's position and was adding his strength to that of the captain in trying to pull back the stick, but he didn't hear Dave telling him to "lay off" as he had become disconnected from his intercom. I found it very difficult to move but I realised that Jack had propelled himself forward because he, like I, thought that Dave was badly injured – his arm trailed down and slightly behind him. Actually he was using the trim wheel to "tail heavy" to try and get out of our perilous dive. Pete (the mid-upper gunner) yelled "Pull her out Dave", and Dave replied "I'm trying to"; I then noticed that the forward escape hatch was being opened by Eddie Jackson (the bomb-aimer). Mike (the engineer) was holding Eddie's lapels and looking at the captain for his order to bale out – or stay put – but Dave was still wrestling with the control column. The aircraft was shuddering violently and there were bangs at the rear of it and how the gunners were getting on I didn't know but I did know that we must be getting awfully close to the ground. I was bracing myself for a violent impact and at the same time scrambling forward to pick up my parachute from under the Type 52 Resistance when suddenly two things happened almost simultaneously – the bomb-aimer who had been half-way out of the escape hatch suddenly tucked in his elbows and went out into the night (and Mike seemed to be perilously near to following him) and then the aircraft shuddered, flattened out and climbed skywards at a most uncomfortable speed, making such awful noises that I believed it was breaking up. After what seemed an eternity we had recovered to such an extent that Dave was asking anybody who was listening if there was any sign of the fighter (now established as being an Me

210) having followed us down – and back up. In fact there was no sign of that or any other aircraft – our antics had taken us miles away from the bomber stream, and we were able to take stock. My codes and other books were scattered around the fuselage and my precious log was quite dirty but most of the movable objects forward of my position, including the navigator's maps, charts, protractor, pencils, rubber and watch, had been sucked out through the hatch. Dave told us that the ailerons had been torn away, severely hampering our left/right movement, and we were still a long way from home but we were still airborne and in spite of the cold draught and the awful smell from the upturned Elsan we pointed our aircraft from somewhere near Orleans northwards towards Waltham, our base in Lincolnshire. We had fallen from 18,000 to 2,000 ft in our little escapade but our admiration for the Lancaster increased with every air mile – a loop, a screaming dive and a rocket-like ascent had been taken in her stride. I thanked God for the vigilance of the rear gunner and the expert recovery action by the captain and Eddie Jackson, whose position was near to the forward escape hatch and who could well have been the only member to survive. Whether or not Eddie did survive I was to have to wait (until the war was over) and see!'

The rest of the crew were unaware of the fate of Eddie Jackson until May 1945 when Arthur Palmer was shown the *Daily Mail* which stated 'Flying Officer Jackson, after baling out of his Lancaster over Orleans on 30 June last year, was sheltered by French farmers and after being passed on to members of the underground in Paris ended his adventures in Buchenwald, having been betrayed to the Gestapo in France by collaborationists. He was put in a block with 800 other prisoners, 500 of which were gypsy children whose parents had been sent to the gas chambers at Auschwitz. From 3 to 14 years of age, they were all boys and completely wild. Some of them killed one man with their hands, tearing him to pieces. Jackson was told he would be classed as a saboteur and executed but he was later transferred to Stalag Luft 3 south of Berlin and eventually liberated by the Russians.'

Arthur Palmer married in 1942 and his crew were introduced to his wife at Finningley in 1943. At the commencement of his operational tour, he held the rank of Sergeant, service number 1516074. He was commissioned in the rank of Pilot Officer with effect from 29 June 1944 although this was not promulgated until July 1944 (service number as commissioned officer 178444); date of demob (retirement) was 27 March 1976 with the rank of Squadron

Leader. The pilot, Dave (or Jack) Rees, called Dave by his crew to differentiate him from Jack Martin the navigator, had completed 45 sorties on bombers in the Middle East before he crewed up in 1943. After completing 30 operations with 100 Squadron (pilots usually did one more operation than other members of the crew) he soon tired of instructional duties and returned to operational flying – this time Mosquitoes.

He did 17 ops, many of them bombing Berlin, thereby completing a total of 92 sorties but on the 17th he was shot-up and crashlanded, his navigator was killed and Dave broke his back and several ribs, among other things. In 1957 Arthur Palmer met Dave quite by accident at the Singapore Swimming Club. He seemed smaller and explained that after breaking his back he was two inches smaller and, being a doctor now in Singapore City, he later explained the telescoping effect on his spine. He had learned to write and speak both Malay and Chinese. It was his great skill and keenness as a bomber pilot that got them safely through their tour of ops.

CHAPTER TWENTY

Our Last Trip: 227 Squadron, Balderton

'On 21 February 1945 we were called in for briefing for what was to be our last raid. We knew that it wasn't to be a long trip because we had been fuelled up with the minimum fuel load. The target was the Mitteland Canal at Gravenhorst. A force of 154 had been detailed to bomb it the night before but all brought back their bombs because the target was obscured by cloud.

'I, A. F. Dales, was the navigator, in Lancaster *'J' Jig PB666*, Flying Officer Green was pilot; W02 James Cassidy (Casey) was the bomb-aimer; Sergeant Ging Roberts was wireless operator; Sergeant Jock Edwards was mid-upper gunner and Sergeant Wally Lancaster was the rear gunner. Sergeant John Ling had been our flight engineer but on a raid shortly before this we had got coned in searchlights and we had come down in an almost vertical dive to escape. The change of pressure had burst both his ear drums so he couldn't fly and we had a "spare bod" that night.

'The officer briefing us told us that the target had been bombed the night before but not damaged badly. He told us that a lot of us might not come back because the night was clear and there was a full moon. It was deadly, in fact almost suicide to fly a mission on a night like this because everything above you is silhouetted but nothing below can be seen. He told us it was extremely important to have the canal blown up, so the raid was on.

'We were briefed, took off and headed for the target, just the same as we had done many times before. We were all happy that this was to be a short trip but felt real apprehension about the night being so moonlit. We got to the target, did our bombing run and dropped our bombs. The defences, flak and searchlights were no worse than we had seen lots of other times. We headed for home and we hadn't gone far when trouble began. We saw several planes burning on the ground and in the distance. All at once a Lanc about a thousand feet below us burst into flames. A few seconds later a Lanc a little below us and to the side burst into flames. We felt sure that we would be next. We were.

'As I recall it, on the first pass the night fighter (an Me 109 I believe) raked us with cannon fire and it blew the front turret off and set fire to the outer starboard motor. The flash fire from the explosion in the front turret was close enough to Casey to burn off all the hair (eyebrow, eyelashes) that wasn't covered by his helmet. He was temporarily blinded but otherwise not hurt. A few seconds later more cannon fire again, this time setting fire to the two port engines and also setting fire to the centre of the fuselage and I think killing the mid-upper gunner (Jock). Pete, our pilot, yelled into the intercom, "Bale out, bale out, we are going down! " There was no argument from the crew – with our aircraft on fire the way it was, there was no incentive to stay with it.

'I had a chest 'chute which I had already grabbed and put on. I headed for the escape hatch in the front. The "D" ring on my chute caught on a projection and pulled my ripcord. My 'chute started to open so I put an arm around it to stop it opening any further. I went past the pilot and engineer to the escape hatch. The bomb-aimer was supposed to open it and jump. He was temporarily blinded so he asked me to open it. I reached down and turned the handle and pushed with my free hand, the door was supposed to jettison but it was jammed. I stood up and stamped on it with my foot but nothing happened. I stamped on it again, this time out went the door and also my foot. My foot went out about 8 or 9 in and slipstream slammed it back against the back of the opening and broke both bones in my leg and bent it at a 90-degree angle along the bottom of the aircraft. I managed to pull it back inside the aircraft.

'I was in a bad predicament. I was holding onto a spar with one hand and holding my 'chute from opening with the other hand and balancing on my one good leg. I knew I couldn't go out head first the way I should, so I hopped as far ahead as I could and dropped through the hole feet first. This is the way to get badly hurt such as a broken back, but I was very lucky and didn't hit the aircraft. As soon as I hit the slipstream I let go of the 'chute and it flew up and hit me in the face and knocked me out. I came to in a few moments and came down on my parachute and after all the noise in the aircraft it seemed very quiet. My first thought was, "Thank God I'm still alive and with only a broken leg." I could see fires of aircraft burning on the ground and everything seemed so very quiet, almost as though I was in a vacuum, then all at once "Wham!" – I hit the ground.

'I tried to get up but could only sit, as all that was holding my leg together was the flesh, and the pain was terrible. I lay back on the ground and almost at once a man from the Dutch underground came. He lit me a cigarette and said he could have helped me but since I couldn't walk there was nothing he could do. All at once he said, "I must go now as the German army is very close", and he vanished into the darkness. A few seconds later a German soldier came running up to me. He was yelling at me and the only word I could catch was "swine, swine" and he let go a burst of machine-gun fire into the ground about a foot from me. I thought for sure that this was to be the end and that he was going to shoot me. But more soldiers came running and one, an officer, was shouting furiously at the soldier. I'm sure he saved my life. The German soldiers then helped to drag me out of this little field, through a ditch to a Dutch farmhouse. The Dutch woman and the others for that matter I think, thought that I was in kind of poor condition as I had three cuts on my face – one cut under one eye, one on my chin and the other cut in my other eyebrow, and my face was covered with blood. There was quite a lot of talking which I didn't understand and then the Dutch woman got a pan of water and cleaned my face off which made me feel a little better but the pain from my leg was very bad.

'There was some more talking that I didn't understand and then the farmer brought a horse and cart with some straw in it. They laid me in it and started out. The pain from my leg was really bad as the cart on the cobble stones was rough and the ends of the broken bones rubbed together at the slightest movement. I was sure I was going to pass out. After what seemed ages but was probably only a few miles we came to a school which they took me into. It had beds and several airmen that had been shot down and had been wounded or hurt. A German doctor came in and put a wire splint on my leg and gave me an injection which helped a little. We weren't allowed to talk and after, I think, three days we were put on a bus and taken to a hospital in Bocholt, Germany. We had baled out near Winterswijk in Holland and three of my crew (Green, Edwards and the engineer) are buried there.

'I spent about a month in this hospital in Bocholt and then just before the Allies captured it I was moved to Groningen in Holland. I was there for a few weeks and just before the Canadian army captured Holland I was moved again, this time to Stalag X, a prison hospital. This prison was located near Schleswig which is close to the Danish border.

'After V-Day I was flown to a Canadian hospital near Hamburg in an old Anson made into an ambulance plane. Then the following day I was flown back to England to a Canadian General Hospital at Cuckfield, Sussex. I was in this hospital for about three months then I was sent back to Canada on the hospital ship *Letitia* and some more hospitals. All told I spend about eleven months in hospitals and had two operations on my leg.'

A force of 167 aircraft dropped 816 tons of bombs on the Mitteland Canal in good weather, marred only by a slight ground haze. Subsequent photographic assessment confirmed that the bomb fall had been concentrated on a vital area where the canal-retaining wall was damaged for a distance of 500 yds; a bridge had collapsed and fields on either side of the canal were again flooded. But, although the bombing had been effective it had been a costly raid, especially for Lancaster 'J' *Jig*, and it was her last trip.

CHAPTER TWENTY ONE

Tale of a Tail Gunner

D uring the phase of Overlord the employment of all elements of the Allied air forces was purely tactical. Heavy and continuous air attacks against communications were ordered by General Eisenhower and heavy bombers were directed on to road and rail centres while light bombers and fighter bombers attacked the bridges across the Loire and in the Paris-Orleans gap. It was estimated that any German troops in immediate reserve stationed between the Seine and the Loire would be committed to battle by 7 June 1944. To stop the Germans from bringing up any reinforcements, several heavy bombing attacks were made on key road and rail centres in this area on 6 and 7 June 1944. The targets chosen were Vire, Châteaudun, St Lô, Lisieux, Argentan, Caen, Condesur-Noireau, Coutances and Achères. One of those taking part in the latter raid was Pilot Officer Gordon J. Ritchie of 429 (Bison) Squadron, Royal Canadian Air Force.

'I was a rear gunner on 429, RCAF, stationed at Leeming in Yorkshire flying Halifaxes. On the night of 7/8 June we were

Crew of 429 Squadron (RCAF) Leeming, Yorkshire. At dispersal, just prior to start, for trip to Bourg Leopold, 27 May 1944. Left to right: John Mangione, mid-upper gunner; Gilbert Steere, flight engineer; Dave Banning, air gunner; Gordon Ritchie, rear, gunner; Second Lieutenant W.B. Anderson, pilot.

The two gunners of V-Victor (Impatient Virgin). On left Gordon Ritchie, rear gunner, on right John Mangione, mid-upper.

detailed to attack Achères, a marshalling yard behind the German lines. Our pilot, Squadron Leader W.B. Anderson had just been appointed flight commander and had taken us through some rather dicy dos – Berlin, Leipzig, the Ruhr, etc, and was given word just prior to take-off that he had been awarded the Distinguished Flying Cross.

'As we crossed the French Coast at Dieppe, all hell broke loose as the flak guns opened up on us. The pilot caught a rather large fragment through his side and gave us the order to bale out – we were at 18,000 ft and the aircraft went into a vertical dive as the pilot slumped over the control column. I had the turret swung out on the beam looking for fighter attacks from below and immediately attempted to centralise it, but I overcorrected in my rush and got it into a position where I could tear myself out of the turret leaving one of my flying boots as I extricated myself and picked up my parachute. I squeezed through the narrow opening between the fuselage and the tail wheel oleo jack. Now anyone who was a rear gunner knows how difficult that is normally but when the aircraft is in a dive and heading for eternity, the impossible can be done. Once through, I was crawling forward to the escape hatch, my face being forced into the floor when I realised that someone was pulling the aircraft out of the dive. I plugged my intercom in and learnt that the flight engineer, Flight Sergeant Gilbert Steere, had pulled the injured pilot from the cockpit and was straightening the aircraft. The mid-upper, Flight Sergeant Mangione from Ottawa, and I went forward to

Flight Sergeant Gordon Ritchie receiving medal from King George VI at Leeming, July 1944.

						Time Carried Forward —	111:40	152:10
Date	Hour	Aircraft Type and No.	Pilot	Duty	Remarks (including results of bombing, gunnery, exercises, etc.)		Flying Times Day	Night
2-6-44	14:25	HALIFAX III AL-"V"	S/L ANDERSON	REAR GUNNER	FIGHTER AFFIL. BOMBING		1:05	
4-6-44	01:15	HALIFAX III AL-"V"	S/L ANDERSON MOTARKEY	REAR GUNNER	OPS. AS ORDERED "PAS DE CALAIS" (D-NIGHT)			4:00
5-6-44	22:20	HALIFAX III AL-"V"	S/L ANDERSON	REAR GUNNER	OPS. AS ORDERED "CAEN AREA"			4:30
7-6-44	23:15	HALIFAX III AL-"V"	S/L ANDERSON	REAR GUNNER	OPS. AS ORDERED "PARIS AREA"			4:15

Our last trip with "Andy", we were hit by flak crossing the coast of France over Dieppe, the B.A., W.Ag and navigator bailed out over enemy territory, Andy had a devil of a job by a pc. of flak, he gave the order to bail out, the engineer, mid-upper and I stayed behind, Andy, with the help of the engineer succeeded in straightening the a/c, we jettisoned the load near Dieppe and headed for England. The mid-upper and I pulled Andy from the cockpit to the rear hatch and clipped his chute on to the static line and pushed him out. He died later from his wounds, then the rest of us bailed out, I landed on the edge of a mine field in Oxfordshire.

JUNE TOTAL

DAY FLYING 1:05
NIGHT FLYING 12:45
JUNE TOTAL 13:50

CERTIFIED CORRECT 30 JUNE 44
"B" FLIGHT COMMANDER
G.F. Keluchile
                                    ?/L

					Total Time	112:45	164:55

						Time Carried Forward —	127:40	187:50
Date	Hour	Aircraft Type and No.	Pilot	Duty	Remarks (including results of bombing, gunnery, exercises, etc.)	Flying Times Day	Night
1/8/44	19:05	HALIFAX III "O"	F/O SLOSKI	REAR GUNNER	OPS. AS ORDERED "L'HEY" (DAY) (V1/S BOMB SITES) (OIL STORAGE)	3:20	
3/8/44	17:50	HALIFAX III "O"	F/O SLOSKI	REAR GUNNER	OPS. AS ORDERED "FORET DE NIEPPE"	3:50	
5/8/44	10:35	HALIFAX III "O"	F/O SLOSKI	REAR GUNNER	OPS. AS ORDERED "ST LEU DESSERENT"	5:05	
8/8/44	18:50	HALIFAX III "O"	F/O SLOSKI	REAR GUNNER	OPS. AS ORDERED "CHANTILLY"	4:30	
12/8/44	21:25	"N"	F/O SLOSKI	REAR GUNNER	OPS. AS ORDERED "BRUNSWICK"		5:40
					COOKS TOUR OF GERMANY BREMEN HANOVER/WILHELMS COMPASSES "/L		
					(LA FALAISE) (DAY)		
14/8/44	12:40	HALIFAX III "O"	F/O SLOSKI	REAR GUNNER	OPS. AS ORDERED "AISY" SUPPORT ARMY	4:25	
15/8/44	21:50	HALIFAX III "O"	F/O SLOSKI	REAR GUNNER	OPS. AS ORDERED GARDENING (LA ROCHELLE) BAY OF BISCAY		6:25
18/8/44	19:05	HALIFAX III "H"	F/O SLOSKI	REAR GUNNER	OPS. AS ORDERED "BOIS ST. REMY" (DAY) (V1/S BOMB SITES)	3:36	
21/8/44	15:40	HALIFAX III "O"	F/O SLOSKI	REAR GUNNER	AIR TO AIR 500 RDS.	:50	
23/8/44	11:30	HALIFAX III "O"	F/O SLOSKI	REAR GUNNER	FIGHTER AFFIL. (BREST PENINSULA)	1:05	
25/8/44	23:20	HALIFAX III "O"	F/O SLOSKI	REAR GUNNER	OPS. AS ORDERED "ST MATHIEU" DIVERTED MARKET HARBORO		5:25
26/8/44	15:55	HALIFAX III "U"	P/O BARLOW	PASSENGER	MARKET HARBRO — BASE	:45	

SCREENED

CERTIFIED CORRECT 28 August
"B" FLIGHT COMMANDER

WING COMMANDER
COMMANDING
429 SQUADRON R.C.A.F.

AUGUST TOTAL

DAY FLYING 27:25
NIGHT FLYING 17:30
AUGUST TOTAL 44:55

					Total Time		

Top 'B' Flight – 429 Squadron, Leeming. Page from Flying Log-Book of Flight Sergeant Ritchie.

Bottom 'B' Flight— 429 Squadron, Leeming, Yorkshire. Page from Flying Log Book of Ritchie showing his last nine operations before being screened. Certified correct 28 August 1944.

render what aid we could, in the meantime the navigator, bomb-aimer and wireless operator had baled out over France.

'The pilot was in very bad shape but still alive, and we administered morphine to try and ease his pain. We had switched on some lights in the aircraft to see what we were doing, not realising we had inadvertently switched on our navigational lights. We jettisoned our bomb load near Dieppe and headed for England. During this period there was such a concentration of shipping in the channel that they had orders to shoot at anything overhead, so that posed another problem, however, we had more to worry about than that, not the least of which was what we were going to do when we arrived over England.

'During this time the flight engineer was flying the aircraft sitting in a bucket seat wearing a chestpack parachute and consequently unable to see out of the aircraft, relying solely on the artificial horizon to keep us somewhat straight and level. It was anything but a smooth flight back. The skipper rallied a few times and we had hopes he might pull through, it was only his great constitution that kept him alive so long. He was a big man and weighed over 200 lb and had played professional football in Canada. We dragged him over the two main spars back to the rear escape hatch, which required a great deal of effort, and we were quite fatigued after that little task. We attached his "D" ring to the snap on the static line and prepared to release him out of the escape hatch. (The static line is a length of strapping about thirty yards long attached to the aircraft to allow a person who is incapable of pulling his own ripcord to bale out.) We were in touch with several airfields in England after our "Mayday" call but had no idea in what part of England we were. We advised them we were about to let the skipper out, I was the last person to speak to him and told him what we

Pilot Officer Gordon Ritchie, DFM (on right) with his new skipper, Flying Officer Michael Sloski, with whom he finished his tour of ops.

Gordon Ritchie with model of Halifax bomber at his home in Dollard-des-Ormeaux, Quebec, Canada.

were doing. He asked for a little time and then said – "OK, let me go.", and so we slid him out.

'Then it was time for the rest of us to leave, the flight engineer being quite anxious about the possibility of running out of petrol. The mid-upper and I went forward to the front hatch but it didn't look too appealing, so back to the rear hatch. After another trip forward and back, neither one looked too inviting but I decided that it was now or never. I slid my feet out and the slipstream took my one remaining boot and my heated slippers – and summoning what courage I could, out I went. What a relief when the 'chute opened, and I have to admit, heavenly to be out of the aircraft with all the noise, blood and clatter. My next concern was where I was going to land. We estimated we were at 12,000 ft at bale out.

'I landed in my stockinged feet on a wire fence before being blown into a field. The first thing I did was reach for a cigarette. I had one of those "Victory" lighters and with my hand shaking I flicked the wheel right off the lighter. So there I was, sitting in a field with a cigarette in my mouth and nothing to light it with. Looking behind, I saw a small white sign with red lettering "Beware of the Mines". This was near Wallingford in Oxfordshire, talk about jumping out of the frying pan into the fire!! I decided I had to move, so I crawled slowly in a straight line to the edge of the field. I then moved in the direction of our burning Halifax, LW128 AL-V (*Impatient Virgin*), which had crashed while I was descending, but as I approached the aircraft across freshly ploughed fields in my stockinged feet, mud oozing up between my toes, the ammunition started to explode with tracers going in all directions. So I made a quick detour. I tried several houses without success, I could not convince some of the people that I was a Canadian airman who had just baled out from a burning aircraft. However, I was directed to a farmer's house and was able to get my cigarette lit. The farmer then drove me to RAF Benson in Oxfordshire. At Benson they were expecting me, for the flight engineer and mid-upper had already arrived. Earlier that morning an American Colonel in a light aircraft had found our pilot and brought him to the mortuary at RAF Benson. We were assured by the station medics that we had done all humanly possible for him.

'Our bomb-aimer and wireless operator, after a few days' freedom, were subsequently taken prisoners by the Germans and were in the same PoW camp until the end of the war. The navigator, with the help of the French Underground was back in England within six weeks. Our skipper, Squadron Leader W.B. Anderson DFC is buried in Brookwood Cemetery in Woking, Surrey. Within a week we were awarded immediate decorations. Gilbert Steere, the flight engineer was awarded the Conspicuous Gallantry Medal, the mid-upper gunner John Mangione and the rear gunner, Gordon J. Ritchie were awarded the Distinguished Flying Medal.'

A Pole in Bomber Command: Sergeant Drozdz

'I was born in March 1920, on a farm in the village of Zastow, which was on the Warsaw boundary, Poland, and was one of a happy family of five boys and two girls. My parents married early, and worked hard, to ensure that their children would each receive a good education. Therefore, following my compulsory state education, I was enrolled at the Technical School of Warsaw, to study aeronautical engineering.

'Aeroplanes had always fascinated me, and on 1 July 1939, I volunteered for, and was accepted in, the Polish Air Force, joining No. 1 Regiment in Warsaw. On 25 August, as war seemed inevitable, we were moved from the city to an airfield in the country, some 30 miles away, awaiting further orders. On 1 September, we heard with dismay that Hitler had indeed declared war on our country – and on the following Sunday afternoon, 3 September, we had our first taste of what Poland could expect. From out of the sky zoomed three German Dorniers and – innocents that we were – we stood and gazed in wonder as from their bellies, there cascaded towards us, long cigar-shaped objects. Their fearful screaming sound made us dive instinctively for cover, and we stood aghast later surveying the wreckage. Our war had begun – violently, and unforgettably.

Sergeant Drozdz.

'The following day, we were moved hurriedly to a base further south in the country, and it was from there that we derived the satisfaction of seeing our own bombers taking off to bomb Glivlice railway, to disrupt German transportation. I witnessed three such operations before we were moved on yet again, still further south. On 18 September, our commander told us in anguished terms that we must now make our choice – to return to our homes, or to attempt to cross into Romania, with the hope of continuing the fight from there. Needless to say, most of us chose the latter – although we were all young men, we had been brought all too quickly to the realisation that to fight back from beseiged and unprepared Poland was futile. That night, in pouring rain, we crossed into Romania just at midnight, with heavy hearts. None of us wanted to leave our beloved country, or our families, but we tried to be realistic.

'But for three weary months, while Romania debated her fate, we were hauled and trekked through one detention centre after another, our hair shaven from our heads, and living meagrely on rough bread and grapes. We became increasingly restless and devised a plan to escape into France. Anything was better than this. In France, our elation was dampened when we were told that France was expected to fall at any time, and, persuaded by a British Air Force officer that we stood a better chance of fighting if we accompanied him to Britain, we threw our lot in with him, and so, on a cold January night, we found ourselves anchored in an overcrowded boat, off Southampton. We landed the following day, 16 January, and were taken to Eastchurch, Kent, where we were sworn into the Royal Air Force. I could not speak nor understand a word of English, but I felt all too well the warmth of the welcome with which we were received. With Hitler's successes in Europe, we were now joining in comradeship with men and boys of our own age, with a mutual aim – the destruction of the enemy. Language was no barrier to that sort of spirit ... our optimism rose. So, I became among the first of many Poles who chose to wage the war from British soil and thousands were to follow me, many to give their lives along with their British comrades, but I believe that many of them had begun to feel as I did myself ... that the cause of keeping Britain free became as dear to us as that cause which brought us here.

'My first few years were spent in training for ground crew duties in various stations all over England – and in learning English. We were warmly received, and through our attendance at church, were often invited into English homes, where we began to understand the British humour, and were made to feel less homesick. But my dearest wish was to fly, and in the Spring of 1944, this wish became reality when I received orders to report to No. 4S, of TT RAF Station St Athan for a flight engineer's course. On 13 July I graduated with Flight Engineer's Wings, and the rank of Sergeant. I shall always remember the elation which I felt that day – now my war had become more personal, for I should be over enemy territory, hitting where it would hurt the most. After initial flying training, I was posted to No. 300 Polish Bomber Squadron, one of the few Polish units to be found in every command of the RAF. There were enough of us now to be "the Polish Air Force". I was posted to Faldingworth, in Lincolnshire, and it was from this base that my 30 sorties over enemy territory took place.

The eagerly awaited first sortie was on 29 November 1944 – target, Dortmund. I cannot express the feelings which surged through me as after the briefing we took off, found and bombed our target, and returned safely from our mission. This was a daylight raid by a force of 311 aircraft and 291 attacked the target. A total of six aircraft were missing from the raid. It seemed a blow for freedom – and I wanted more! I think that fear was always with us, because all sorties were dangerous. The cumbersome, though well loved, Lancaster, was not exactly a lithe bird, and with its full bomb load, a potentially laden arsenal. I saw too many of my friends die in front of me, as enemy flak accurately detonated the 'plane, but one always believed that such a fate was, at least, quick. While we lived, we craved the next assignment. My own 'plane was hit by flak immediately after we had dropped our bomb load on Hamburg, and the 'plane was badly crippled. We limped gingerly home … and examination proved that our lives had hung on a mere inch – the length between a piece of embedded flak and our fuel tank!

Bombing up Sergeant Drozdz's Lancaster with 4,000 lb 'cookie'.

'Besides Dortmund and Hamburg, I was also on missions to Essen, Nuremberg, Munich, Bonn, Gelsenkirchen, Zeitz, Ludwigshaven, Chemnitz, Kassel, Nordhausen and Hanover, but my final sortie proved to be the one which was my own particular goal. On 14 April 1945, we were called to the Briefing Room. There were no latecomers that day – a sort of suppressed excitement was in the air. To our incredulous eyes, the flag on the large map pinpointed the destination for which we had all longed – Berlin! Berlin! The strategic mission of Bomber Command was almost complete. This was one of 15 nuisance raids on the German capital before the Russian forces arrived there by the end of the month. I prayed that nothing might happen to cancel this flight, such as adverse weather conditions. We were all disappointed that the authorities had brought down the number of sorties to complete a tour from 35 to 30, and if this was to be my last, then it couldn't have given me more satisfaction.

'After briefing and normal preparations, take-off came at 18:15 precisely. Our full capacity was 67,000 lb, including a bomb load of 11,000 lb. There were no hitches as we charted our course, climbing over Reading, and then, at Beachy Head, reaching 18,000 ft. I looked down on the fading English landscape, and said a silent "goodbye" – if I should not return, I left her my love and admiration. The blue ribbon of the English Channel now appeared before us and soon, the coastline of the Continent. We had lapsed into silence. It was our unwritten but golden rule. Each man must concentrate on the job at hand, and whatever he felt privately, dedicate himself to the success of the mission, and the welfare of the rest of the crew. The four Merlin engines, with their rhythmic purr, were the only sounds to dominate that strange and enclosed environment. About us and around us were more Lancasters, the light still good enough to discern their darkening silhouettes. Like a drone of deadly wasps, 426 aircraft were heading to their target. The years of World War II have seen devastation such as we could never have dreamed, we earnestly wished we could end it all ... we knew it could only come from the destruction of the enemy. My consolation lay in the fact that this hope of a speedy end to the war was shared by all of us there that night ... I was not alone.

'After we reached the French coast, we changed course, heading due east for Frankfurt. We moved on, uneventfully. The weather started to break – formations of tiny clouds mushroomed around us. Just before Frankfurt, the navigator told our skipper to alter course, so many degrees to the left, and to climb a further 1,000 ft to reach 19,000 ft, which was going to be our bombing height. These manoeuvres were carried out, and then we were heading for Kassel and Misburg – previous targets of ours, but not that night! These changes of course were part of our defensive tactics to throw the enemy into confusion as to our real target. At 52 degrees longitude, we were now on our last leg to the target, with Magdeburg to starboard. The enemy below was prepared – flak became intense, and too many searchlights scoured the sky. Up went one's blood pressure, the crucial time would soon be to hand, as beneath us, we saw that all hell had been let loose. The Pathfinders had done their job well, their flares and red markers had illuminated our targets, and already, streams of fire dotted the earth below. For us, there was no longer any difference between earth and air, both were consumed with fire, light – and death. Just as the flak found its target in front of us, we were caught in the relentless beam of a searchlight ... it pierced the cabin, and made daylight in the cockpit. We couldn't escape it, its brilliance had trapped us and we couldn't shake it away ... we were the target now. But the voice of our skipper was calm as he ordered "3,000 revs, plus 14 boost" – maximum speed! Then the bomb-aimer's voice took over, giving the pilot instructions: "Left, left ... bomb doors open ... left again, now ... steady ... steady ... steady and bombs gone!" We felt the familiar jerk, and a sense of relief. Now, we had to make our way home. Still hazardous. The pilot issued new instructions, we were going down now. 19,000 ft, 18,000 ft, 17,500 ft ... diving rapidly and gaining speed, 200 mph. The flak was still heavy, but it was getting farther and farther behind us. A friendly Lancaster passed us, racing us home. Clouds appeared, and we were anxious. There were still a great many aircraft in the sky, including German fighters, waiting to get us on the way back. But we emerged from the milky clouds, and breathed a sigh of thanks. Coffee was passed round from the flask, and we congratulated the skipper, and each other. I worked on the petrol consumption calculations – everything was working normally. Frankfurt again, and now, we retraced the course which had brought us in.

'At 02:45, we saw the illuminated letters "FH" on the runway beneath, and we were home – this was our greeting when there was no air-raid – Faldingworth.

'We had been in the air for $8\frac{1}{2}$ hours, and had journeyed 1,500 miles, using 1,174 gallons of petrol, of which 440 gallons were left in the tank. Our bombs had been dropped at 22:50 precisely, and later, our cameras were to show that they had been dropped accurately on target. 'R' *Roger*, officially aircraft *PB730*, our regular plane, had been our friend once more – we were all endeared to it. As a flight engineer I felt our AMPG wasn't too good – only 0.875, but we were back – and alive!

'Leave followed, and while we speculated on the chance of getting back, the war came to an end. I was demobbed in 1947, eight years after that naive boy first donned his proud blue uniform, and though I now am happily domiciled in England with an English wife (she and her family lost everything in the 1940 German raid on Coventry) and three teenage children, I will always feel grateful to those compatriots of mine who gave their lives whilst serving with me. Of my 30 sorties, 70 crew (10 aeroplanes) failed to return – one of the most tragic incidents being when two aircraft collided over Wickenby, Lincolnshire, in February 1945 with both crews lost.

'I never saw my parents again, but I have been back to Warsaw twice. The holocaust there was indescribable ... may we never see such a war again. I am completely at home in England – my wife and children are in love with Poland, and proud of their dual heritage. This genuine love between my families often seems to me to be the best thing that came out of it all ...'

CHAPTER TWENTY THREE

Special Duty Operator's Diary: 101 Squadron, Ludford Magna

No. 101 was no ordinary squadron. It had an extra duty which entailed an eighth crew member and special broadcasting equipment, 'Airborne Cigar' or 'ABC' as it was known. The 101 Squadron Lancaster had two extra aerials and the bomb load was reduced by 1,000 lb weight to compensate for the extra (secret) VHF equipment. Their targets were those of the main force or back-up crews and except for 'Airborne Cigar' they did the same job, facing the same enemy and sharing the same risks.

This squadron was the RAF counter to German night-fighter radar. The Germans did not have enough radar to mount sets in individual night fighters. Instead they had giant radar sets called Wurtzburgs on the ground. They worked in pairs, one Wurtzburg tracking a German fighter while the other searched for our aircraft. When they found one they would plot the position and radio a course to the fighter so that he could intercept. The 'specials' of No. 101 Squadron had to intercept those messages and counter them.

Because of this important work each special duty operator had to speak German fluently. They were volunteers from various aircrew trades, ie, engineers, pilots, wireless operators, air gunners, etc, who had responded to requests for German-speaking volunteers for 'special duties', which were not at the time disclosed. Having been accepted, they eventually found themselves on 101

Squadron at Ludford Magna right on top of the Lincolnshire Wolds. Here each special duty operator joined a crew whenever a Battle Order was posted for an operation, as some special operators and their crews would be on it. After the main briefing, the specials had a separate briefing, when each of them was given a specific section of their receiver's waveband; thus the entire waveband was covered. Each special operator would switch his set on at a point determined at briefing, usually about 6 degrees East, and commence searching his section of the waveband. Any incoming signal had first to be identified as German, rather than Polish, Russian, or Czech and when this was done, one, two, or three transmitters were back-tuned so that wavelength and the incoming transmission jammed. How many transmitters were used to jam one signal would depend upon that signal's strength. They could jam up to three different signals at any time. What they were jamming was the German vectoring system which guided their night fighters towards the bomb stream, but they could never jam a signal for more than a few seconds at a time since their transmitters acted as "beacons" and they themselves became the night fighters' chief interest. The German ground stations were able to vector their night fighters onto the jamming signal they were transmitting, by taking bearings on their signals; thus they attracted fighters to themselves and were more vulnerable than the other aircraft in the bomber stream. However, it was not just a case of jamming enemy transmissions but also of broadcasting false information to the German night fighters. Using the call-sign he had just overheard, the 101 special would give the fighter false directions and stir it up as much as possible. Quite often there was quite a panic between the German on the ground and the German fighter in the air with the German-speaking special of 101 Squadron.

All ABC aircraft were spread out among the main stream in order to provide maximum protection, and they were required to keep a log of all signals received and jammed, together with the actual time, and, if possible, details of the actual German dialogue between Ground Control and night fighter pilot. Upon returning to base, they were interrogated together with their crew, and then separately upon their own duties. Among the special operators were men of different nationalities – at least one was German-born, and had been provided with a false British identity to protect him in the event of being shot down in Germany. Another, Sergeant Felix, was Palestinian.

The following raid details are extracts from the Diary of 1896587 Sergeant van Geffen, special duty operator 101 Squadron RAF No. 1 Group, Ludford Magna. These recollections were put down on paper by Sergeant van Geffen immediately after each operation and before catching up on lost sleep. His first and second operations were on 14 October 1944 against Duisburg and we take up his diary on his 11th operation on 6 December 1944.

'*6 December 1944, 11th Op. Abortive. Target*: Merseburg Nr Leipzig 51°17'N 12°08'E. *Crew*: S/Ldr McLeod-Selkirk and crew. *A/c*: I/Item DV298. *Airborne*: 16:48. *Landed*: 22:38. *Time in air*: 5 hrs 50 mins. Heavy icing conditions; forced off track as far west as Bath, instead of Reading: 46 mins behind main bomber stream, flying alone – unable to catch up on bomber stream, even by short cuts off-route briefed to fly. Still 36 mins late and alone, at approximately 06°00'E and decided to abandon attempt to reach target, 290 miles further east, into Germany – icing still troublesome – coldest trip yet – oxygen supply frozen – altered course for base and jettisoned "cookie", 2 x 1,000 lb DAHEs and photo-flare over North Sea – landed with remaining bomb load.

'*15 December 1944, 11th Op. Target*: Ludwigshafen (Mannheim) 49°23'N 02°36'E. *A/c*: I/Item DV298. *Crew*: S/Ldr McLeod-Selkirk and crew. *Airborne*: 14:32. *Landed*: 21:07. *Time in air*: 6 hrs 35 mins. This was 5th attempt at 11th op so it was about time we got it done! Arrived early and had to orbit over target, waiting for PFF Markers. We were briefed to expect night fighter intruders to follow us back to base to bomb and attack us whilst landing, but they didn't materialise – I didn't mind! Target was chemical and munition works and we know we didn't miss it … short story.

'*17 December 1944, 12th Op. Target*: Ulm 48°22'N 10°05'E, Marshalling yards, chemical works firefighting equipment manufacturers. *A/c*: I/Item DV 298. *Crew*: S/Ldr McLeod-Selkirk. *Airborne*: 15:05. *Landed*: 23: 15. *Time in air*: 8 hrs 10 mins. This was third briefing for this target – the first two being scrubbed owing to the weather conditions. This was first ever attack on Ulm, weather dicy all the way to target. We flew at 2,000 ft most of the way, with visibility limited to the wing-tips – climbed to and bombed from 10,000 over target. Two other Lancs 1,000 ft above us seemed to think we were the targets! Their "cookies" only missed us by half a wing span.

'*28 December 1944, 13th Op. Target*: Bonn (Ruhr) 50°46'N 07°10'E. Reinforcements – Transport Junction. *A/c*: I/Item DV298. *Crew*: S/Ldr McLeod-Selkirk and crew. *Airborne*: 15:18. *Landed*: 20:55.

Time in air: 5 hrs 37 mins. This raid was in support of General Hodges' US Army fighting in the Liège area of Belgium after retreating before General Von Runstedt's surprise Christmas offensive – Sgt King, also doing his 13th op, did not return.

'*29 December 1944, 14th Op. Target*: Buer (Ruhr) 51°36'N 07°02'E – Oil Plants. *A/c*: W²/William NG139. *Crew*: S/Ldr Gundry-White and crew. *Airborne*: 15:02. *Landed*: 21:11. *Time in air*: 6 hrs 09 mins. Easy trip for us, in spite of reports of moderate flak. Arrived over target early and had to orbit, waiting for PFF main fuselage door blew open; tried to shut it, but couldn't and had to put up with the cold – bombed from 19,000 ft, some aircraft from 101 Squadron were shot-up by flak ('R' Roger came home minus a wing-tip). Heard a few weeks later that the pilot was awarded the DFC.

'*2 January 1945, 15th Op. Target*: Nurnberg 49°28'N 11°12' E. Tanks – Diesel engines – Aircraft works. *A/c*: I/Item DV298. *Crew*: S/Ldr McLeod-Selkirk and crew. *Airborne*: 15:24. *Landed*: 23:42. *Time in air*: 8 hrs 20 mins. *Track Mileage*: 1,4. Arrived early over target, and orbited four times in target area, waiting for PFF – the sky was full of Lancasters and Halifaxes on the way out to the target, I've never seen so many aircraft in a stream before! Had a very busy time on the set, and worked my longest watch so far: $3\frac{3}{4}$ hrs – all 101 Sqdn aircraft returned safely, which surprised me as we lost nine last time we went to this target.

'*28 January 1945, 16th Op. Target*: Zliffenhausen – Stuttgart 48°50'N 09°09'E – Heinkel Jetpropulsion a/c factory. A/c: X/X-Ray ME310. *Crew*: F/O Schenk and crew. *Airborne*: 19:48. *Landed*: 02:57. *Time in air*: 7 hrs 10 mins. Flew with this crew who were doing their

Ludford Magna, November 1944. Sergeant van Geffen (with pipe) with crew.

first op, as my skipper was in hospital – the previous night brought the heaviest fall of snow I've ever seen, and we had the pleasure of clearing the runways during the day; it was 4 ft deep in parts! Skirted Paris on the way to and from the target: bombed from 18,000 ft, where the temperature was 40°C below 0°! We were seen by an Me 110 nightfighter and had to corkscrew to lose him.

'2 February 1945, 17th Op. Abortive. Target: Wiesbaden Nr Frankfurt 50°04'N 08°13'E – Rest area for Wehrmacht troops. A/c: H/How DV302. Crew: F/Lt McClenaghan and crew. Airborne: 20:48. Landed: 23:10. Time in air: 2 hrs 20 mins. Navigator reported "Gee" u/s over base, immediately after take-off; checked ABC equipment, which was also u/s. Proceeded out over North Sea, and jettisoned bombs before returning to base. Four other a/c from 101 Sqdn failed to take off! Two were bogged down, another unable to pass them, and the fourth had Magneto trouble from the previous night raid on Ludwigshafen. Three 101 Sqdn a/c failed to return, included in the crews were Frank Smith who came here with me, P/Os Kenny and Fenske and F/Lt Harrison – two days later F/Lt Harrison and his W/Op were reported to have landed at Croydon – breach of security was responsible for our losses. Sgts Felix and Wells completed their tour on this trip.

'3 February 1945, 17th Op. Target: Bottrop – Ruhr 51°32'N 07°01'E. Coke plants, for synthetic oil. A/c: D/Dog NF983. Crew: F/Lt McClenaghan and crew. Airborne: 16:25. Landed: 21:41. Time in air: 5 hrs 15 mins. Rather a sticky target, situated near Essen – had to fly near several ack-ack defence areas. Bombed from 17,000 ft and results were fairly good – saw several Lancasters go down and were ourselves investigated by fighters – felt more shaky on this trip than ever before – learned the next day that we now have to do 36 ops for a tour instead of 30. At the rate the Russians are moving westwards now, we'll soon be giving them some close support bombing at places like Magdeburg and Dresden – maybe even Cologne! (Joke Ha! Ha!).

'20 February 1945, 18th Op. 454a/c & PFF. Target: Dortmund, Ruhr 51°40'N 07°38'E – Railway marshalling yards. A/c: N²/Nan ME305. Crew: F/Lt Woods and crew. Airborne: 21:28. Landed: 03:59. Time in air: 6 hrs 30 mins. As my own crew are now flying in a non-ABC aircraft, it looks as though I shall be flying with anybody, and everybody for a while – just half-way through my tour now, whereas I thought I'd reached that stage on 2 January! This isn't a job – it's a career, at this rate! A fairly quiet trip, with nothing but the usual barrage flak to bother us. Bombed from 20,000 ft – weather conditions fairly good. S/Ldr Warner, awarded DFC for operations over Belgian Salient at Xmas (when he was shot down), didn't return from this trip.

'*21 February 1945, 19th Op. 327a/c plus PFF. Target*: Duisburg, Ruhr. 51°28'N 06°49'E. Marshalling yards – supplies, transportation – centre for Western Front. *A/c*: S/Sugar DV245. *Crew*: F/Lt Andrews and crew. *Airborne*: 19:55. *Landed*: 01:54. *Time in air*: 6 hrs 0 mins. This is the fourth time I've been to Duisberg – if I go again I don't think we'll need a navigator!! Weather good, but target obscured by cloud – bombed from 17,000 ft. Saw an Me 262 fighter (jet-propelled) and a Ju 88, both of them were uncomfortably close, and we had to corkscrew to dodge them. I saw my log-book floating around in mid-air for a while – have arranged to fly with F/Lt McClenaghan in future; have flown with him twice before while S/Ldr McLeod-Selkirk was ill.

'*23 February 1945*. The boys went out last night to Pforzheim and two crews didn't come back, they were F/Lts Watts and McClenaghan – if the latter had been flying in his own aircraft, instead of in S/Ldr McLeod-Selkirk's brand new kite, which doesn't carry ABC special equipment, I should have been flying with him – seems I'm lucky.

'*3 March 1945*. Night-intruders shot up the airfield and village for two hours.

'*5 March 1945, 20th Op. Target*: Chemnitz (Nr Dresden) 15°40'N 13°00'E, Railway repair shops (world's largest) and supplies centre. *A/c*: D/Dog NF983. *Crew*: F/O Cooke and crew. *Airborne*: 16:29. *Landed*: 02:49. *Time in air*: 10 hrs 20 mins. *Air Mileage*: 2,080 miles. This raid was in support of the Russian offensive approximately 100 miles further east; it was the deepest penetration to date for me, and we were over Germany for at least five hours (Chemnitz is almost due south of Berlin). Weather conditions over target made good bombing results impossible, due to 10/10ths cloud and icing – we'll probably have to go again! One of our aircraft, from 101 Sqdn shot down a Ju 88, all 101 Sqdn a/c safe but F/O Blackburn had to land in France.

'*7 March 1945, 21st Op. Target*: Dessau – secondary target: Remscheid (Ruhr) 51°36'N 12°00'E 51°10'N 07°07'E. *A/c*: R/Roger LL772. *Crew*: F/O Henn and crew. *Airborne*: 17:02. *Landed*: 23:29. *Time in air*: 6 hrs 30 mins. Oil leak developed in port-outer engine, which was expected to fail – Dessau being only 60-odd miles from Berlin, we bombed Remscheid, in the Ruhr, as we foresaw the possibility of losing another engine before getting back. S/Ldr

Gibbons didn't return from Dessau. I was supposed to fly with F/O Robinson, but he went sick just before briefing; F/O Henn (whose special operator, Rudy Mahr, was flying with S/Ldr Gibbons) took his place – Rudy and I tried to change, so that he could fly with his own crew, but it was too late to alter arrangements ... Now Rudy is missing, instead of me. (Second time lucky!)

'*8 March 1945 22nd Op. Target*: Kassel, Central Germany 51°20'N 09°29'E. Railway marshalling yards and workshops – tank factories and jet-propulsion aircraft works. *A/c*: X/X-Ray ME310. *Crew*: F/Lt Wagner and crew. *Airborne*: 17:25. *Landed*: 01:02. *Time in air*: 7 hrs 35 mins. Nice quiet trip – little or no flak and few fighters – temperature 35° below at bombing altitude (20,000 ft) reports indicate a "good prang" in spite of cloud – saw several rockets on their way to London. Hamburg was also bombed and we saw it burning from a distance.

'*12 March 1945*. Obtained permission from F/Lt Harrison to fly with him today as a passenger on today's raid on Dortmund. I have never been able to see a target area being bombed, as I'm always too busy. Didn't have much luck though – the port inner engine developed an oil leak as we were taking-off and we had to feather the prop within ten minutes of being airborne. We went out over the North Sea to jettison our bomb load but couldn't get above 3,000 ft and so had to land at Carnaby, Yorkshire with a 4,000 lb "cookie", being unable to find base due to ground haze. Spent two days in Bridlington waiting for aircraft to be repaired and then as we were all broke, spent two days at RAF Lisset. Finally took off and returned to base on Friday afternoon, 16 March. Upon returning learned that S/Ldr McLeod-Selkirk had "phoned up" asking for me to fly with him on a raid on Gelsenkirchen. Sgt Toy went in my place and they were seen to blow-up over Germany – the only aircraft we lost that night. That's my third lucky break in as many weeks – how many more?'

Luck did hold for Sergeant van Geffen and he successfully completed 22 operational missions. The awareness of those years spent with No. 101 squadron is something he will never forget and it is still fresh in his mind after almost four decades.

CHAPTER TWENTY FOUR

An Erk in Bomber Command

Ralph Dargue had an early interest in aviation and at the age of nine had his first flight in an Avro 504 from a rugby ground near Whitley Bay. His first flight as a paying passenger was with Alan Cobham's circus in 1935. Thereafter he haunted aerodromes such as Abbotsinch, Renfrew, Croydon and Hendon. In 1936 he eagerly wished to join the Royal Air Force Apprentice School but was defeated by his guardian's view, 'Just Tommies with dirty hands!' The following year he passed the Civil Service entrance and went into the Customs.

He continued with interest in aviation (model building) and volunteered for the Royal Air Force at Ad Astral House on 6 September 1939, but was held in reserve by the Customs. He volunteered again at Gorbals, Glasgow in January 1940 and was offered duty in MTBs or 12 years with the Cavalry, no vacancies being available in the RAF. In March 1940 he was called forward and offered Radio Operator (Ground) but declined this as electricity was his worst subject at school. Called to Padgate for attestation as Flight Mech. in June 1940 and sent with only half-kit on coal-heaving at a front-line aerodrome, he was routed to West Kirby in August 1940 for square-bashing, then on to St Athan for rigger's course in September, a year after initial volunteering! He answered a call for aircrew volunteers in October and was accepted at Uxbridge as Observer. He was posted to 83 Squadron Scampton (Hampdens), end of January 1941; to fitter's course in mid-summer, then called from Scampton to ACRC, London in October 1941; taken off aircrew training with defective vision soon afterwards and posted to No. 2 (C) OTU, Catfoss January 1942. Posted overseas

(Canada) February 1942 to 36 OTU, Greenwood, Nova Scotia (Hudsons and Mosquitoes). Posted 9 AFU, Errol August 1944 (Masters and Harvards) with training as EVT Instructor in February 1945 before posting to 96 Squadron, Leconfield (Halifaxes) in March 1945. He was again posted overseas to 22 APC, Indian Air Force (Harvards), May 1945 and to 82 Squadron, SEAAF, Madras area (Mosquitoes), July 1945. Unit disbanded at St Thomas Mount, India on 15 March 1946, with most personnel going to Japan. Air Staged from Poona to Holmsley South and demobilisation, April 1946. That same month he returned to Customs under Essential Works Order. In November 1955 entered Ministry of Supply and remained there until he retired in January 1982.

During his RAF service Ralph Dargue served on many bomber airfields in Nos. 4 and 5 Groups, Bomber Command and the following are his recollections of life on those wartime bomber airfields:

'After a day and night journey from St Athan in late January 1941, Campbell, Dobbie and I arrived at RAF Scampton somewhat unsteady and begrimed, having had a cold water wash and shave but no breakfast at Lincoln Station while awaiting transport. We were directed to 83 Squadron Orderly Room, kitbags and all, and sent to see the Squadron Commander, or his second dickie. We waited outside his office and as a peaked cap emerged, flattened ourselves against the corridor wall. I thought I had the presence of mind to snap up a salute, only to be told, "Don't salute me, you fool; I'm the Station Warrant Officer!".

'As AC1, Flight Mech(A) we were assigned to Maintenance Flight, and my second memory of the unit is the Flight Sergeant looking at the flashes on my shoulder and saying, "I don't like VRs". As I was a volunteer ahead of my callup date, I couldn't see his point, and we were hardly eye-to-eye from then on. I spent nearly all my time sweeping the hangar floor wondering why I had spent so much time at No. 4 School of Technical Training, but was allowed after about five weeks to take part in 30 hour inspections. I was encouraged on odd occasions to give a "2–6" on the doors of the C type hangar, and to help steady the rear-end of aircraft during engine run-ups. The Hampden (or Flying Tadpole) was so flexible that the slender rear fuselage used to "whip" threateningly under ground-effect vibration of the twin-rudders, and two lowly creatures were made to face and embrace the fins while the 900 HP Pegasus engines were being given a thorough check. In February/March the slipstream could be freezing and soon penetrated overalls and uniform. A hat or spectacles could not be worn in such conditions and it was a lucky man who could still believe that his ears were attached to his head after five to ten minutes of this treatment.

'We had at least one aircraft which limped back after a flare had gone off "in the tube" and it says a lot for the strength of the Hampden "spine" that it could land without breaking up in that condition. I also attended numerous funeral parades, possibly to improve my drill standard, or because I had a pale and woeful expression, and helped to clear human wreckage out of lower gunner positions.

'The intruder raids were a source of interest, though I slept through the attacks even when a small stick straddled the hangars and the duty store basher was killed at the door; curiosity at the noise had drawn him to his death.

'A naval Chief Petty Officer was brought in to set the fuses on the "cigars" after the mine dump blew up one evening as the aircraft were being readied for operations and all we retrieved was the Armament Corporal's cap badge and part of his head. A rolled-steel joist from the dump structure was twisted like a corkscrew and spun its way through the opposite walls of a cottage at the edge of Ermine Street; luckily it had been emptied of its occupants. Some Hampdens were dispersed at that time on the other side of the road with their wings filling the gaps in the hedges for camouflage.

'I remember that the squadron had a Harrow (high-wing monoplane) which was used to ferry ground crews and their tools to places such as St Eval when some aircraft were deployed to bomb the ships at Brest Naval Base. We had a storm in March/April 1941 and I never saw anything looking so forlorn and u/s as that Harrow completely on its back with its fixed undercarriage in the air where the pickets had been ripped out of the ground. As the corkscrew portion of the "anchors" must have been some 4 ft long, it could only have been a massive "blow" to achieve such damage. As far as I can remember the poor old beast lay in that attitude until after October 1941, probably beyond economical repair.

'The brick-built barracks and station buildings were comfortable and more in keeping with my idea of what an operational station should be after the huts of previous (training) existence. There was little entertainment for the erks on the camp other than occasional housey-housey or getting drunk on NAAFI beer, so that Lincoln was resorted to as regularly as spare time would allow. I spent nearly all my pay in bookshops as there was little else to do, the cinemas and teashops being overcrowded with airmen from all the neighbouring airfields, and all the decent places declared as out of bounds. There was friendly rivalry between 49 and 83 Squadron personnel as both units had been awarded VCs.

LAC Ralph Dargue

'A programme was carried through to fit cable cutters to the armoured leading edges of Hampden mainplanes, the theory being that at a strike the cable would obligingly slide along the sheathing to be chopped by the cartridge-fired chisel! (This was a big "invention" after the Dortmund-Ems episode.)

'I spent a lot of time on aircraft night guard patrols. No. 83 Squadron covered two "legs" of the airfield perimeter with a sandbagged MG pit at one corner, and 49 covered the other sides. It was normally wet (and cold) on such a duty and the Orderly Officer had the thankless task of checking around the parked aircraft to see if any airman was sheltering under an engine nacelle. The duty fell to a corporal and six men doing two hours on and four hours off.

'The Ju 88 which attacked in May 1941 flew low over the airfield. Corporal Inkpen had heard the engines (which most people could recognise by the "beat") and had all six standing-to with himself in the gun pit. As the dark shape flew over the regular flare path, he opened up with both Lewises and emptied all the ammo at the intruder. Of the 2 x 97 rounds fired only four actually hit the aircraft, one by luck striking an oxygen bottle (in the tail of an 88) which exploded, rupturing the controls. The Junkers hit the ground near the boundary fence and burned for most of the night. At first light two of the guards approached the smouldering wreck; one man suddenly yelled, "There's a body there!", dropped his weapon and scuttled towards the guard hut as fast as his shaking legs would carry him. He retrieved his rifle from his rather amused mate, and they stood guard, bravely together, until the Corporal and the orderly officer arrived. The swastika was cut off the fin and hung in No 4 Hangar as a trophy with Corporal Inkpen's name stencilled on it with the date. A few days later I was posted to a fitter's conversion course and so missed the funeral of the German crew, and the adulatory parade for the corporal and his six brave men.

'In spite of seeking a posting to another unit at the end of the course, I returned to 83 Squadron after eight weeks to the over-sceptical eye of the efficient Flight Sergeant in No. 4 Hangar, who promptly sent me to base workshops with never a look at an aircraft but more than occasionally returning to gardening fatigues, funeral parades and work on setting up the airfield defence cable rockets (ie, ditch digging). It could be said that this Senior NCO had little concept of man-encouragement, though he had the tidiest work-control board in his office that I have ever seen.

'The squadron had absorbed a lot more humanity and there was little spare barrack room accommodation available. Like many others I was given the dubious honour of sleeping in tents at Hackthorne on a site with few facilities but directly in line with the main flare path. The occasional intruder still beat up the airfield when aircraft were returning from raids, and many cannon shells and MG bullets whistled through the branches above our heads. For some strange reason other than compassion the Flight Sergeant allocated me to a billet at a farm near Nettleham with a macdonald bed in an attic. I never completely unpacked my kit during this second posting as there was nowhere to keep anything, and took only washing kit in a side pack along with overalls to the hangars each day, doing all ablutions before returning to the farm. A truck collected dispersed airmen from the village at 07:00 and deposited us back again at 20:30 – otherwise it was a long walk back. The farmer offered nothing, not even a drink of water, so I tended to put in all my free evenings in the "Education Office", offering basic German phrases to some aircrew using a Hugo Pocket German and leaflets I had found in various aircraft during cleaning. As a handful of junior WAAF officers attended (out of curiosity?), their attention was minimal but it kept me from going berserk, I suppose. One erk who had a most appalling Birmingham accent and couldn't pronounce the diphthongs, and a corporal SP did make some attempts at learning, so the time was not entirely wasted. A very young WOP/AG Sergeant Read also attended – for company I suspected – and in a quiet moment he told me that only three others remained with him of the original Hampden aircrews. He had been in a crash himself, and carried a piece of shiny black leather in his wallet – it was the burnt skin off his nose!

'One job I had at the workshops was the trimming up of pre-welded auxiliary bomb carriers. These were fitted under the outer mainplanes and supported 4 x 25 lb anti-personnel bombs. On one night an aircraft returned with its full load, having missed the targets in the fog, and the crew got out to stand around the aircraft awaiting transport back to quarters and debrief. The bomb-aimer had inadvertently left the switches in the "Armed" condition, so that while an airman was doing internal checks and an armourer was clearing the racks, the weapons were still fused. Unfortunately the armourer dropped one heavy pack which exploded on impact. It blew off the port mainplane, firing the main fuel tanks and all the pyrotechnics, killing the aircrew and ground tradesmen outright. A fitter named Stevenson, who had recently shared a tent with me at Innsworth, was a little late on the scene because he had snapped a boot lace as he was coming from the crew shelter, and he received the effect of the blast at about 50 yards. This threw him over backwards and it was just unlucky that the back of his head hit a piece of contractors' rubble which broke his neck; he would have otherwise survived with only bruises, and it was a particularly unpleasant duty to be on *his* funeral parade.

'On the same night a pilot from 49 Squadron panicked and took the wrong level or turn on his circuit, so colliding with a Hampden from 83; both fell and exploded killing all the crew members. Another 83 crew were caught coming over the coast by an intruder, so that apart from losses over enemy territory and the North Sea, it was a pretty disastrous night for the station. In addition, another Hampden had failed to get airborne the night before, so the next morning we had to retrieve it – and its bomb load – from a perimeter hedge; the crew were lucky and lived to fly again. I noticed on the ensuing funeral parades that the Scampton churchyard was filled and that a neighbouring piece of land had been consecrated to receive the overflow of crosses. Also I noted that someone had put fresh flowers on the German graves with the message "To Some Mother's Son." Magnanimity or sentimentality in wartime; I wonder!

'After the *debacle* in Crete, airfield defence came into prominence. A few riflemen rode around in open three-ton trucks with canvas flapping down the sides and twin Lewis guns mounted on the back. There was also the big experiment in anti-intruder weaponry, and in company with many others trained as tradesmen but who could be spared from gardening duties, I helped to dig shallow trenches around two-thirds of the 83 perimeter. These were to take electric cables with small posts at every 100 yds. The post carried a small electrically-fired rocket which had a coil of wire in a tin on the ground, the idea being to throw up a screen of wires in the path of an attacking aircraft. The rocket was to deploy a small parachute which would delay the drop of the wires. We laboured mightily and then some fool either connected the wrong wire or pulled a switch accidentally. A few rockets went off singeing some of the tradesmen and left a tangle of wires all over the flarepath area. The next days' fatigues were spent in searching the grass for bits of wire which could have fouled undercarriages or propellers.

'Many of the tradesmen were given additional grenade-throwing practice, five rounds at the butts and some fieldcraft under the instruction of a Sergeant from the Royal Norfolk Regiment. His favourite command was: "At 11 o'clock, 800 yards, by bushy-top tree; halfway up field, cow; halfway up cow, bull; Aim! Fire! "

'One of my last parades at Scampton was to be photographed with most of the squadron. I have a photograph to this day of many good men and true swamping a Hampden. The faces were so young! My connection with Scampton ceased in October 1941 when I was posted to the Aircrew Receiving Centre at Lords Cricket Ground in London. I had volunteered and been accepted for Observer in August 1940 – the mills of God, indeed! I had started there with such high hopes and found mainly disappointments. My next visit to Scampton was in 1979 as a Project Officer (MOD) to witness the packing of liferafts and survival aids to new scales in the Vulcan pannier.

'For some reason I shall never understand, I was sent with a Corporal (Engines & Airframe) and an LAC Fitter 2E to Waddington in September 1941 to activate a damaged Hampden which had been forced to land there on return from a raid. The aircraft was parked on the far side of the airfield and no overnight accommodation could be offered so we slept when we could in our day clothes in the dispersal hut. For meals and ablutions we had to trudge across to the main site and on the second day I found myself on a charge for being improperly dressed at the dining hall. Apparently the mess officer, who happened to be Roy Fox, the band leader, had made a decree that airmen should have their hands properly scrubbed (he sometimes inspected fingernails) and wear gym shoes at main meals. How anyone could get from the flights, get cleaned up and don soft shoes – assuming he had them – eat, and then get back to work in an hour was beyond human comprehension, and the two SPs who flanked this wingless wonder looked plainly embarrassed at his orders. The charge sheet never reached Scampton while I was there, so must have been torn up by someone with a mite of wisdom. Fortunately we got the aircraft repaired in two and a half days and so could leave Waddington to its miseries (I understand that the airfield and the village received more than a fair amount of enemy attention) and its petty "bull".

'I had waited a year to be called to aircrew training in which time, thanks to indifferent feeding, general conditions and possibly some increase of nervous tension, my eyesight had deteriorated significantly so that within two weeks of arrival at Lords Cricket Ground, I was discharged from any commitment to observer training. The establishment at Abbey Lodge was skeletal, except on the medical side, so I was more or less obliged to stooge around the West End in the evenings and passed most of the days in the Reference Library at St Pancras Town Hall. There was no "Careers Guidance" or choice of future role, and while I slept on the floor of what had been Miss Evelyn Laye's flat off Hall Road, it took time for me to be returned to "basic trade". However it came as no surprise to be put on a train at King's Cross on New Year's Day 1942 bound for Catfoss, East Yorkshire, a place no one seemed to have heard of previously.

'I don't know how I got to the guard room from Beverley in a blinding snowstorm, but it was well after midnight when, with a few other new arrivals, I was shown into an unheated Nissen hut containing metal beds but no blankets or mattresses. From that chilly reception I have a feeling I never recovered in the ensuing weeks as little pleasant seemed to happen from then on.

'Some thought that Catfoss had been an Auxiliary Air Force summer camp prewar and certainly the smallness and lack of substantial camp buildings could attest to such a condition, but now the strength was past the 2,500 mark while the dining hut could seat about 250 at a time. One shuffled from a queue at the ablutions block and the "heads" to the dining hut through the snow and sleet which rarely stopped blowing across that treeless part of Holderness, so that at least $1\frac{1}{2}$ hours was needed for a meal-break away from the workplace. The camp apparently boasted only one Bellman hangar and there were no huts on the flights so that men and their toolboxes were crammed under engine covers for some protection against the weather. Fitters cursed the cold as they worked under the canvas hoods on the Bristol engines, and the best, though limited, shelter for other trades was inside the aircraft themselves.

'I never saw the total camp. It was a matter of trudging through a field to a road and then along to Brandesburton to some asbestos huts on the outskirts of the village. At the end of the day it was the duty of the first man in to try to get a stove going, and we soon used up all the nearest farmer's spare fencing timbers. The blankets and our clothes were perpetually damp and the only water that was not frozen was warmed in a bucket on the tortoise stove. About 20 men used the same bucket for some attempts at shaving! In the early morning we slithered through the slush to the flight (a small hut about 6 ft x 6 ft for the Sergeant, all his records and some tea-making equipment) to report, then across a concrete runway to the main camp site to line up for ablutions and breakfast. This was repeated throughout my stay with a break after the eighth day.

'The weather let up from time to time to permit some flying with a mixture of Blenheims and Beaufighters; there were 13 crashes in 11 days, most of them fatal, and things seemed to happen in threes. Once on the return of a Beau from an airtest, I saw it on to the hardstanding and then caused a watching LAC to faint. I had forgotten that the propeller arcs were so close together and as I went forward to open the hatch, I had walked *through* the airscrew swept area during the final tick-over. When told, I nearly fainted myself but I have no other recollections of the Beaufighter as such!

'In the time that I was at Catfoss I had two free half-days. On the first I learned that I could get a bath at a big mansion just outside the village, and this turned out to be the local asylum. It seemed strange but appropriate, but at least provided the one place where I could be warm and clean even in a few inches of water with a stiff brush and some carbolic soap. On leaving the building I heard some poor inmate give vent to a line of crazy laughter, but somehow the manic mirth had the undertone of knowledge that perhaps it was better to be crazy inside than to be driven just about crazy on the outside! On the other half-day I visited Beverley and had the one decent meal of the month in a small cafe near to the minster, and afterwards could pause for a while as an organist practised in a big church. Bach was never quite so satisfying! The only other entertainment, it seemed, was provided by two London "girls" who had set up in the safety of Brandesburton, but somehow the prospect of standing in line in the snow and sleet with an equally browned-off lot of airmen had little personal appeal, even in an area of such dismal human contact.

'One day towards the end of the month I had been delayed more than usual over at the dining hall area and was told that the sergeant had sent the hounds out for me. His news was that he had a list of 13 overseas postings; one man had been admitted to hospital and as I was the last arrival on the flight, my name had been "volunteered". Although things were reported to be going badly in the Far East I wasn't sure whether it came as a blow or as a relief, and then spent the next two days trying to get my clearance from sections of the camp which I had never seen. Nor in that time had I seen any officer, least of all an orderly officer in the dining hall, and as far as I could tell, no one ever inspected the Brandesburton huts.

'My records had not yet arrived from ACRC at London so the medical officer pumped about five doses of vaccine into my already overladen arteries, the MO at Abbey Lodge having done the same treatment for the same reasons only three months earlier. Eventually I got a lift into Beverley and caught a train to York with a connection to Newcastle. At 1 am I had to walk with all my kit about two miles from the central station before pressing my mother's door bell. When she opened the door I fell inside, and she, poor soul, thought I was drunk. Indeed I was – on vaccine fever – and spent the first four days of embarkation leave in bed with a raging temperature. The leave passed all too quickly and sadly for my mother, who had known happier times in Singapore before my father's death there in the early 1930s, but at least it enabled me to get my uniform and clothes cleaned and repaired, then I was off to Catfoss again leaving a pale figure looking very small and vulnerable on the receding platform. There was no need to spend a night at Catfoss (memories of the Nissen hut were still keen) as the other members of the group were present. We were shunted down to a church hall at Hornsea from where we moved out to West Kirby on the morning train. The future looked bleak, but at least it couldn't be any worse than Catfoss! I had been back at Errol for just over two weeks after attending an EVT Instructor's Course at Snitterfield when I was posted on about 7 March 1945 to 4096 Servicing Echelon at Leconfield, East Yorkshire.

'This was an Expansion Programme station and currently housed 640 Squadron with Halifaxes, who were regularly on operations. One of these sticks in my mind and was the attack on Wurms through cloud only a short time and distance ahead of advancing American troops, who rapidly occupied the town behind the moving pattern of bombs.

'We were housed in decent barracks and could work in substantial hangars our main task being the acceptance and conversion of new Halifaxes to carry 1 or 13 stretchers or multiple troop seats in preparation for movement to the Far East. This was my first experience of four-engined (or indeed any) heavy aircraft, and I must admit to being more than overawed by the sheer size of components, especially the massive Messier undercarriages, and the height of the upper surfaces of the wings. Work was going well enough under efficient though unfamiliar organisation and though I never saw the outside world in the time I was there, I could find no complaint with my lot in the fairly affable company of airmen and junior NCOs now earmarked for a second overseas tour. Just before the end of the month we were suddenly sent on leave, even though many of our jobs were incomplete, and were as hastily recalled after about eight days absence. The buzz was that the Halifaxes were being ditched and that the squadron was to use Dakotas, and we soon found that organisational chaos was reigning at full blast. We paraded in the hangar from which the Halifaxes were rapidly disappearing and were shunted around in groups or by the nominal roll from one corner to another, am and pm, as the senior NCOs simultaneously issued conflicting orders that echoed from the walls to create an absolute babel. Men flocked here and there and this prompted Bob Dane, a fellow Corporal, to remark from a vantage point, "Just look at them – a flock of bloody sheep! Go on! Baa, Baa!" This bleating was soon being chorused in different styles by the disgusted erks, and only added to the confusion.

'Eventually after about 36 hours half the airmen were collected and marched off by the admin NCOs to go more or less directly (we were later informed) to embarkation at Gourock. Much later I learned that a relative was the Squadron Movements Officer with 96 Squadron Dakotas – in Rangoon! The rest of us continued for a few more days of bleating on parades until about 12 April when we were suddenly assembled with full kit and marched across the airfield to Arram, whence we went *en masse* to an overseas pool at Morecambe, each with prospects of joining some draft or other as the peculiarities of RAF Records and Postings required. Some of us passed non-stop through the Straits of Gibraltar on the *Chitral* on 8 May, while there was dancing in the streets we had left behind.'

CHAPTER TWENTY FIVE

Destination Hanover

During the latter part of September and early October 1943, four heavy raids were made against Hanover. The first raid was on 22/23 September and took place in clear weather conditions. From the 716 bombers despatched with 2,357 tons of bombs, 658 attacked the target. But many of the bombs fell over five miles away from the true aiming point and only the southern suburbs were hit at all. Flight-Lieutenant 'Taff' Jenkins and his crew in Halifax 'N' Nuts HR924 from No. 10 Squadron, Melbourne,

Farouk III, 'Taff' Jenkins and crew with most of ground crew. Aircrew left to right, Flight Sergeant Monty Banks, flight engineer; Flight Sergeant Eric Saddington, bomb-aimer; Pilot Officer A.L. Fuller (RAAF), mid-upper gunner; Flight-Lieutenant J.G. Jenkins, DFC, pilot; Pilot Officer R. N. Hurst, DFM (RCAF) rear gunner; Pilot Officer J. Whatley, wireless operator; Pilot Officer J. Ryan, navigator. Photo taken at RAF Melbourne, No. 10 Squadron, on completion of tour, January 1943.

Yorkshire took part in the first raid. The crew were Flight-Lieutenant 'Taff' Jenkins, pilot; Sergeant J. Ryan, navigator; Sergeant E. Saddington, bomb-aimer; Sergeant 'Monty' Banks, flight engineer; Sergeant J. Whatley, wireless operator; Flight Sergeant R. Hurst, rear gunner and Flight Sergeant Les Fuller, mid-upper gunner. This was their 14th operation and they were a very experienced crew.

At the briefing in the afternoon the Commanding Officer, Wing Commander Edmunds announced that a special honour had been paid to No. 10 Squadron in that one of their Halifaxes was to be fitted with a cine camera which would operate automatically when the bombing run commenced and film, in colour, the inferno below, during the passage over the target area. It was revealed that 'N' *Nuts* had been selected to carry the camera in the flare chute. They took off at 18:50 and the flight was uneventful. As they approached the target area nearly 200 searchlights probed the sky for the bombers. Many bombers were being engaged with fighters which on this occasion had not been misled by diversionary attacks on Oldenburg and Emden.

As they approached the target area the atmosphere inside 'N' *Nuts* grew tense as they waited for the commencement of the bomb-aimer's patter. With the desperate struggles going on all around them they had completely forgotten about the cine-camera. However, it was not the bomb-aimer's voice they heard, but the rear gunner's. The latter's Canadian voice came unexpectedly over the intercom. 'Fighter below – an Me 110'. It appeared to be manoeuvring in preparation for an attack but it was unusual for a 'curve of pursuit' attack and the rear gunner watched, waiting for further development. Flight Sergeant Les Fuller, the mid-upper gunner peered into the darkness but could not see the fighter. He waited, expecting the fighter to reposition on one of the beams, or quarters, to launch an attack. Suddenly the rear gunner announced that they were going to be attacked as the fighter moved swiftly to a position directly underneath 'N' Nuts and some 400 yds off. Flight Sergeant Hurst tried to get his guns to bear on the enemy by extending the hydraulic jacks in his turret to the full but the fighter was too far forward for him. 'Dive, dive!' shouted the rear gunner. The pilot responded immediately but just an instant too late. A devastating burst of fire streamed upwards and raked the fuselage, seemingly from tail to nose. The burst of fire struck on the downward dive of their combat manoeuvre. The Me 110 had carried out a near perfect *Schräge Musik* with upward firing cannon – a far cry from the classical curve of pursuit attacks which were the type the gunners expected. The Halifax and Lancaster were very vulnerable to attacks from below.

After what seemed a prolonged dive the pilot levelled the bomber out, much to the relief of the crew and the rear gunner reported that they had lost the fighter. Once it had been ascertained that there were no injuries the pilot regained his bombing course before it was too late. The alternative would have been to circle Hanover and virtually begin all over again. The new bombing run was started but on the run-in the bomb doors would not open; obviously the fighter had done some damage and this was confirmed when it was found that the H$_2$S also was not functioning. On investigation it was discovered that the perspex cover, shaped like half an egg, had been shot completely away from the floor of the fuselage, leaving a large gaping oval hole about 5 ft x 3 ft through which the probing searchlights and the incipient inferno below could be seen. There was hydraulic fluid in the floor area around the mid-upper turret which had leaked from a fractured pipe. The flight engineer found a projectile from the attack embedded in the bullet-proof plate glass protective panel positioned directly behind the pilot's head and when he withdrew it the round was still hot enough to burn his finger and thumb, causing him to drop it. Unable to drop their bombs it was decided that the only course left open to them was to carry on over the target and return with the main bomber force, thereby retaining the protection of Window, which was still being dropped through a chute at regular intervals by the wireless operator.

'Les' Fuller, the mid-upper gunner, takes up the story: 'The flight over the target area, which was now beginning to burn fiercely, proved an apprehensive one for us as we feared further enemy interceptions. The night fighters, having been informed of the route being flown out of the city, began laying a lane of powerful flares, on a grand scale, to silhouette the bombers as they left illuminated Hanover and re-entered the surrounding darkness of night. Each flare lit up an extensive area of the sky and two separate lines, placed a considerable distance apart, laterally, so that each bomber had to fly between them presented a frightening challenge, running the gauntlet thus, whilst the fighters orbited above, to spot a Lancaster or Halifax, outlined against the descending flares from either side of the enlightened lane. We were particularly vulnerable in our damaged aircraft, the extent of which was unknown and it was our intention to avoid any combat manoeuvres, which might prove detrimental to the Halifax, if it was in a more suspect condition than we imagined. The lane extended in length as the main stream of bombers flew out of the target area and more flares drifted down on their parachutes from the fighters above and looked like an elongated airborne flare path, illuminating the darkness beyond Hanover.

'Flight Sergeant Hurst, the rear gunner, and I manipulated our turrets continually and together with the flight engineer, when he could, searched the luridly lit sky, for lurking fighters, whilst we flew along the flare way. Fortunately, none was seen, in spite of their obvious presence and eventually, after a seemingly long time, we reached the end of the lane, which was then burning out and once again were wrapped in the night's protective cloak of darkness. It was a great relief to escape from the brightly burning target area and the illuminated lane, marking our route out and on this particular operation the lines of flares were positively conspicuous, more so than on any of our previous or later raids. Running the gauntlet that night, so soon after the fighter attack and resultant damage to the Halifax, was a memorable and fearful experience.

'We were now in a position to try and assess the situation and decide what was to be done with the 4,000 pounder in the bomb bay and the load of incendiaries, housed in the mainplane. The door operating equipment was tried again, but without any success; the doors remained firmly closed. The "cookie" could not be released safely whilst they were shut; nevertheless, it was suggested that we try and drop the bomb on to the two long hinged panels, joining at the centre, hoping that the great weight would force them apart. However, the pilot and engineer thought that the risk was too great and there was no guarantee that the idea would work and a loose bomb in the bay, under the floor, and laid on the doors, would increase the dangers on landing.

'The H$_2$S equipment was out of action; the scanning section, set in the floor aft of the mid-upper turret, had been shot away, leaving a gaping hole in the floor. On testing the undercarriage, the discovery was made that it was not functioning properly, for the wheels had not descended, so unless we could correct the fault, it would mean a belly landing, if we made it back to Melbourne. This latest misfortune, combined with the bomb door problem, placed us in an unenviable position. After discussing the situation as we flew along, the pilot, in summing up, warned us that we would probably have to bale out on return to base. In our own minds we had, each of us, feared the worst without saying it openly and the statement, coming from the captain, provided plenty to think about.

'The fusilade of cannon shells must have damaged the hydraulics operating the undercarriage and bomb doors. Meantime, the flight engineer, who had been thinking profoundly about these two problems, raised our hopes by revealing that there was a pipe in the system, which, if cut in an emergency, would cause the bomb doors to open under the influence of their weight and he set about there and then to select the right one from the collection. The means of cutting the pipe was found in the form of a special small hacksaw blade, taken from the flight engineer's Pandora (escape kit carried by aircrew) and we waited hopefully during the sawing operation and nervously, in case something unforeseen happened. In a few minutes the pipe was soon cut, but nothing happened – the bomb doors remained closed.

'Someone then suggested hacking a hole in the plywood floor and, through the opening made, possibly forcing the long doors open, so that the bomb could be dropped safely, even if we try and shake it off, assuming this was feasible. In desperation it was agreed to try this and I was selected to do the cutting with the turret axe, one of which was provided in each turret. I was to vacate the mid-upper turret and the flight engineer would search around and above from the astrodome for fighters, as much as possible, whilst watching the instruments and recording the readings at required intervals. Unfortunately, the floor area necessary for the opening was remote from the oxygen supply connection, so it meant working without the gas which was essential at operational height. Setting to work with the axe, which was really a hatchet with a 15 in long handle, I soon realised it was going to be a difficult task, even though it was a specially designed and sharp tool. The keen blade made little impression on the tough laminated timber. Before long, the lack of oxygen took its toll and, combined with the physical exertion, compelled me to return to the oxygen connection and plug in for a time, to rejuvenate myself and relieve the chronic headache that had developed, along with impaired vision. The plywood, which was some 4 in thick, resisted the hatchet blows to an aggravating extent, because the successive layers had their grains running at right angles to each other for strength and many chops with the axe were necessary to make even a slight impression on the floor. I had visualised the cutting of a large hole in the flooring when commencing, thinking the job would be fairly easy, but eventually had to settle for a smaller opening, sufficient only to pass my flying-boot covered foot.

'Informing the crew that I was about to try and tread the bomb free, I put my foot into the hole and on to the long steel cylinder and pushed first and then stood on it, but nothing budged. The bomb held fast on its mountings as solidly as a rock and I knew that nothing that I could do was going to drop it the short distance on to the bomb doors and open them by virtue of the bomb's weight. I informed the pilot that it seemed hopeless trying to dislodge the 4,000 pounder and reconsidering the element of risk involved, he decided to abandon the idea and press on back to base. It was now realised that we would have to bale out of the bomber or attempt a belly landing at Melbourne or at the Emergency Landing Unit at Carnaby, with the load of explosives and incendiaries on board. Neither alternative was pleasant to look forward to, so we tried to forget about our return to terra firma for the time being and concentrate on getting back to base first.

'Having failed to jettison the bomb load, I returned to my turret and continued the search for fighters that could still appear and attack, right up to the time of landing at Melbourne. At this stage, my intercom plug had somehow become wet or damp, possibly with coming into contact with oil from a fractured hydraulic pipe or from some other moisture on the floor, and when I plugged in a loud squeaking noise became audible to all the crew. Associating this interference with my return to the turret, the pilot told me to disconnect and stay off the system; consequently I lost contact with the crew and for some time was unaware of what was said or was happening within the aircraft, because from the mid-upper turret I could only see outside, whatever my night vision permitted. Meantime, we flew through the night and eventually arrived back to base, where radio contact was made with Flying Control. I left the turret now we were over Melbourne, dried my intercom plug thoroughly and connected up again, to find out what was happening, but the squeak was still there and interfered with the crews' conversation, so again I had to "go off the air".

'However, I soon found out that we had been ordered by the CO to abandon 'N' Nuts. It had been decided that because the 4,000 pounder was still on board and the undercarriage damaged, the risk was too great to attempt a belly landing. Apart from the very probable loss of crews' lives, if the aircraft exploded on touching down, there was the destruction of the runway to consider, which would mean diverting the other bombers when they returned and, also, the squadron would be put out of action for some time, so considering these factors, the decision to bale out was the obvious and sensible one.

'We had about 25 minutes' flying time left, before the supply of fuel ran out, so the skipper confirmed to Flying Control that the aircraft would be abandoned, in accordance with orders, and turned back towards the coast in the direction of Hull, instructing us to prepare for baling out, informing each member of the order in which he was to leave the Halifax. The front escape hatch was to be used in preference to the side entrance in the fuselage on the port side. The pilot could ensure by utilising the forward exit, which was reasonably visible to him, that all the crew had gone before he switched on "George", the automatic pilot, and left the aircraft himself. The vision of plunging headlong out into the inky darkness of the night, at 2 am in the morning, was a frightening thought and the only consolation and spur to going through with it, was the knowledge that it offered the best prospects for survival.

'We were now circling Patrington, near Hull, preparatory to abandoning 'N' Nuts and Flying Control, through the system, had alerted the Army Ground Defence Units in the area. As we circled at 8,000 ft altitude, with navigation lights on, the powerful searchlights below were switched on and soon picked the Halifax up in a cone. Standing near the open hatch, I could see the long dazzling pale yellow shafts of light, tapering up from the ground, half a league beneath us, piercing the darkness and, entering through the opening in the floor, around which we stood waiting. We shared out our cigarettes to make sure that everyone had some to smoke, once safely on terra firma. The rear gunner was the first to leave, by falling out head-first into space, down the searchlight beams. One instant he was there, in the opening, entering the slipstream and the next, he was whipped away into the atmosphere and gone – it was like an illusion or a scene from a bad dream. Nevertheless, we had subconsciously conditioned ourselves to the ordeal of dropping out into space and we virtually queued to take our turn to get it over with as quickly as possible. It was a consolation that we could not see the ground, a mile and a half below.

'As I waited my turn I thought of the lecture we had received some four months earlier at the Heavy Conversion Unit at Riccall. I checked my parachute pack and decided to fall forward into the opening and dive out headlong. Just as I was about to leave the aircraft I was alarmed to see that a ground defence post had started firing at us with a machine-gun. At this juncture I knelt on the floor and rolled forward through the aperture and out into space. As I dropped through the cool fresh air, with the roar of the engines still in my ears, I started counting away the recommended ten seconds, before pulling the ripcord, and on reaching five I tugged at the handle on the pack and flung it away, rather than wait unnecessarily longer, to get the first part of the ordeal over. On hurtling out of the Halifax, I had noticed a bright stream of tracer shooting up from the darkness below, obviously aimed at our machine and confirming that the ground defence posts regarded it as a hostile bomber. I soon forgot about this perplexing incident when the released bundle of silk opened with a shocking jolt and the two heavy webbing straps, running up the cord lines to the huge 'chute taking shape above, snapped taut and smacked forcibly against both of my ears, making them sting.

'The atmosphere grew strangely silent as the engine noise quickly faded away in the distance. The searchlights seemed to have gone out as I descended in the darkness, although there was no feeling or impression of moving downwards at all, but only that I was spinning backwards and forwards as the lines above were twisting and untwisting. The open 'chute, like a gigantic white silken umbrella, billowed out overhead and the cone of long cord lines tapering down to the harness, which pulled tightly around my cradled body, rendered me nearly helpless, suspended in the air. At intervals, loud cracking noises were evident aloft, when air was being expelled from pockets in the swelling silk canopy. As I gazed into the darkness below me I wondered where I would land and I felt comforted that I still had on my Mae West, should I fall in water. My luck held and I landed in a rough ploughed field but I landed with such force that I hit the back of my head on a large lump of soil and momentarily knocked myself out. When I came to and had recovered my breath I released my harness and put the webbing around the base of the nearest tree and locked it to prevent it from blowing away.

'I did not expect to see any lights in the blackout, so looking around in the obscurity, I decided to walk across the ploughed land with hopes of arriving at a farmhouse or village. Walking was difficult in my fur-lined flying boots but once on grassed land it was much better and I had not proceeded very far before being challenged, out of the shadows, by a soldier. A fixed bayonet, placed perilously close to my throat, caused me to shout "RAF" to the sentry's challenge. It was all I could manage because of the unexpected interception, which had proved somewhat startling.

When the guard had checked me over in the light of his torch, he informed me that their post had been warned of the presence of baled out aircrew in the vicinity and members on duty were, in fact, out looking for us. He took me to a hut, which was part of the gun-post and another soldier made some tea for me, whilst I quickly told the small group what had occurred to drop me from the clouds among them. They seemed amazed to have an operational aircrew among them.

'When more of these ground defence men came in off duty, they admitted firing at us. They had thought our Halifax was a Dornier 217 and in the searchlight beams had seen black objects dropping out of the underside of the fuselage and, assuming these were bombs, they commenced shooting at us with machine guns. Fortunately, a radio message sent out from their headquarters, informing all posts in the area that the circling machine was an RAF bomber, returning from a raid, damaged and that the crew were baling out, was received, so the firing stopped immediately, without any harm being done. These same men then proudly informed me that they had shot down a Dornier 217 several nights earlier and had thought our aircraft was another.

'I remained in the hut and drank tea, whilst the Army headquarters were informed, by radio, that I had been picked up and a message came back, for my benefit, that some other members of the crew had been found already in various places, when they had landed safely in the area. An instruction came through a little later that I was to be transported to the headquarters, to join up with the rest of the crew, who had all been accounted for now and were being conveyed there also. While questioned by the Army personnel I informed them where to find my parachute. As a reward I told them they could have it, thinking it would make some underclothes for their wives and girlfriends. I thought the RAF would have no further use for it. However, I was wrong, because squadron personnel from the parachute section came over later and collected all the 'chutes, which were returned to use after inspection for damage and repacking. When we arrived at headquarters we were given a hot meal and a bed for the night before being returned to the squadron.

'The luckiest member of the crew was probably Flight Sergeant Hurst, the rear gunner. He landed close to the edge of a cliff, from the best of his judgement in the darkness; he could clearly hear the sound of the sea beating on the shore below him, in the quiescent stillness of the night, so moved away from the sound of the waves, to get inland to safety. After walking for some minutes, he came to a barbed wire fence, laid in the military manner, and managed, with great difficulty and numerous tears, to get through it. Continuing for a reasonable distance, he again ran into a similar barrier and following a further struggle, succeeded in battling through the entanglement. Proceeding once more, he shortly came up to a third fence, like the others and once more crawled through the twisting circles of jagged wire. Beyond this, he arrived at a roadside fence, formed of timber and hedging, and at the point where he climbed over onto the verge of the highway, he saw a large warning notice which read:"Danger, Mined Land – Keep Out". It was a shocking discovery to the rear gunner to find he had walked and crawled through a mined field; but at least it explained the presence of the barbed wire barriers, which, needless to say, kept puzzling him, as each one of them barred his way.

'The sequel was that when the RAF requested the return of the parachute, if possible a team of Army specialists in land mining technique travelled up from London to retrieve the 'chute.

'Sergeant "Monty" Banks landed on the tiled roof of a large outhouse and bumped and rolled down the sloping surface, the billowing 'chute fortunately retarding, to some extent, the pace at which he was gravitating. Coming to the edge of the roofing, he dropped down onto the village policeman, at that moment passing by on his beat. The unfurled fabric and cordage of the 'chute soon followed the airman and within seconds, the two men were covered by the white canopy and floundering in the folds to extricate themselves from the massive silk envelope. The bewildered constable had no idea of what had happened but after a struggle, many strong words and hurried explanation by the shaken flight engineer, the situation was retrieved by the understanding and sympathetic PC who helped the aeronaut gather in and bundle up the parachute and stow it away safely, temporarily. When this had been accomplished, the pair of them went to the constable's home, where, apparently, they finished off half a bottle of whisky during a more detailed narration of the operation over Hanover during the night.

'The skipper was the only one of the seven of us who retained his grip on the ripcord handle when he pulled it to open the 'chute and he proudly showed his trophy, still firmly grasped, when we came together. The rest of us dropped the handles into space, following the action of pulling the ripcord. I clearly remember flinging mine away, probably in jubilation when the 'chute opened and realising it was of no further use then. You were supposed to return the handle to the Parachute Section and the penalty for failing to do so was the purchase of drinks for the personnel belonging to this department.

'It was a very curious fact that each of the crew who baled out head first found an 'L' shaped tear in his battle-dress trousers, at the front, about halfway up the thigh on the right leg and those who went out feet first, had a similar rip in the seat of their pants, also on the right hand side. We discussed this strange occurrence numerous times together, but failed to find a satisfactory solution to the mystery. I was the only one to sustain cuts on the ears, which were not serious and there seemed no plausible explanation as to why I alone should have suffered thus.

'The next morning Wing Commander Edmunds entered our room. He asked how we were feeling and where was the film? "What film?" "The coloured film of course." Then it registered exactly what he was referring to. The film had been left in the Halifax which had crashed off Patrington, Yorkshire. It was a bitter blow to the Wing Commander and some strong words were spoken for a few seconds but then the CO, who was very human, cut short his reproof and admitted that in similar circumstances he would probably have forgotten all about the cine camera. We journeyed back to Melbourne and on arrival were debriefed in the usual way. Afterwards we went to the mess for lunch and then to bed for some well-earned sleep. Next day we had to report to the station medical officer for a check-up and on being found fit were granted four days' survivors' leave. The rear gunner and I, being from the Dominions, spent the furlough together at Bridlington, whilst the others went home to their families, to recover from the Hanover ordeal. Before going on leave, the Squadron Adjutant, Flight-Lieutenant "Paddy" Keene, a great friend of all aircrew, made application for each of us for membership of the "Caterpillar Club" and each of us received a membership card, plus a small gold caterpillar, with ruby eyes, in the form of a brooch, with name and rank engraved on the reverse side.

'One of the consequences of this operation on Hanover, was the growing suspicion that the night fighters were homing on the newish H_2S equipment which we were now using, because on several occasions we had been intercepted whereas other crews, without H_2S, had not been troubled by fighters; out of discussions held among ourselves, this possibility emerged and soon became a firm belief. The skipper reported the matter one morning at crew conference and the Intelligence Officer present agreed to submit the theory to Group Headquarters, for their consideration. Later on it was announced, when we were all assembled in the briefing room, that an investigation had been carried out on this question and it was considered extremely unlikely that the Germans had equipment capable of homing on H_2S. However, some months later, at the completion of our tour, it was revealed officially one morning, again at crew conference, that night fighters were now known in fact, to be homing on H_2S, so it was gratifying in the end to learn that we had been correct in our surmise, although it was bad news for the crews who, at this stage, were nearly all using this navigational aid.

'After our visit to the medical officer, following the Hanover raid, I went with the crew to the dispersal area where our own Halifax, 'O' Oboe, was parked, with the ground crew busily preparing the aircraft for the next operational sortie. Together, we examined the bomb bay and the operating mechanism, to study their construction and see what I had been up against in my attempt to open the doors manually. As soon as we saw the arrangement of the robust mechanicals for opening and closing the doors and the fixings for the bombs, it was realised how hopeless was the task I had tried to accomplish, on the way back from the target. Unfortunately, we had paid little attention to the bomb door system, because the details did not seem to concern us, so when the crisis arrived, I wasted my time and effort in a futile attempt to achieve the impossible.

'On our return from leave, we carried on flying by night, slowly and hopefully notching up the operations towards the required seemingly excessive number of 26 or thereabouts, constituting a tour; then one day we learnt that an appellation had been bestowed upon our pilot by the other crews, and whilst still at the squadron, often heard operational anecdotes retold about "Bring 'em back alive Jenkins" – a well-earned and suitable sobriquet.'

CHAPTER TWENTY SIX

Reflections

J.C. (Andy) Andrew joined the Royal Air Force on 17 May 1943 and after enlistment was sent on a flight engineer's course at No 4 school, St Athan. After passing out as a flight engineer he was then sent on a conversion course on four-engined bombers at Stradishall, Suffolk where he crewed up. The crew were: Flying Officer G.T. Jarratt, pilot; Sergeant J.C. Andrew, flight engineer; Flight-Lieutenant J. Wiseman, bomb-aimer; Warrant Officer A.K. Webster, navigator; Sergeant Compton, mid-upper gunner; Sergeant D.A. Powlson, rear gunner; Sergeant J. Jones, wireless operator.

After a few hours on Stirlings the crew were then posted to a Lancaster Finishing School at Hemswell and finally on to No. 460 Squadron RAAF at Binbrook. They were one of the lucky crews and

Crew of 'S' Sugar at RAF Binbrook. Standing: Flying Officer G.T. Jarratt, pilot; Sergeant J.C. Andrew, flight engineer; Sergeant R.C. Compton, mid-upper gunner; Flying Officer J.L. Wiseman, bomb-aimer. Squatting: Flight Sergeant A.K Webster, navigator; Sergeant D.A. Powlson, rear gunner; Sergeant J. Jones, wireless operator.

completed their tour. The first op was on 18/19 July 1944 to Gelsenkirchen. The last sortie was a daylight raid of 3 hours 50 minutes duration and the target was Emmerick. This was their 31st sortie. The crew did an extra op because the bomb-aimer had missed one through illness and so that they could keep the same crew did an extra one so that they could finish together.

Sergeant Andy Andrew was demobbed on 27 March 1947 and over three decades later looks back on his wartime days spent as a flight engineer with No. 460 Squadron, Royal Australian Air Force: 'There are many wartime incidents that aircrew experienced which at the time formed a background to a somewhat nerve-racking career. Upon reflection, some 36 years on, these such incidents stand out like slippery stepping stones in a dicy course of duty. Many had a tour or more of operations where these moments formed a major part of their experience, while many had a quieter time of it, but these moments were just as disquietening as the "regulars", and sometimes perhaps more stomach freezing, especially to a fresh crew. Leaving the runway in a four-engined bomber, with its deadly load of bombs and aviation fuel, and then gaining a safety height of 500 ft was an achievement, giving a grand feeling of relaxation as a steady climbing speed was reached. It was similar at Binbrook, where the Lancaster next to move onto the runway for take-off watched as the previous one seemed to disappear in the valley and slowly rise again, and the thoughts of "our turn next" went through the mind.

'Being a flight engineer on a Lancaster had the advantage that I could see most of what happened and enjoy the interesting views of land formations, as also the cloud patterns, and sometimes beautiful, tell-tale herringbone wake of shipping on the sea as well, of course, as the barrage of flak, searchlights, and enemy night fighters.

'One such opportunity came whilst climbing prior to setting course for the target. Occasionally my skipper would go to Manchester and back, rather than circle over North Lincolnshire. This lovely summer evening was clear of heat haze and cloud, giving a crystal clear view. Turning to return eastwards, we had the sinking sun to rearwards and there lay a perfect picture of the eastern seaboard of England, a view which was very much admired by my skipper, George Jarratt from Sydney, Australia, and of course myself. It was a perfect map from the Tyne down past Flamborough Head, the River Humber, Wash, Norfolk and Suffolk bulge and around to the Thames Estuary, all readable, and it took us about 15 to 20 minutes duration. Our height was probably 9 or 10,000 ft.

'8/9 August 1944 was an evening take-off for, I believe, Aire-sur-Lys and just the reverse we almost immediately ran into a heavy belt of storm clouds. Trying to battle through the storms and set course looked an impossible task. All the instruments went berserk. The continuous flashes of lightning were far from pacifying and indeed the traces of "St Elmo's Fire" were constantly dancing up and down and across the windows. There were great arcs from one gun to the other, in fact the whole aircraft was covered with "sparks" and the outer circle of the propellors were like huge catherine wheels. Added to this we started icing up. Huge masses of ice made the aircraft extremely difficult to handle and indeed the weight of ice became too great for climbing. Suddenly we found a "funnel of clear air". We tried to turn and keep in this area, but the inability to turn quickly gave us no chance. We then began to lose height but were able to keep fairly level. Suddenly down we went, from about 12,000 ft flat to possibly 6,000 ft, the ice then began to crack off and we were able to continue on our way. On our return we discovered that base had recalled us soon after take-off but we and a few others did not receive these instructions. It was probably the core of the storm in the clear patch but I have no wish to see one again.

'We often hear the expression "they were waiting for us". One such occasion was on 20/21 July 1944. An earlier stream of bombers had a target some miles beyond Courtrai, which we were to bomb. The theory was that the German aircraft would have to land for re-arming and refuelling during the period we were to attack the target. A clear sky gave rise to apprehension and this was justifiable when perhaps 15 or 20 minutes short of the target. Night fighters, seemingly hundreds of them, came from all directions and apparently as fresh as daisies. Leaving the target area we had an escort of enemy aircraft. A sudden frantic chorus from the rear and mid-upper gunners gave us concern but we were unable to comprehend their message. On looking around and upwards, we saw the immense image of a Lancaster bearing down on us. The only action we were able to take was downwards. He was too close to attempt a turn as this would have meant a collision. As the Lancaster slid away the turrets both opened up and I obsesrved there were no markings whatever and that it was painted jet black. We later learned the Germans used any salvaged RAF aircraft to infiltrate our bomber stream. The Luftwaffe escorted us back to our bases and created havoc with Lancasters waiting to land – no lights anywhere. At first we went to Finningley, who in turn directed us to Leicester East.

Ground and aircrew of 'S' Sugar at Binbrook, the mount of Sergeant Andy Andrew.

'The navigator was unable to find the location of this place and the wireless operator was not able to raise them on his radio. By this time I was more than a little concerned about our fuel position, practising absolutely every means of economy, in an attempt to give the navigator the chance to guide us to this mystery place, which was so elusive. Eventually the skipper had great difficulty in holding the wallowing Lanc at about 135 mph!! Suddenly there was a shout, and someone spotted an airfield below. Using "Darkie" emergency radio wavelength we discovered it to be Lichfield. Like our throats, the fuel tanks were almost dried out. When we told them we were coming in to an emergency landing we were asked to go away as their training (OTU) Wellingtons had been on a cross-country flight. We warned all and sundry that we were coming in and anyone who got in our way did so at their peril. Again we were "warned off" so firing all Very cartridges available and flashing all available identification lights I could lay my hands on we made a beeline direct to the runway. We managed the runway OK and then ran off somewhere across the airfield, where the engines coughed and died where we stood. Needless to say, very strong words indeed were exchanged with the Control Officer and anyone else who dared to criticise our action. The telephone to Binbrook was in danger of melting. In our opinion the Control Officer had no known father and I still say so. His temper was further aggravated when the skipper demanded an armed guard to keep everyone at a reasonable distance and not allow photography, as we carried "Village Inn", a highly secret addition which, originally, we used in the experiments. I would have liked to have taken that Duty Officer in our rear turret for a few ops.

'Another exciting trip which I will never forget was on 12 August 1944. In 'K' King it was our ninth trip in ten days. The target was

Brunswick and a beautiful bombers' (and fighters') moon!! We felt really naked in that clear sky and were wide awake watching for fighters and anything else which might happen. Soon after crossing the coast the radio packed up and then some navigation aids also went to sleep. Caught in flak, one particular piece of "scrap" tore through the side of the fuselage, chopped off the hydraulic pipes to the rear turret, made a hole in the rear gunner's door, ripped open all his clothing on his thigh, hit the turret guns and decided to leave us no souvenir as it disappeared through the perspex!! The result was an almost useless turret. Pressing on to the target we dodged the attentions of enemy aircraft. Almost in the target area the rear gunner ran short of oxygen so down we went to ease his position. A fully-loaded Lancaster in full dive took all the skipper's and my strength to overcome and this we finally managed by a rocking movement on the control column and slid sideways. As I remember we were rather low by this time but on target and then much later climbed back up to a more reasonable operating area of sky, the rear gunner now with emergency oxygen bottle as standby. Having deviated on our way out of the target, the navigator was a little uncertain of our exact position. Fortunately the clear skies gave him the opportunity to obtain a fix and we made for home. A pack of three German fighters appeared to be on their way to entertain us – an Me 110, an Me 109 and an Fw 190. The 109 made a few passes at us, the 190 probably engaged himself to another of our bombers and the 110 stood off. Suddenly a "light" was attracted to us and evasive action gave no sign of eluding it. As this something

'Q' Queenie of 460 (RAAF) Squadron stands in readiness on dispersal—Binbrook, July 1944.

came very much closer we climbed at maximum and escaped. The 110 suddenly showed itself down below our starboard wing and was obviously intent on studying our welfare. He opened up and as we corkscrewed the mid-upper gunner who was waiting got a brief view of the 110 and made no mistake. The rear gunner watched him fall out of the sky and hit the deck. Whilst wandering around the sky somewhere in Germany the navigator managed to assess our approximate position and gave us a course for home. Straight across the Zuider Zee at probably only 3–4,000 ft and what a reception!! It seemed every flak ship had gone there to wait for us, but we escaped and thought of the eggs and bacon and drink of tea for which we felt well ready. In only a few days the 110 was confirmed and credited to us as a definite kill. We also learnt that the fiery object we saw was one of the early air-to-air missiles.

'One of the occasional lecture/conferences we liked to attend gave us advice about radar-predicted flak batteries and the evasion of such. By making the right move at the right time it was possible to be one step ahead each time, too close for comfort, but nonetheless effective as we proved. Shortly afterwards in daylight we set off for Trossy-St Maximin, a huge quarry with built-in rocket and flying bomb V1 and V2 storage. As we approached Reading the rear gunner reported oil streaks on his perspex. On investigation I decided it was a high pressure oil leak on the starboard inner engine and the only action was to feather same. This delayed our mission and on approach to the target area we came across Lancaster AS-S from Kirmington with the same dead motor as ourselves. Our bombing runs were successful as there was a violent explosion on target, and we began our run-out. Suddenly a salvo of flak exploded very close to our rear end. Being so accurate we reasoned it was the radar predicted and took the necessary action. After a few abortive attempts they left us and concentrated on AS-S. The second salvo caught them and we saw four or five parachutes open – obviously they were not aware of the ferocity of this new flak system. It was frighteningly deadly. On return the ground staff discovered a fractured H/oil pressure pipe and so the motor remained in very good condition.

'Having been crewed up and trained for operations for quite some weeks while we instructed the rest of the squadron on the use of "Village Inn", it was a mixed and nervous feeling to be going to our first operational briefing. It was 18/19 July 1944 and our first initiation was a huge red area on the map of Europe, with tapes which led to the very centre – Happy Valley and the target was to

The Duke of Gloucester, prior to taking position of Governor General in Australia. With the Duke of Gloucester is Wing Commander Douglas being presented to Flying Officer Jarratt and crew. Binbrook, 26 July 1944.

be Gelsenkirchen. The area was well known as a 35 mile, 60,000 AA guns, etc, test of luck and patience. On approach an Fw 190 slid across our nose, the pilot looking away from us, having no idea we were so near. The sky was full of fireworks with no safe and clear way of slipping through quietly. Unfortunately the bombs failed to release and having no option we continued on course. Reaching the turning point we felt we ought to contribute to the night's effort and so swung the aircraft round and went back to the starting point and did a repeat performance. Dodging and weaving our way in I marvelled at how the aircraft handled, in spite of the heavy bomb load, and never gave a moment's cause for concern. At 21,500 ft it was like being in a class-type of car and the sweet sound of the four Merlins, synchronised so well, gave a confidence and a memory never to be forgotten. In fact the thousands of people who still go out and look up when they hear the sound of a Lancaster proves the attractive and individual personality of the Rolls-Royce engines.

'On 4 October 1944 and in 'S' ND970 we were selected to go mining in the Baltic, a trip known as "gardening" and the location was, I believe, near Malmo in the Kategat Sea lanes. Only two other aircraft operated that night so we were loners, each to their own area. We had to "sow" our mines only a short distance offshore and at very low height. In order to prove we were in the correct location the camera was transferred to the H$_2$S screen position and took pictures of the "map" shown thereon. Having left a blacked-out Britain and passed the blacked-out Danish and Norwegian areas it was a wonderful feast for sore eyes to be so close and low to a fully lit neutral town enjoying nightlife to the full, with glaring neon signs on the theatres and cinemas. Street lights and buses and trams added to the volumes of cars, etc, was like looking at a film about another world. Here, in a blacked-out Europe, was a jeweller's shop of glittering jewels of all colours, reds, greens, yellows and diamonds. It was as if one could smell the gammon cooking, taste the beers and wines and hear the laughter and gaiety of a carefree nation. Then we had to think of that tiring long haul back home, hoping we would arrive safely. Setting course, as low as possible, we crossed Denmark and at last we were over water again. Relaxed and contented, the alarm can be imagined as tracer suddenly appeared from below and passed silhouetted against the engines and airframe! A narrow neck of land with a machine gun nest warned us never to relax and be complacent. Fortunately we enjoyed our eggs and bacon on return!

The variety is illustrated by two successive day outings to Paulliac, near Bordeaux in lower France by the Bay of Biscay. It was beautiful summer weather, and in order to dodge the German radar we had to drop down "on to the water" as we passed the "first and last" at Land's End. Skimming the waves to within a few miles short of the target gave us a chance to open the windows and enjoy the fresh air of the Atlantic Ocean. At the earlier stage we had difficulty judging our height until a Lancaster not far away flew straight in and exploded. This gave us a good indication and we had no more problem having adjusted the altimeter to keep us a "safe low". Endless water all the way down the "bay" was broken only by the sight of a lifeboat poised momentarily on the crest of the wave. I think possibly five or six bodies lay in this 15-seater boat. Our surprise visit was complete and climbing to 6,000 ft, there was a perfect view of the refinery/storage target and also the harbour and town. On the return we hedge-hopped all the way over France giving us a thrilling and close up view of the countryside. We saw people ploughing with oxen, a few dogs, waves from the French people and some German army vehicles, otherwise mostly empty roads. Some of the boys crossed the Channel coast and found some German MTBs. They were having a rare old time giving chase to them, the odd one perhaps trying to get rid of them with "hung up" bombs. After the strain of night ops this proved a real tonic. Apart from over England and the target I think the whole trip was done at less than 1,000 ft.

'On 5 October 1944 and in 'Z' *PB152* the target was to be Saarbrucken. It was anticipated that weather problems might arise on our return and so it was. Our diversion was to Shipdham in Norfolk, a USAAF Base. On arrival we found the American's Control unused to handling a lot of Lancs just back from a night op. Our CO, Group Captain Hughie Edwards VC, was on one of his occasional ops and went in to take control. Soon we were safely on the deck and directed to our parking area in a very efficient and orderly manner by the US ground staff. Being dark and early morning we just found ourselves any empty beds or chairs and had an hour or two. In the light of morning the whole camp made us welcome and did wonders in feeding and seeing to our needs. After breakfast we made our way to see to our aircraft and what a sight met our eyes – one huge arc of Lancasters all neatly lined up around the inner edge of the perimeter track. There were about 100 of them from Binbrook, Kelstern and Waltham. The sight of these was matched by the crowds of Americans, in fact the whole camp turned out to look. The Liberators of the USAAF were being prepared for a mid-morning take-off on ops. We were being refuelled and one can imagine the amount of activity taking place. The Americans gazed in awe at the "Night Hawks" whilst we took an interest in their aircraft and all that was to be seen, including armrests and ashtrays in the aircraft!! We bade them farewell as they took off on their "mission". This was one time the Americans showed admiration for the RAF Bomber Command and we all felt proud to be part of it.

'It was a beautiful Saturday afternoon on 7 October 1944 in 'T' *ND959* and a full turn out of RAF and USAAF. Hundreds of Lancs and Halifaxes littered the cloudless sky as far as the eye could see, wending their individual way to Emerich on the Rhine. Equally, "hundreds" of Forts and Libs in their neat formations were to attack a target on the opposite side of the Rhine. Escorted by fighters providing cover, the picture of the sheer weight of power now available by the Allies against the Germans could not have been more evident. This was the last trip for us and two more crews with whom we were very friendly. At take-off it was a moving and "lump in the throat" feeling to see so many from the station lining the runway to wish us luck and wave us off. Three crews on their last trip together must have been unique. On the return trip we lost the race and were the second crew to reach home, probably because we paid our last flying respects to Lincoln Cathedral which meant so much to so many aircrew. In the evening we took our dispersal ground crew to Grimsby for a thank you celebration to recognise those hours spent waiting and working to keep the aircraft airworthy.

'I would like to stress the admiration for all the WAAFs who, with great cheerfulness, drove the crew buses and lorries, sometimes under extremely dark and inclement conditions, dodging the lethal props of taxiing aircraft, finding the dispersal points far and wide and bleary-eyed after being called out at all hours because "Ops are back on". I remember their cheerfulness and blessings, also disappointments at the non-return of a crew. They did a job which once would have been thought impossible for women to do. Later, as an MT type, I did this for one night in an emergency and it frightened me to think of all the near mishaps these girls must have had. Another outstanding memory was a WAAF we called "Smiling Morn". As she served our flying meals she always had a smile for us and brightened up that Sergeants' mess at Binbrook.

'And what of the aircrew's unsung frights? Like the whistling of HE bombs passing close on their way down and heard even above the roar of the engines; the 4 lb stick incendiaries bouncing off the props and airframe, like a shower of confetti, but rattling with a dull clunk while we wondered where the 4,000 lb "cookie" was that usually comprised the bomb load; being "coned" in a nest of hornets who waited to sting; trying to keep the flight engineer's log up to date, especially the fuel side of it and at the same time straining the eyes for hidden nightfighters in the black depth of night; one sudden sight of a Lanc or Halifax weaving in a do or die attempt to dodge a nightfighter; being in a strange area at night and trying to land on the wrong aerodrome doing a left hand circuit while everyone else is right hand; and seeing the scrap floating about as a heavy bomber explodes and you picture yourself as the only bomber with 5 Merlins!!

'Can you capture the picture of a Lancaster in the finals approaching and trying to land as a steamroller trundles past the end of the runway; or the frantic flashing of Aldis lamps and equally frantic puffs of smoke from the roller with the fly-wheel going like the clappers and the driver white-faced and prepared to bale out; or the Group Captain in his Tiger Moth watching take-off procedures to try and improve the efficiency (any Lancaster nearby trying to dip his backside and give a groupie the full benefit of slipstream)? Then there was the time the bomb-aimer's hatch fell on the runway on take-off and, waiting till the last aircraft had taken off, landed with a max all up weight, retrieved same, then took off again with no extra fuel hoping we could complete the trip with what remained (fortunately we did but it involved a lot of calculations for economy flying); and the antics of the "mad" Australians who let their pants down in the mess and forgot their worries at the occasional flight parties. They were a good crowd whom I felt proud and privileged to know and fly with.'

Part Three

CHAPTER TWENTY SEVEN

Airmen of RAF Bomber Squadrons Who Were Awarded the Victoria Cross

The following citations accompanied the supreme awards for valour gained by airmen of RAF Bomber Squadrons in the World War II. The Victoria Cross is usually conferred for a single act of heroism, for example, the valour of Jackson. One VC was awarded in effect for four years of courage and for target marking, that awarded to Cheshire. In the case of Reid, the station commander of RAF Syerston and Wing Commander Reg Stidolph, the commanding officer of No. 61 Squadron, both agreed that after the incredible conditions Reid and his crew experienced on the Düsseldorf raid, the Victoria Cross was the only award they could cite him for.

It was their qualities and actions that went towards the winning of a VC: the determination to press on and fulfil a briefed mission in spite of unimaginable hazards; the resolve to get an aircraft and crew back to base, or anyway, back to home territory where all could live to fight again; sacrifice – the sacrifice of a man's life for his fellows, as in such stories as those of Swales, Thompson, and others. In all cases their devotion to duty in the face of overwhelming odds is unsurpassed in the annals of the Royal Air Force.

In the belief that these narratives represent some of the most vivid, moving and authentic writing to emerge from World War II, these citations are reproduced in full. It should be noted, however, in fairness to them, that the compilers were invariably writing in the heat of battle, often with necessarily incomplete knowledge of the action, and where, as in some cases, there are minor errors and omissions, no excuse is necessary.

Donald Edward Garland and **Thomas Gray**, 12 Squadron AASF (Extract from *The London Gazette*, 11 June 1940.) 'Flying Officer Garland was the pilot and Sergeant Gray was the observer of the leading aircraft of a formation of five aircraft that attacked a bridge over the Albert Canal which had not been destroyed and was allowing the enemy to advance into Belgium. All the aircrews of the squadron concerned volunteered for the operation, and, after five crews had been selected by drawing lots, the attack was delivered at low altitude against this vital target. Orders were issued that this bridge was to be destroyed at all costs. As had been expected, exceptionally intense machine-gun and anti-aircraft fire was encountered. Moreover, the bridge area was heavily protected by enemy fighters. In spite of this, the formation successfully delivered a dive-bombing attack from the lowest practicable altitude. British fighters in the vicinity reported that the target was obscured by the bombs bursting on it and near it. Only one of the five aircraft concerned returned from this mission. The pilot of this aircraft reports that besides being subjected to extremely heavy anti-aircraft fire, through which they dived to attack the objective, our aircraft were also attacked by a large number of enemy fighters after they had released their bombs on the target. Much of the success of this vital operation must be attributed to the formation leader, Flying Officer Garland, and to the coolness and resourcefulness of Sergeant Gray, who in most difficult conditions navigated Flying Officer Garland's aircraft in such a manner that the whole formation was able successfully to attack the target in spite of subsequent heavy losses. Flying Officer Garland and Sergeant Gray did not return.'

Roderick Alastair Brook Learoyd, 49 Squadron. (Extract from *The London Gazette*, 20 August 1940.) 'Acting Flight-Lieutenant Roderick Alastair Brook Learoyd. This officer, as first pilot of a Hampden aircraft, has repeatedly shown the highest conception of his duty and

Donald Edward Garland. Thomas Gray.

Roderick Alastair Brook Learoyd.

complete indifference to personal danger in making attacks at the lowest altitudes regardless of opposition. On the night of 12 August 1940, he was detailed to attack a special objective on the Dortmund/Ems Canal. He had attacked this objective on a previous occasion and was well aware of the risks entailed. To achieve success it was necessary to approach from a direction well known to the enemy, through a lane of especially disposed anti-aircraft defences, and in the face of the most intense point-blank fire from guns of all calibres. The reception of the preceding aircraft might well have deterred the stoutest heart, all being hit and two lost. Flight Lieutenant Learoyd nevertheless made his attack at 150 ft, his aircraft being repeatedly hit and large pieces of the main plane torn away. He was almost blinded by the glare of many searchlights at close range, but pressed home this attack with the greatest resolution and skill. He subsequently brought his wrecked aircraft home and, as the landing flaps were inoperative and the undercarriage indicators out of action, waited for dawn in the vicinity of his aerodrome before landing, which he accomplished without causing injury to his crew or further damage to the aircraft. The high courage, skill and determination, which this officer has invariably displayed on many occasions in the face of the enemy sets an example which is unsurpassed.'

John Hannah, 83 Squadron. (Extract from *The London Gazette*, 1 October 1940.) '652918 Sergeant John Hannah No. 83 Squadron. On the night of 15 September 1940, Sergeant Hannah was the wireless operator/air gunner in an aircraft engaged in a successful attack on enemy barge concentration at Antwerp. It was then subjected to intense anti-aircraft fire and received a direct hit from a projectile of an explosive and incendiary nature, which apparently burst inside the bomb compartment. A fire started which quickly enveloped the wireless operator's and rear gunner's cockpits, and as both the port and starboard petrol tanks had been pierced, there was grave risk of the fire spreading. Sergeant Hannah forced his way through to obtain two extinguishers and discovered that the rear gunner had had to leave the aircraft. He could have acted likewise, through the bottom escape hatch or forward through the navigator's hatch, but remained and

John Hannah.

fought the fire for ten minutes with the extinguishers, beating the flames with his log book when these were empty.

'During this time thousands of rounds of ammunition exploded in all directions and he was almost blinded by the intense heat and fumes, but had the presence of mind to obtain relief by turning on his oxygen supply. Air admitted through the large holes caused by the projectile made the bomb compartment an inferno and all the aluminium sheet metal on the floor of this airman's cockpit was melted away, leaving only the cross bearers. Working under these conditions, which caused burns to his face and eyes, Sergeant Hannah succeeded in extinguishing the fire. He then crawled forward, ascertained that the navigator had left the aircraft, and passed the latter's log and maps to the pilot.

'This airman displayed courage, coolness and devotion to duty of the highest order and by his action in remaining and successfully extinguishing the fire under conditions of the greatest danger and difficulty, enabled the pilot to bring the aircraft to its base.'

Hughie Idwal Edwards, 105 Squadron. (Extract from *The London Gazette*, 22 July 1941.) 'Acting Wing Commander Hughie Idwal Edwards, DFC, No. 105 Squadron. Wing Commander Edwards, although handicapped by physical disability resulting from a flying accident, has repeatedly displayed gallantry of the highest order in pressing home bombing attacks from very low heights against strongly-defended objectives.

'On 4 July 1941, he led an important attack on the Fort of Bremen, one of the most heavily defended towns in Germany. This attack had to be made in daylight and there were no clouds to afford concealment. During the approach to the German coast several enemy ships were sighted, and Wing Commander Edwards knew that his aircraft would be reported and that the defences would be in a state of readiness. Undaunted by this misfortune he brought his formation 50 miles overland to the target, flying at a height of a little more than 50 ft, passing through a formidable balloon barrage. On reaching Bremen he was met with a hail of fire, all his aircraft being hit and four of them being destroyed. Nevertheless he made a most successful attack, and then with the greatest skill and coolness withdrew the surviving aircraft without further loss.

Hughie Idwal Edwards.

'Throughout the execution of this operation, which he had planned personally with full knowledge of the risks entailed, Wing Commander

Edwards displayed the highest possible standard of gallantry and determination.'

James Allen Ward, 75 (New Zealand) Squadron. (Extract from *The London Gazette*, 5 August 1941.) 'NZ 401793 Sergeant James Allen Ward, Royal New Zealand Air Force, No. 75 (NZ) Squadron. On the night of 7 July 1941, Sergeant Ward was second pilot of a Wellington returning from an attack on Munster. When flying over the Zuider Zee at 13,000 ft, the aircraft was attacked from beneath by a Messerschmitt 110, which secured hits with cannon shell and incendiary bullets. The rear gunner was wounded in the foot but delivered a burst of fire which sent the enemy fighter down, apparently out of control. Fire then broke out near the starboard engine, and, fed by petrol from a split pipe, quickly gained an alarming hold and threatened to spread to the entire wing. The crew forced a hole in the fuselage and made strenuous efforts to reduce the fire with extinguishers and even the coffee in their vacuum flasks, but without success. They were then warned to be ready to abandon the aircraft.

'As a last resort, Sergeant Ward volunteered to make an attempt to smother the fire with an engine cover which happened to be in use as a cushion. At first he proposed to discard his parachute, to reduce wind resistance, but was finally persuaded to take it. A rope from the dinghy was tied to him, though this was of little help and might have become a danger had he been blown off the aircraft. With the help of the navigator, he then climbed through the narrow astro-hatch and put on his parachute. The bomber was flying at a reduced speed, but the wind pressure must have been sufficient to make the operation one of extreme difficulty. Breaking the fabric to make hand and foot holds where necessary, and also taking advantage of existing holes in the fabric, Sergeant Ward succeeded in descending 3 ft to the wing and proceeding another 3 ft to a

position behind the engine, despite the slipstream from the airscrew, which nearly blew him off the wing. Lying in this precarious position, he smothered the fire in the wing fabric and tried to push the cover into the hole in the wing and on to the leaking pipe from which the fire came. As soon as he moved his hand, however, the terrific wind blew the cover out and when he tried again it was lost. Tired as he was, he was able with the navigator's assistance to make successfully the perilous journey back onto the aircraft.

James Allen Ward.

'There was now no danger of the fire spreading from the petrol pipe, as there was no fabric left nearby, and in due course it burnt itself out. When the aircraft was nearly home some petrol which had collected in the wing blazed up furiously but died down quite suddenly. A safe landing was then made despite the damage sustained by the aircraft. The flight home had been made possible by the gallant action of Sergeant Ward in extinguishing the fire on the wing in circumstances of the greatest difficulty and at the risk of his life.'

John Dering Nettleton.

John Dering Nettleton, 44 (Rhodesia) Squadron. (Extract from *The London Gazette*, 28 April 1942.) 'Acting Squadron Leader John Dering Nettleton, No 44 (Rhodesia) Squadron. Squadron Leader Nettleton was the leader of one of two formations of six Lancaster heavy bombers detailed to deliver a low-level attack in daylight on the diesel engine factory at Augsburg in southern Germany on 17 April 1942. The enterprise was daring, the target of high military importance. To reach it and get back, some 1,000 miles had to be flown over hostile territory.

'Soon after crossing into enemy territory his formation was engaged by 25 to 30 fighters. A running fight ensued. His rear guns went out of action. One by one the aircraft of his formation were shot down until in the end only his and one other remained. The fighters were shaken off but the target was still far distant. There was formidable resistance to be faced. With great spirit and almost defenceless, he held his two remaining aircraft on their perilous course and after a long and arduous flight, mostly at only 50 ft above the ground, he brought them to Augsburg. Here, anti-aircraft fire of great intensity and accuracy was encountered. The two aircraft came low over the roof tops. Though fired at from point-blank range, they stayed the course to drop their bombs true on the target. The second aircraft, hit by flak, burst into flames and crashlanded. The leading aircraft, though riddled with holes, flew safely back to base, the only one of the six to return.

'Squadron Leader Nettleton, who has successfully undertaken many other hazardous operations, displayed unflinching determination as well as leadership and valour of the highest order.'

Leslie Thomas Manser, 50 Squadron. (Extract from *The London Gazette* 23 October 1942.) 'Flying Officer Leslie Thomas Manser, Royal Air Force Volunteer Reserve (Deceased), No. 50 Squadron. Flying Officer Manser was captain and first pilot of a Manchester aircraft which took part in the mass raid on Cologne on the night of 30 May 1942. As the aircraft was approaching its objective it was caught by searchlights and subjected to intense and accurate anti-aircraft fire. Flying Officer Manser held on his dangerous course and bombed the target successfully from a height of 7,000 ft. Then he set course for base. The Manchester had been damaged and was still under heavy fire. Flying Officer Manser took violent evasive action, turning and descending to under 1,000 ft. It was of no avail. The searchlights and flak followed him until the outskirts of the city were passed. The aircraft was hit repeatedly and the rear gunner was wounded. The front cabin filled with smoke; the port engine was over-heating badly.

Leslie Thomas Manser.

'Pilot and crew could all have escaped safely by parachute. Nevertheless, Flying Officer Manser, disregarding the obvious hazards, persisted in his attempt to save aircraft and crew from falling into enemy hands. He took the aircraft up to 2,000 ft. Then the port engine burst into flames. It was ten minutes before the fire was mastered, but then the engine went out of action for good, part of one wing was burnt, and the airspeed of the aircraft became dangerously low.

'Despite all the efforts of pilot and crew, the Manchester began to lose height. At this critical moment, Flying Officer Manser once more disdained the alternative of parachuting to safety with his crew. Instead, with grim determination, he set a new course for the nearest base, accepting for himself the prospect of almost certain death in a firm resolve to carry on to the end. Soon, the aircraft became extremely difficult to handle and, when a crash was inevitable, Flying Officer Manser ordered the crew to bale out. A sergeant handed him a parachute but he waved it away, telling the non-commissioned officer to jump at once as he could only hold the aircraft steady for a few seconds more. While the crew were descending to safety they saw the aircraft, still carrying their gallant captain, plunge to earth and burst into flames.

'In pressing home his attack in the face of strong opposition, in striving, against heavy odds, to bring back his aircraft and crew and, finally, when in extreme peril, thinking only of the safety of his comrades, Flying Officer Manser displayed determination and valour of the highest order.'

Rawdon Hume Middleton, 149 Squadron. (Extract from *The London Gazette*, 15 January 1943.) Aus 402745 Flight Sergeant Rawdon Hume Middleton, Royal Australian Air Force (Missing), No. 149 Squadron. Flight Sergeant Middleton was captain and first pilot of a Stirling aircraft detailed to attack the Fiat works at Turin one night in November 1942. Great difficulty was experienced in climbing to 12,000 ft to cross the Alps, which led to excessive consumption of fuel. So dark was the night that the mountain peaks were almost invisible.

'During the crossing Flight Sergeant Middleton had to decide whether to proceed or turn back, there being barely sufficient fuel for the return journey. Flares were sighted ahead and he continued the mission and even dived to 2,000 ft to identify the target despite the difficulty of regaining height. Three flights were made over Turin at this low altitude before the target was identified. The aircraft was then subjected to fire from light anti-aircraft guns. A large hole appeared in the port main 'plane which made it difficult to maintain lateral control. A shell then burst in the cockpit, shattering the windscreen and wounding both pilots. A piece of shell splinter tore into the side of Flight Sergeant Middleton's face, destroying his right eye and exposing the bone over the eye. He was probably wounded also in the body or legs. The second pilot received wounds in the head and both legs which bled profusely. The wireless operator was also wounded in the leg.

'Flight Sergeant Middleton became unconscious and the aircraft dived to 800 ft before control was regained by the second pilot, who took the aircraft up to 1,500 ft and released his bombs. There was still some light flak and the aircraft was hit many times. The three gunners replied continuously until the rear turret was put out of action. Flight Sergeant Middleton had now regained consciousness and, when clear of the target, ordered the second pilot back to receive first aid. Before this was completed the latter insisted on returning to the cockpit, as the captain could see very little and could speak only with loss of blood and great pain.

Rawdon Hume Middleton.

'Course was set for base and the crew now faced an Alpine crossing and homeward flight in a damaged aircraft with insufficient fuel. The possibilities of abandoning the aircraft or landing in northern France were discussed but Flight Sergeant Middleton expressed the intention of trying to make the English coast, so that his crew could leave the aircraft by parachute. Owing to his wounds and diminishing strength, he knew that, by then, he would have little or no chance of saving himself. After four hours, the French coast was reached and here the aircraft, flying at 6,000 ft, was once more engaged and hit by intense light anti-aircraft fire. Flight Sergeant Middleton was still at the controls and mustered sufficient strength to take evasive action. After crossing the Channel there was only sufficient fuel for five minutes' flying. Flight Sergeant Middleton ordered the crew to abandon the aircraft while he flew parallel with the coast for a few miles, after which he intended to head out to sea. Five of the crew left the aircraft safely, while two remained to assist Flight Sergeant Middleton. The aircraft crashed in the sea and the bodies of the front gunner and flight engineer were recovered the following day. Their gallant captain was apparently unable to leave the aircraft and his body has not been traced.

'Flight Sergeant Middleton was determined to attack the target regardless of the consequences and not to allow his crew to fall into enemy hands. While all the crew displayed heroism of a high order, the urge to do so came from Flight Sergeant Middleton, whose fortitude and strength of will made possible the completion of the mission. His devotion to duty in the face of overwhelming odds is unsurpassed in the annals of the Royal Air Force.'

Hugh Gordon Malcolm, 18 Squadron. (Extract from *The London Gazette*, 27 April 1943.) 'Acting Wing Commander Hugh Gordon Malcolm (Deceased), No. 18 Squadron. This officer commanded a squadron of light bombers in North Africa. Throughout his service in that theatre his leadership, skill and daring were of the highest order.

'On 17 November 1942, he was detailed to carry out a low level formation attack on Bizerta airfield, taking advantage of cloud cover. Twenty miles from the target the sky became clear, but Wing Commander Malcolm carried on, knowing well the danger of proceeding without a fighter escort. Despite fierce opposition, all bombs were dropped within the airfield perimeter. A Junkers 52 and a Messerschmitt 109 were shot down; many dispersed enemy aircraft were raked by machine-gun fire. Weather conditions became extremely unfavourable and as a result, two of his aircraft were lost by collision; another was forced down by enemy fighters. It was due to this officer's skilful and resolute leadership that the remaining aircraft returned safely to base.

Hugh Gordon Malcolm.

'On 28 November 1942, he again led his squadron against Bizerta airfield which was bombed from a low altitude. The airfield on this occasion was heavily defended and intense and accurate anti-aircraft fire was met. Nevertheless, after his squadron had released their bombs, Wing Commander Malcolm led them back again and again to attack the airfield with machine-gun fire. These were typical of every sortie undertaken by this gallant officer; each attack was pressed to an effective conclusion however difficult the task and however formidable the opposition.

'Finally, on 4 December 1942, Wing Commander Malcolm, having been detailed to give close support to the First Army, received an urgent request to attack an enemy fighter airfield near Chouigui. Wing Commander Malcolm knew that to attack such an objective without a fighter escort – which could not be arranged in the time available – would be to court almost certain disaster; but believing the attack to be necessary for the success of the Army's operations, his duty was clear. He decided to attack. He took off with his squadron and reached the target unmolested, but when he had successfully attacked it, his squadron was intercepted by an overwhelming force of enemy fighters. Wing Commander Malcolm fought back, controlling his hard-pressed squadron and attempting to maintain formation. One by one his aircraft were shot down until only his own aircraft remained. In the end he, too, was shot down in flames.

'Wing Commander Malcolm's last exploit was the finest example of the valour and unswerving devotion to duty which he constantly displayed.'

Guy Penrose Gibson, 617 Squadron. (Extract from *The London Gazette*, 28 May 1943.) 'Acting Wing Commander Guy Penrose Gibson, DSO, DFC, Reserve of Air Force Officers, No. 617 Squadron.

This officer served as a night bomber pilot at the beginning of the war and quickly established a reputation as an outstanding operational pilot. In addition to taking the fullest possible share in all normal operations, he made single-handed attacks during his "rest" nights on such highly defended objectives as the German battleship *Tirpitz*, then completing in Wilhelmshaven. When his tour of operational duty was concluded he asked for a further operational posting and went to a night fighter unit instead of being posted for instructional duties. In the course of his second operational tour, he destroyed at least three enemy

Guy Penrose Gibson.

bombers and contributed much to the raising and development of new night-fighter formations.

'After a short period in a training unit he again volunteered for operational duties and returned to night bombers. Both as an operational pilot and as leader of his squadron, he achieved outstandingly successful results and his personal courage knew no bounds. Berlin, Cologne, Danzig, Gdynia, Genoa, Le Creusot, Milan, Nuremberg and Stuttgart were among the targets he attacked by day and by night. On conclusion of his third operational tour, Wing Commander Gibson pressed strongly to be allowed to remain on operations and he was selected to command a squadron then forming for special tasks. Under his inspiring leadership, this squadron has now executed one of the most devastating attacks of the war – the breaching of the Mohne and Eder dams. The task was fraught with danger and difficulty. Wing Commander Gibson personally made the initial attack on the Mohne Dam. Descending to within a few feet of the water and taking the full brunt of the anti-aircraft defences he delivered his attack with great accuracy. Afterwards he circled very low for 30 minutes drawing the enemy fire on himself in order to leave as free a run as possible to the following aircraft which were attacking the dam in turn. Wing Commander Gibson then led the remainder of his force to the Eder Dam, where, with complete disregard for his own safety, he repeated his tactics, and once more drew on himself the enemy fire so that the attack would be successfully developed.

'Wing Commander Gibson has completed 170 sorties, involving more than 600 hours' operational flying. Throughout his operational career, prolonged exceptionally at his own request, he has shown leadership, determination and valour of the highest order.'

Arthur Louis Aaron, 218 Squadon. (Extract from *The London Gazette*, 5 November 1943.) 'Flight Sergeant Arthur Louis Aaron, DFM, Royal Air Force Volunteer Reserve No. 218 Squadron. On the night of 12 August 1943, Flight Sergeant Aaron was captain and pilot of a Stirling aircraft detailed to attack Turin. When approaching to attack, the bomber received devastating bursts of fire from an enemy fighter. Three engines were hit, the windscreen shattered, the front and rear turrets put out of action and the elevator control damaged, causing the aircraft to become unstable and difficult to control. The navigator was killed and other members of the crew were wounded. A bullet struck Flight Sergeant Aaron in the face, breaking his jaw and tearing away part of his face. He was also wounded in the lung and his right arm was rendered useless. As he fell forward over the control

Arthur Louis Aaron.

column, the aircraft dived several thousand feet. Control was regained by the flight engineer at 3,000 ft. Unable to speak, Flight Sergeant Aaron urged the bomb-aimer by signs to take over the controls. Course was then set southwards in an endeavour to fly the crippled bomber, with one engine out of action, to Sicily or North Africa.

'Flight Sergeant Aaron was assisted to the rear of the aircraft and treated with morphia. After resting for some time he rallied and, mindful of his responsibility as captain of the aircraft, insisted on returning to the pilot's cockpit, where he was lifted into his seat and had his feet placed on the rudder bar. Twice he made determined attempts to take control and hold the aircraft to its course but his weakness was evident and with difficulty he was persuaded to desist. Though in great pain and suffering from exhaustion, he continued to help by writing directions with his left hand. Five hours after leaving the target the petrol began to run low, but soon afterwards the flare path at Bone airfield was sighted. Flight Sergeant Aaron summoned his failing strength to direct the bomb-aimer in the hazardous task of landing the damaged aircraft in the darkness with undercarriage retracted. Four attempts were made under his direction; at the fifth attempt Flight Sergeant Aaron was so near to collapsing that he had to be restrained by the crew and the landing was completed by the bomb-aimer.

'Nine hours after landing, Flight Sergeant Aaron died from exhaustion. Had he been content, when greviously wounded, to lie still and conserve his failing strength, he would probably have recovered, but he saw it as his duty to exert himself to the utmost, if necessary with his last breath, to ensure that his aircraft and crew did not fall into enemy hands. In appalling conditions he showed the greatest qualities of courage, determination and leadership, and, though wounded and dying, he set an example of devotion to duty which has seldom been equalled and never surpassed.'

William Reid, 61 Squadron. (Extract from *The London Gazette*, 14 December 1943.) 'Acting Flight-Lieutenant William Reid, RAFVR, No. 61 Squadron. On the night of 3 November 1943, Flight-Lieutenant Reid was pilot and captain of a Lancaster aircraft detailed to attack Düsseldorf. Shortly after crossing the Dutch coast, the pilot's windscreen was shattered by fire from a Messerschmitt 110. Owing

William Reid.

to a failure in the heating circuit, the rear gunner's hands were too cold for him to open fire immediately or to operate his microphone and so give warning of danger; but after a brief delay he managed to return the Messerschmitt's fire and it was driven off. During the fight with the Messerschmitt, Flight-Lieutenant Reid was wounded in the head, shoulders and hands. The elevator trimming tabs of the aircraft were damaged and it became difficult to control. The rear turret, too, was badly damaged and the communications system and compasses were put out of action. Flight-Lieutenant Reid ascertained that his crew were unscathed, and saying nothing about his own injuries, he continued his mission.

'Soon afterwards, the Lancaster was attacked by a Focke Wulf 190. This time, the enemy's fire raked the bomber from stem to stern. The rear gunner replied with his only serviceable gun, but the state of his turret made accurate aiming impossible. The navigator was killed and the wireless operator fatally injured. The mid-upper turret was hit and the oxygen system put out of action. Flight-Lieutenant Reid was again wounded and the flight engineer, though hit in the forearm, supplied him with oxygen from a portable supply. Flight-Lieutenant Reid refused to be turned from his objective and Düsseldorf was reached some 50 minutes later. He had memorised his course to the target and had continued in such a normal manner that the bomb-aimer, who was cut off by the failure of the communications system, knew nothing of his captain's injuries, or of the casualties to his comrades. Photographs show that, when the bombs were released, the aircraft was right over the centre of the target.

'Steering by the pole star and the moon, Flight-Lieutenant Reid then set course for home. He was growing weak from loss of blood. The emergency oxygen supply had given out. With the windscreen shattered, the cold was intense. He lapsed into semi-consciousness. The flight engineer, with some help from the bomb-aimer, kept the Lancaster in the air despite heavy anti-aircraft fire over the Dutch coast. The North Sea crossing was accomplished. An airfield was sighted. The captain revived, resumed control and made ready to land. Ground mist partially obscured the runway lights. The captain was also much bothered by blood from his head wound getting into his eyes. But he made a safe landing although one leg of the damaged undercarriage collapsed when the load came on.

'Wounded in two attacks, without oxygen, suffering severely from cold, his navigator dead, his wireless operator fatally wounded, his aircraft crippled and defenceless, Flight-Lieutenant Reid showed superb courage and leadership in penetrating a further 200 miles into enemy territory to attack one of the most strongly defended targets in Germany, every additional mile increasing the hazards of the long and perilous journey home. His tenacity and devotion to duty were beyond praise.'

Cyril Joe Barton, 578 Squadron. (Extract from *The London Gazette*, 27 June 1944.) 'Pilot Officer Cyril Joe Barton (168669) RAFVR No. 578 Squadron (Deceased). On the night of 30 March 1944, Pilot Officer Barton was captain and pilot of a Halifax aircraft detailed to attack Nuremberg. When some 70 miles short of the target, the aircraft was attacked by a Junkers 88. The first burst of fire from the enemy made the intercommunication system useless. One engine was damaged when a Messerschmitt 210 joined in the fight. The bomber's machine guns were out of action and the gunners were unable to return the fire. Fighters continued to attack the aircraft as it approached the target area and, in the confusion caused by the failure of the communications system at the height of the battle, a signal was misinterpreted and the navigator, air bomber and wireless operator left the aircraft by parachute.

'Pilot Officer Barton faced a situation of dire peril. His aircraft was damaged, his navigational team had gone and he could not communicate with the remainder of the crew. If he continued his mission, he would be at the mercy of hostile fighters when silhouetted against the fires in the target area, and if he survived he would have to make a $4\frac{1}{2}$ hours journey home on three engines across heavily-defended territory. Determined to press home his attack at all costs, he flew on and, reaching the target, released the bombs himself. As Pilot Officer Barton turned for home the propeller of the damaged engine, which was vibrating badly, flew off. It was also discovered that two of the petrol tanks had suffered damage and were leaking. Pilot Officer Barton held to his course and, without navigational aids and in spite of strong head winds, successfully avoided the most dangerous defence areas on his route. Eventually he crossed the English coast only 90 miles north of his base. By this time the petrol supply was nearly exhausted. Before a suitable landing place could be found, the port engine stopped. The aircraft was now too low to be abandoned successfully. Pilot Officer Barton therefore ordered the three remaining members of

Cyril Joe Barton.

his crew to take up their crash stations. Then, with only one engine working, he made a gallant attempt to land clear of the houses over which he was flying. The aircraft finally crashed and Pilot Officer Barton lost his life, but his three comrades survived.

'Pilot Officer Barton had previously taken part in four attacks on Berlin and 14 other operational missions. On one of these, two members of his crew were wounded during a determined effort to locate the target despite the appalling weather conditions. In gallantly completing his last mission in the face of almost impossible odds, this officer displayed unsurpassed courage and devotion to duty.'

Geoffrey Leonard Cheshire, 617 Squadron. (Extract from *The London Gazette*, 8 September 1944.) 'Wing Commander Geoffrey Leonard Cheshire DSO, DFC (72021), Royal Air Force Volunteer Reserve, No. 617 Squadron. This officer began his operational career in June 1940. Against strongly-defended targets, he soon displayed the courage and determination of an exceptional leader. He was always ready to accept extra risks to ensure success. Defying the formidable Ruhr defences, he frequently released his bombs from below 20,000 ft. Over Cologne in November 1940, a shell burst inside his aircraft, blowing out one side and starting a fire; undeterred, he went on to bomb the target. About this time, he carried out a number of convoy patrols in addition to his bombing sessions.

'At the end of his first tour of operational duty in January 1941, he immediately volunteered for a second. Again, he pressed home his attacks with the utmost gallantry. Berlin, Bremen, Cologne, Duisburg, Essen and Kiel were among the heavily-defended targets which he attacked. When he was posted for instructional duties in January 1942, he undertook four more operational missions. He started a third tour in August 1942, when he was given command of a squadron. He led the squadron with outstanding skill on a number of missions before being appointed in March 1942, as a station commander. In October 1943, he undertook a fourth operational tour, relinquishing the rank of Group Captain at his own request so that he could again take part in operations. He immediately set to work as the pioneer of a new method of marking enemy targets involving very low flying. In June 1944, when marking a target in the harbour of Le Havre in broad daylight and

Geoffrey Leonard Cheshire.

without cloud cover, he dived well below the range of the light batteries before releasing his marker-bombs, and he came very near to being destroyed by the strong barrage which concentrated on him. During his fourth tour which ended in July 1944, Wing Commander Cheshire led his squadron personally on every occasion, always undertaking the most dangerous and difficult task of marking the target alone from a low level in the face of strong defences.

'Wing Commander Cheshire's cold and calculated acceptance of risks is exemplified by his conduct in an attack on Munich in April 1944. This was an experimental attack to test out the new method of target marking at low level against a heavily-defended target situated deep in Reich territory. Munich was selected, at Wing Commander Cheshire's request, because of the formidable nature of its light anti-aircraft and searchlight defences. He was obliged to follow, in bad weather, a direct route which took him over the defences of Augsburg and thereafter he was continuously under fire. As he reached the target, flares were being released by our high-flying aircraft. He was illuminated from above and below. All guns within range opened fire on him. Diving to 700 ft, he dropped his markers with great precision and began to climb away. So blinding were the searchlights that he almost lost control. He then flew over the city at 1,000 ft to assess the accuracy of his work and direct other aircraft. His own was badly hit by shell fragments but he continued to fly over the target area until he was satisfied that he had done all in his power to ensure success. Eventually, when he set course for base, the task of disengaging himself from the defences proved even more hazardous than the approach. For a full twelve minutes after leaving the target area he was under withering fire, but he came safely through.

'Wing Commander Cheshire has now completed a total of 100 missions. In four years of fighting against the bitterest opposition he has maintained a record of outstanding personal achievement, placing himself invariably in the forefront of the battle. What he did in the Munich operation was typical of the careful planning, brilliant execution and contempt for danger which has established for Wing Commander Cheshire a reputation second to none in Bomber Command.'

George Thompson, 9 Squadron. (Extract from *The London Gazette*, 20 February 1945.) '1370700 Flight Sergeant George Thompson, RAFVR, No. 9 Squadron Bomber Command (Deceased). This airman was the wireless operator in a Lancaster aircraft which attacked the Dortmund-Ems Canal in daylight on 1 January 1945. The bombs had just been released when a heavy shell hit the aircraft in front of the mid-upper turret. Fire broke out and dense smoke

George Thompson.

filled the fuselage. The nose of the aircraft was then hit and an inrush of air, clearing the smoke, revealed a scene of utter devastation. Most of the perspex screen of the nose compartment had been shot away, gaping holes had been torn in the canopy above the pilot's head, the intercommunication wiring was severed, and there was a large hole in the floor of the aircraft. Bedding and other equipment were badly damaged or alight; one engine was on fire.

'Flight Sergeant Thompson saw that the gunner was unconscious in the blazing mid-upper turret. Without hesitation he went down the fuselage into the fire and the exploding ammunition. He pulled the gunner from his turret and, edging his way round the hole in the floor, carried him away from the flames. With his bare hands, he extinguished the gunner's burning clothing. He himself sustained serious burns on his face, hands and legs. Flight Sergeant Thompson then noticed that the rear gun turret was also on fire. Despite his own severe injuries he moved painfully to the rear of the fuselage where he found the rear gunner with his clothing alight, overcome by flames and fumes. A second time Flight Sergeant Thompson braved the flames. With great difficulty he extricated the helpless gunner and carried him clear. Again he used his bare hands, already burnt, to beat out flames on a comrade's clothing.

'Flight Sergeant Thompson, by now almost exhausted, felt that his duty was not yet done. He must report the fate of the crew to the captain. He made the perilous journey back through the burning fuselage, clinging to the sides with his burnt hands to get across the hole in the floor. The flow of cold air caused him intense pain and frostbite developed. So pitiful was his condition that his captain failed to recognise him. Still, his only concern was for the two gunners he had left in the rear of the aircraft. He was given such attention as was possible until a crash-landing was made some forty minutes later. When the aircraft was hit, Flight Sergeant Thompson might have devoted his efforts to quelling the fire and so have contributed to his own safety. He preferred to go through the fire to succour his comrades. He knew that he would then be in no position to hear or heed any order which might be given to abandon the aircraft. He hazarded his own life in order to save the lives of others. Young in years and experience, his actions were those of a veteran.

'Three weeks later Flight Sergeant Thompson died of his injuries. One of the gunners unfortunately also died, but the other owes his life to the superb gallantry of Flight Sergeant Thompson, whose signal courage and self-sacrifice will ever be an inspiration to the Service.'

Robert Anthony Maurice Palmer, 109 Squadron. (Extract from *The London Gazette*, 23 March 1945.) 'Acting Squadron Leader Anthony Maurice Palmer, DFC (115772), RAFVR, No. 109 Squadron (Missing). This officer has completed 110 bombing missions. Most of them involved deep penetration of heavily-defended territory; many were low-level 'marking' operations against vital targets; all were executed with tenacity, high courage and great accuracy. He first went on operations in January 1941. He took part in the first 1,000 bomber raid against Cologne in 1942. He was one of the first pilots to drop a 4,000 lb bomb on the Reich. It was known that he could be relied upon to press home his attack whatever the opposition and to bomb with great accuracy. He was always selected, therefore, to take part in special operations against vital targets.

'The finest example of his courage and determination was on 23 December 1944, when he led a formation of Lancasters to attack the marshalling yards at Cologne in daylight. He had the task of marking the target, and his formation had been ordered to bomb as soon as the bombs had gone from his, the leading aircraft. The leader's duties during the final bombing run were exacting and demanded coolness and resolution. To achieve accuracy he would have to fly at an exact height and air speed on a steady course, regardless of opposition. Some minutes before the target was reached, his aircraft came under heavy anti-aircraft fire, shells burst all around, two engines were set on fire and there were flames and smoke in the nose and in the bomb bay. Enemy fighters now attacked in force. Squadron Leader Palmer disdained the possibility of taking avoiding action. He knew that if he diverged the least bit from his course, he would be unable to utilise the special equipment to the best advantage. He was determined to complete the run and provide an accurate and easily seen aiming-point for the other

Robert Anthony Maurice Palmer.

bombers. He ignored the double risk of fire and explosion in the aircraft and kept on. With his engines developing unequal power, an immense effort was needed to keep the damaged aircraft on a straight course. Nevertheless, he made a perfect approach and his bombs hit the target.

'His aircraft was last seen spiralling to earth in flames. Such was the strength of the opposition that more than half of his formation failed to return.

'Squadron Leader Palmer was an outstanding pilot. He displayed conspicuous bravery. His record of prolonged and heroic endeavour is beyond praise.'

Edwin Swales.

Edwin Swales, 582 Squadron. (Extract from *The London Gazette*, 24 April 1945.) 'Captain Edwin Swales, DFC (6101V) SAAF No. 582 Squadron (Deceased). Captain Swales was "master bomber" of a force of aircraft which attacked Pforzheim on the night of 23 February 1945. As "master bomber", he had the task of locating the target area with precision and of giving aiming instructions to the main force of bombers following in his wake. Soon after he had reached the target area he was engaged by an enemy fighter and one of his engines was put out of action. His rear guns failed. His crippled aircraft was an easy prey to further attacks. Unperturbed, he carried on with his allotted task; clearly and precisely he issued aiming instructions to the main force. Meanwhile the enemy fighter closed the range and fired again. Almost defenceless, he stayed over the target area issuing his aiming instructions until he was satisfied that the attack had achieved its purpose. It is now known that the attack was one of the most concentrated and successful of the war.

'Captain Swales did not, however, regard his mission as completed. His aircraft was damaged. Its speed had been so much reduced that it could only with difficulty be kept in the air. The blind-flying instruments were no longer working. Determined at all costs to prevent his aircraft and crew from falling into enemy hands, he set course for home. After an hour he flew into thin-layered cloud. He kept his course by skilful flying between the layers, but later heavy cloud and turbulent air conditions were met. The aircraft, by now over friendly territory, became more and more difficult to control; it was losing height steadily. Realising that the situation was desperate Captain Swales ordered his crew to bale out. Time was very short and it required all his exertions to keep the aircraft steady while each of his crew moved in turn to the escape hatch and parachuted to safety. Hardly had the last crew member jumped when the aircraft plunged to earth. Captain Swales was found dead at the controls.

'Intrepid in the attack, courageous in the face of danger, he did his duty to the last, giving his life that his comrades might live.'

Ian Willoughby Bazalgette, 635 Squadron. (Extract from *The London Gazette*, 17 August 1945.) 'Acting Squadron Leader Ian Willoughby Bazalgette, DFC (118131), RAFVR, No. 635 Squadron (Deceased). On 4 August 1944, Squadron Leader Bazalgette was "master bomber" of a Pathfinder squadron detailed to mark an important target at

Ian Willoughby Bazalgette.

Trossy St Maximin for the main bomber force. When nearing the target his Lancaster came under heavy anti-aircraft fire. Both starboard engines were put out of action and serious fires broke out in the fuselage, and the starboard main-plane. The bomb-aimer was badly wounded. As the deputy "master bomber" had already been shot down the success of the attack depended on Squadron Leader Bazalgette, and this he knew. Despite the appalling conditions in his burning aircraft, he pressed on gallantly to the target, marking and bombing it accurately. That the attack was successful was due to his magnificent effort. After the bombs had been dropped the Lancaster dived, practically out of control. By expert airmanship and great exertion Squadron Leader Bazalgette regained control. But the port inner engine then failed and the whole of the starboard mainplane became a mass of flames.

'Squadron Leader Bazalgette fought bravely to bring his aircraft and crew to safety. The mid-upper gunner was overcome by fumes. Squadron Leader Bazalgette then ordered those of his crew who were able to leave by parachute to do so. He remained at the controls and attempted the almost hopeless task of landing the crippled and blazing aircraft in a last effort to save the wounded bomb-aimer and helpless gunner. With superb skill, and taking great care to avoid a small French village nearby, he brought the aircraft down safely. Unfortunately, it then exploded and this gallant officer and his two comrades perished.

'His heroic sacrifice marked the climax of a long career of operations against the enemy. He always chose the more dangerous and exacting roles. His courage and devotion to duty were beyond praise.'

Norman Cyril Jackson, 106 Squadron. (Extract from The London Gazette, 26 October 1945.) '905192 Sergeant (now Warrant Officer) Norman Cyril Jackson, RAFVR No. 106 Squadron. This airman was the flight engineer in a Lancaster detailed to attack Schweinfurt on the night of 26 April 1944. Bombs were dropped successfully and the aircraft was climbing out of the target area. Suddenly it was attacked by a fighter at about 20,000 ft. The captain took evading action at once, but the

Norman Cyril Jackson.

enemy secured many hits. A fire started near a petrol tank on the upper surface of the starboard wing, between the fuselage and the inner engine.

'Sergeant Jackson was thrown to the floor during the engagement. Wounds which he received from shell splinters in the right leg and shoulder were probably sustained at that time. Recovering himself, he remarked that he could deal with the fire on the wing and obtained his captain's permission to try to put out the flames. Pushing a hand fire-extinguisher into the top of his life-saving jacket and clipping on his parachute pack, Sergeant Jackson jettisoned the escape hatch above the pilot's head. He then started to climb out of the cockpit and back along the top of the fuselage to the starboard wing. Before he could leave the fuselage his parachute pack opened and the whole canopy and rigging lines spilled into the cockpit. Undeterred, Sergeant Jackson continued. The pilot, bomb-aimer and navigator gathered the parachute together and held on to the rigging lines, paying them out as the airman crawled aft. Eventually he slipped and, falling from the fuselage to the starboard wing, grasped an air intake on the leading edge of the wing. He succeeded in clinging on but lost the extinguisher, which was blown away.

'By this time, the fire had spread rapidly and Sergeant Jackson was involved. His face, hands and clothing were severely burnt. Unable to retain his hold he was swept through the flames and over the trailing edge of the wing, dragging his parachute behind. When last seen it was only partly inflated and was burning in a number of places. Realising that the fire could not be controlled, the captain gave the order to abandon aircraft. Four of the remaining members of the crew landed safely. The captain and rear gunner had not been accounted for. Sergeant Jackson was unable to control his descent and landed heavily. He sustained a broken ankle, his right eye was closed through burns and his hands were useless. These injuries, together with the wounds received earlier, reduced him to a pitiable state. At daybreak he crawled to the nearest village, where he was taken prisoner. He bore the intense pain and discomfort of the journey to Dulag Luft with magnificent fortitude. After ten months in hospital he made a good recovery, though his hands require further treatment and are only of limited use.

'This airman's attempt to extinguish the fire and save the aircraft and crew from falling into enemy hands was an act of outstanding gallantry. To venture outside, when travelling at 200 miles an hour, at a great height and in intense cold, was an almost incredible feat. Had he succeeded in subduing the flames, there was little or no prospect of his regaining the cockpit. The spilling of his parachute and the risk of grave damage to its canopy reduced his chances of survival to a minimum. By his ready willingness to face these dangers he set an example of self sacrifice which will ever be remembered.'

Leonard Henry Trent, 487 (RNZAF) Squadron. (Extract from *The London Gazette*, 1 March 1946.) 'Squadron Leader Leonard Henry Trent, DFC (NZ2481), Royal New Zealand Air Force, No. 487 (RNZAF) Squadron, Bomber Command. On 3 May 1943, Squadron Leader Trent was detailed to lead a formation of Ventura aircraft in a daylight attack on the power station at Amsterdam. This operation was intended to encourage the Dutch workmen in their resistance to enemy pressure. The target was known to be heavily defended. The importance of bombing it, regardless of enemy fighters or anti-aircraft fire, was strongly impressed on the air crews taking part in the operation. Before taking off, Squadron Leader Trent told the deputy leader that he was going over the target, whatever happened.

'All went well until the eleven Venturas and their fighter escort were nearing the Dutch coast. Then one bomber was hit and had to turn back. Suddenly large numbers of enemy fighters appeared. Our escorting fighters were hotly engaged and lost touch with the bombing force. The Venturas closed up for mutual protection and commenced their run up to the target. Unfortunately, the fighters detailed to support them over the target had reached the area too early and had been recalled. Soon the bombers were attacked. They were at the mercy of 15 to 20 Messerschmitts which dived on them incessantly. Within four minutes six Venturas were destroyed. Squadron Leader Trent continued on his course with the three remaining aircraft. In a short time two more Venturas went down in flames. Heedless of the murderous attacks and of the heavy anti-aircraft fire which was now encountered, Squadron Leader Trent completed an accurate bombing run and even shot down a Messerschmitt at point-blank range. Dropping his bombs in the target area, he turned away. The aircraft following him was shot down on reaching the target. Immediately afterwards his own aircraft was hit, went into a spin and broke up. Squadron Leader Trent and his navigator were thrown clear and became prisoners of war. The other two members of the crew perished.

'On this, his 24th sortie, Squadron Leader Trent showed outstanding leadership. Such was the

Leonard Henry Trent.

trust placed in this gallant officer that the other pilots followed him unwaveringly. His cool, unflinching courage and devotion to duty in the face of overwhelming odds rank with the finest examples of these virtues.'

Arthur Stewart King Scarf, 62 Squadron. (Extract from *The London Gazette*, 21 June 1946.) 'Squadron Leader Arthur Stewart King Scarf (37693) (Deceased), Royal Air Force, No. 62 Squadron. On 9 December 1941, all available aircraft from the Royal Air Force Station, Butterworth, Malaya, were ordered to make a daylight attack on the advanced operational base of the Japanese Air Force at Singora, Thailand. From this base, the enemy fighter squadrons were supporting the landing operations. The aircraft detailed for the sortie were on the point of taking off when the enemy made a combined dive-bombing and low level machine-gun attack on the airfield. All our aircraft were destroyed or damaged with the exception of the Blenheim piloted by Squadron Leader Scarf. This aircraft had become airborne a few seconds before the attack started.

'Squadron Leader Scarf circled the airfield and witnessed the disaster. It would have been reasonable had he abandoned the projected operation which was intended to be a formation sortie. He decided however, to press on to Singora in his single aircraft. Although he knew that this individual action could not inflict much material damage on the enemy he, nevertheless, appreciated the moral effect which it would have on the remainder of the squadron, who were helplessly watching their aircraft burning on the ground. Squadron Leader Scarf completed his attack successfully. The opposition over the target was severe and included attacks by a considerable number of enemy fighters. In the course of these encounters, Squadron Leader Scarf was mortally

wounded. The enemy continued to engage him in a running fight, which lasted until he had regained the Malayan border. Squadron Leader Scarf fought a brilliant evasive action in a valiant attempt to return to his base. Although he displayed the utmost gallantry and determination, he was, owing to his wounds, unable to accomplish this. He made a successful forced-landing at Alor Star without causing any injury to his crew. He was received into hospital as soon as possible but died shortly after admission.

'Squadron Leader Scarf displayed supreme heroism in the face of tremendous odds and his splendid example of self sacrifice will long be remembered.'

Arthur Stewart King Scarf.

Andrew Charles Mynarski, 419 Squadron (RCAF). (Extract from *The London Gazette*, 11 October 1946.) 'Pilot Officer Andrew Charles Mynarski (Can/J.87544) (Deceased), Royal Canadian Air Force, No. 419 Squadron (RCAF). Pilot Officer Mynarski was the mid-upper gunner of a Lancaster aircraft, detailed to attack a target at Cambrai in France, on the night of 12 June 1944. The aircraft was attacked from below and astern by an enemy fighter and ultimately came down in flames. As an immediate result of the attack, both port engines failed. Fire broke out between the mid-upper turret and the rear turret, as well as in the port wing. The flames soon became fierce and the captain ordered the crew to abandon the aircraft.

'Pilot Officer Mynarski left his turret and went towards the escape hatch. He then saw that the rear gunner was still in his turret and apparently unable to leave it. The turret, was in fact, immovable, since the hydraulic gear had been put out of action when the port engines failed, and the manual gear had been broken by the gunner in his attempt to escape. Without hesitation, Pilot Officer Mynarski made his way through the flames in an endeavour to reach the rear turret and release the gunner. Whilst so doing, his parachute and his clothing up to the waist, were set on fire. All his efforts to move the turret and free the gunner were in vain. Eventually the rear gunner clearly indicated to him that there was nothing more he could do and that he should try to save his own life. Pilot Officer Mynarski reluctantly went back through the flames to the escape hatch. There, as a last gesture to the trapped gunner, he turned towards him, stood to attention in his flaming clothing and saluted, before he jumped out of the aircraft. Pilot Officer Mynarski's descent was seen by French people on the ground. Both his parachute and clothing on fire. He was found eventually by the French, but was so severely burnt that he died from his injuries.

'The rear gunner had a miraculous escape when the aircraft crashed. He subsequently testified that, had Pilot Officer Mynarski not attempted to save his comrade's life, he could have left the aircraft in safety and would, doubtless have escaped death.

'Pilot Officer Mynarski must have been fully aware that in trying to free the rear gunner he was almost certain to lose his own life. Despite this, with outstanding courage and complete disregard for his own safety, he went to the rescue. Willingly accepting the danger, Pilot Officer Mynarski lost his life by a most conspicuous act of heroism which called for valour of the highest order.'

Andrew Charles Mynarski.

Index

Index of places

St Tudwals 71
Salisbury Plain 1
San Polo d'Enza 136
Saracen's Head 65
Sardinia 134
Scampton 14, 37, 136,
137, 166, 167, 171, 172,
173
Schleswig 128, 146
Schweinfurt 118, 130, 219
Shellingford 71
Sheringham 75, 77
Shipdham 196
Sicily 211
Singapore City 142, 175
Singora 222
Skellingthorpe 80, 81, 84,
88, 102–105, 112, 113,
125
Skipton-on-Swale 3, 39
Snaith 21, 24, 35
Snitterfield 175
Social Circle 76
Solihull 76
Spa 69
Spezia 134, 137
Stafford 76
Sterkrade 100
Stettin 54, 111, 113
Stockton-on-Tees 76
Stradishall 189
Stuttgart 95, 99, 136, 162,
210
Suda Bay 112
Suffolk 189, 191
Surrey 125, 152
Sussex 146
Sweden 56
Swinderby 8, 9, 29
Switzerland 90, 127, 133
Sydney 101, 190
Syerston 8, 13, 67, 200

Teesside Airport 9
Thailand 222
Tholthorpe 29, 30
Topcliffe 4, 5
Toulouse 106
Trappes 98
Trossy-St-Maximin 194,
219
Truro 125
Turin 207, 210

Ulm 161
United Kingdom 16
Upper Heyford 8
Uxbridge 166

Vaires 139
Vierzon 139
Villeneuve St George 97
Vire 147
Vitry-le-Francois 139

Waddington 1, 6, 9, 20,
29, 31, 33, 36, 37, 46,
67, 88, 172, 173
Walcheren 67
Wallingford 152
Waltham 139, 141, 197
Warsaw 153, 158
Warwickshire 125
Wattisham 54
Wellesbourne Mountford
90
West Ham 120
West Kirby 166, 175
Whitley Bay 166
Wickenby 158
Wiesbaden 163
Wigsley 66
Wilhelmshaven 67, 94, 209
Winnipeg 88
Winterswijk 145
Winthorpe 88
Woking 152
Woodhall Spa 47, 83
Wurms 175

York 61, 175
Yorkshire 18, 92, 93, 94,
100, 147, 148, 165, 173,
175, 187

Zastow 153
Zeitz 156
Zliffenhausen 162

Index of units
Advanced Air Striking
Force 18
No 2(C) OTU 166
No 4 SOTT 167
No 9 AFU 167
No 22 APC 167
No 36 OTU 167

SQUADRONS
No 7: 19
No 9: 67, 215
No 10: 94, 177, 178
No 12: 48, 50, 51, 53, 55,
200
No 18: 208
No 35: 27, 31, 32
No 44: 205
No 49: 107, 110, 170, 171,
201
No 50: 29, 80, 83, 84, 86,
102, 106, 125, 205
No 57: 88, 90, 135, 137
No 58: 41
No 61: 84, 86, 111, 112,
113, 211
No 62: 222
No 75: 204
No 82: 167
No 83: 14, 83, 166, 167,
169, 202
No 96: 101, 167, 176
No 97: 119
No 100: 139
No 101: 93, 159, 162, 163,
165
No 103: 30, 34, 62, 76
No 106 (RAFVR) 219
No 109: 217
No 149: 16, 17, 207
No 158: 92–98, 101
No 207: 115
No 218: 210
No 227: 88, 143
No 300 (Polish) 155
No 311 (Czech) 15
No 408 (RCAF) 13
No 419 (RCAF) 223
No 420 (RCAF) 23, 30
No 429 (RCAF) xi, xii,
147, 148
No 460 (RAAF) 189, 190,
193
No 463 (RAAF) 31, 33, 38
No 467 (RAAF) 37, 45,
46, 67, 68, 133
No 487 (RNZAF) 221
No 576: 38
No 578: 124, 213
No 582 (SAAF) 218
No 617: 209, 214
No 635: 218